CONTENTS

D0141197

PART IV Evaluation
        Case Studies
        (International)

DESIGNING FOR DESIGNERS

LESSONS LEARNED FROM SCHOOLS OF ARCHITECTURE

DESIGNING FOR DESIGNERS

LESSONS LEARNED FROM SCHOOLS OF ARCHITECTURE

JACK L. NASAR
WOLFGANG F. E. PREISER
AND
THOMAS FISHER

FAIRCHILD PUBLICATIONS, INC.
NEW YORK

Director of Sales and Acquisitions: Dana
    Meltzer-Berkowitz
Executive Editor: Olga T. Kontzias
Acquisitions Editor: Joseph Miranda
Assistant Acquisitions Editor: Jaclyn Bergeron
Senior Development Editor: Jennifer Crane
Development Editor: Michelle Levy
Art Director: Adam B. Bohannon
Production Manager: Ginger Hillman
Associate Production Editor: Jessica Rozler
Cover Design: Adam B. Bohannon
Cover Art: *front cover*: © Larry Kanfer
    Photography, www.kanfer.com;
    back cover: Courtesy of École des Beaux Arts
Text Design: Andrew Katz

Copyright © 2007
Fairchild Publications, Inc.

Library of Congress Catalog Card Number:
2006939040

ISBN: 978-1-56367- 459-4

GST R 133004424

Printed in the United States of America
TP 13

ACKNOWLEDGMENTS

We thank the contributing authors to this book, whose patience was tested over the years this project evolved, and the people whose photographs, images, and documentation are reproduced in this book.

For their help with the post-occupancy evaluations (POEs) we thank Jamie Carpenter, Anoa Changa, Scott Conlon, Brett Davis, Martti Eckert, Ramiere Fitzpatrick, Danield Garza, Matthew Hinkle, Matt Holdren, David Horstman, Michael Jimson, Thomas Lodge, Peter Marsh, Michael McBeth, Jill Morelli, Chanel Norton, Patrick Sage, Katrina Scales, Laura Shinn, Justin Snyder, Jennifer Vanni, Stephen Zellinger (Ohio State), Mark Gillem, Jon Norman, Iris Tien, Jess Wendover (Berkeley), Ozgur Mert, Dede Price (Cincinnati), Samia Rab (Hawaii), Arturo Barin, Lara Blankenburg, Curtis Clay, Charles Davis, Gloria Day, Amy Fatlan, Scott Klimek, Paul Kramer, Erin Lavin, Lyria Martin, Sean May, Catherine McCulloch, Wendell Moore, Keith Nowakowski, Marina Panos, Chris Requena, Shauna Shepston, Stacey Thomas, Scott Utter, Matthew Wei, Russell Weisbard, Hub White, Neda Zarraby, Nicol Zeller (Illinois), Linda Groat (Michigan), Amy Anderson, Holly Bristol, Jean Chicoine, Danielle Folchert, Lisa Guerra, Sara Haster, Lance Hiatt, Anthony Johnson, Heather Keele, Becky Kunkel, Sachi Miura, Mandy O'Loughlin, Diane Sherlock, Kim Stiebinger (Nebraska), Kwallek's interior design students, Kokyung Soon (Texas), Jodie Gaven, Gledhills Construction, Allan Lamb, Phil McCamley, Strategic FM, Allan Lamb, University of Sydney's Facilities Management, and Office and Mariana Vurmeska (Sydney). The POE of Dokuz Eyul was supported in part by a research grant from the Dokuz Eyul University Scientific Research Project.

We also thank the many people we worked with at Fairchild Books for their support. Joe Miranda saw the potential in the book and handled its acquisition. Jason Moring, Development Editor, gave us editorial guidance. We also thank Jennifer Crane, Senior Development Editor, Adam Bohannon, Director of Creative Services & Production, Jessica Rozler, Associate Production Editor; and we are especially grateful to Michelle Levy, Development Editor, for her diligent editorial advice and guidance.

Lastly, we join the contributors in thanking the hundreds of students, faculty, staff, and others who took part in the POEs of their schools. We created this book for you and future occupants, and welcome your comments and critical feedback.

JACK L. NASAR
WOLFGANG F. E. PREISER
THOMAS FISHER

PREFACE

The idea and inspiration for this book have concerned the editors for some time. We all share a commitment to building knowledge for design, whether through evaluative studies, competitions, or design juries.

Jack Nasar developed his interest in design evaluation in the 1960s and 1970s, having visited Pruitt Igoe in its disastrous heyday as an undergraduate, and later as a graduate studying with Oscar Newman. He focused his research on visual quality, wrote a dissertation on the perceived appearance of residential streetscapes (Nasar, 1979), and continued to refine measurement methods and knowledge about environmental meanings in different contexts (Nasar 1994, 1998, 1999). A Critic at Large for *Landscape Architecture Magazine,* and former architectural critic for *The Columbus Dispatch,* Nasar brings knowledge gleaned from environmental design research to the evaluation of proposed projects. Using shared meanings, one can make places more legible, meaningful, and functional to users.

Wolfgang Preiser wrote his Master's thesis on dormitory quality profiling (Preiser 1969) and has carried on development of evaluation techniques over the past 30 years (Preiser, Rabinowitz, and White 1988; Preiser and Vischer 2005). The National Council of Architectural Registration Boards (NCARB) contracted with Preiser to write "Improving Building Performance" as part of their Professional Development Monograph Series (NCARB Professional Development Program, 2003). Now, to earn recertification or continuing education credits, every architect can study and be tested on the topic of building performance assessment.

Thomas Fisher, former editor of *Progressive Architecture (P/A),* has been committed to a critical, evaluative stance in publishing. For years, he moderated the research awards as part of the *P/A* Awards program, and instituted and edited the Practice section of the magazine, providing a critical look at the nature of architectural practice. As editorial director of the magazine, he also encouraged publication of articles about projects after they had been inhabited for at least a year, with input from users and janitors, as well as the architects and clients of buildings. Since then, Fisher has emphasized the importance of research, co-editing the British journal *Architectural Research Quarterly* and co-chairing a research committee as part of the American Institute of Architects' (AIA) Large Firm Roundtable's Dean's Forum. A recent essay by him in *Harvard Design Magazine,* entitled "Architects Behaving Badly," looks at the missed opportunities that come from not integrating the wealth of available environment-behavior research into mainstream architectural practice.

Our collaboration goes back more than 30 years. During Fisher's tenure as editor of *Progressive Architecture,* Preiser served on the Progressive Architecture Design Awards Jury in 1979, and later received the Applied Research Award and Citation in 1985 and 1989, respectively. In the early 1980s, Preiser joined a series of Environmental Design Research Association (EDRA) conference symposia run by Nasar on environmental aesthetics. Those symposia served as the basis for Nasar's (1988) edited book *Environmental Aesthetics: Theory, Research and Applications* (Cambridge University Press), which included a chapter by Preiser. For years, Preiser and Nasar, who taught in universities less than 100 miles apart, exchanged class lectures, followed by discussion over coffee or lunch. These discussions led to the Nasar and Preiser co-edited book *Directions in Person-Environment Research and Practice.*

One discussion, when Preiser's school was undergoing a renovation and Nasar's was planning a new building, turned to the architecture of schools of architecture. They saw a need for a knowledge base to guide such designs; and they decided to collaborate on a project toward that end. They planned to conduct systematic evaluations of contemporary facilities serving schools of architecture to learn what to do and what to avoid.

That led to grant applications to the National Endowment for the Arts and the Graham Foundation for a book on the architecture of schools of architecture, which eventually evolved into the present book. The lessons learned from those discussions and applications helped refine the book you are now reading.

FOREWORD

THE CURIOUS PROBLEM
OF THE ARCHITECTURE OF
SCHOOLS OF ARCHITECTURE

PHILIP LANGDON

In the 1980s, after I quit my job at a newspaper and started writing books, magazine articles, and newsletters on design and planning, I noticed how strangely, how radically, the quality of architecture schools varied. It wasn't the differences among professors, students, or curricula that caught my attention. It was the buildings in which the schools were housed; they were so disparate in character and not infrequently disappointing.

At the University of Michigan, where I'd once spent a glorious sabbatical from the newspaper business, courtesy of the National Endowment for the Arts, I was puzzled by the architecture school. It stood, almost mute, on Ann Arbor's automobile-scale North Campus, prompting hardly any response. In nine months of attending classes and getting to know professors and students at Michigan, I don't think I heard more than two conversations about the building. The Art and Architecture building was just *there*. Its exterior was clad mostly in glass and brownish brick, except for one portion covered in Cor-Ten steel that left rusty stains on the concrete at its base.

The building had been designed by Robert S. Swanson, nephew of Eero Saarinen, who master-planned the campus—a lifeless, low-slung expanse that contrasted poorly with the old central campus near downtown Ann Arbor. Swanson described the building as "not precious...easily modified, essentially loft space," a verdict that has proven accurate in the years since it opened in 1974. "It's a fairly simple set of boxes with an exposed steel frame—vaguely Miesian—that has lent itself easily to reworking," says Douglas Kelbaugh, the current dean. "We've had some fun making many interventions, modifications, and changes, and hope to add another 12,000 square feet on the roof in the future. Faculty and students have done much of the design and construction work." The structure's 90-by-360-foot open studio space bears the distinction, Kelbaugh believes, of being the largest in the nation; it has been reconfigured more than once. The building also features "a large high-bay space for hands-on building and environmental research, full-scale fabrication and construction, for which the college has always been known," Kelbaugh points out.

It's fair to say that in most respects, Michigan's architecture building functions well. The trouble is, it just doesn't make much impression. I've never heard people express *delight* about it or declare that it influenced their outlook. This seems an odd omission—a serious flaw—in a school whose purpose is to educate architects and, one might think, to be a source of inspiration.

A different kind of decision, in some ways better, in some ways worse, was made at the first architecture school I became familiar with: the State University of New York at Buffalo. In the late 1960s, when SUNY started its architecture school, rather than erecting brand new facilities, the university assigned the architectural school to Hayes Hall, a large structure already a century old. The building, with its rough-textured walls of gray limestone, had served successively as an insane asylum, a county almshouse, and a county hospital before it was converted to educational purposes in the 1920s. I got to know the building in the late 1970s, when on many a Monday afternoon I would rush from the downtown office of *The Buffalo News* to the Hayes Hall auditorium to hear architecture lectures that were open to the public.

Hayes Hall rose from a generous slope of lawn in the city's green northeastern corner, and I always enjoyed approaching it. The building had a dignified yet not imperious presence, its central roof topped by an elaborate tower that had been added in the 1920s, closely patterned after James Gibbs's St. Martin-in-the-Fields Church in 1720s London. The tower provided Hayes Hall with what one architect calls a "late Wrenaissance" touch. The building stretched for quite a distance, with well modulated projections and recesses, and the interior was easy to figure out, but the spaces themselves were mundane. The auditorium was a problem unsolved; its seating was steeply raked, with the entrance at its base. As a result, anyone leaving before the end of a lecture would walk behind or next to the speaker and make a decidedly conspicuous exit. I recall George Anselevicius, the chairman of the architecture department, chastising students about cutting out early because it was rude and disruptive. SUNY-Buffalo's building was in some respects the reverse of Michigan's: It made a favorable impression from outdoors but was less successful once you penetrated the interior.

I discovered in time that many architects have misgivings about the buildings in which they received their education. "On arriving at Berkeley, my heart sank when I realized that the ugliest building by far was Wurster Hall, the home of the College of Environmental Design," recalls Michael Mehaffy, an Oregon-based architect who has worked in the United States and England. "It was something—brutal concrete exterior, merciless repetitive grid, horrible appearance when wet, aged badly, etc. The interior was barely habitable. Chris Alexander used to point out features of the building that

Fig. F.1.
Vaulted
Ceiling in
the School
of Applied
Design.

were working particularly horribly—very basic stuff, like rectangular seminar rooms with windows on the narrow end, which made speakers utterly
invisible in the glare; bare concrete walls with dreadful acoustics, and so on."
Washington, D.C., architect Dhiru Thadani, recalls attending Catholic University, which was housed in "a banal, modern building that expressed the
vertical and horizontal structure, with brick and glass infill panels. It was the
lowest denominator of 'building,'" Thadani says, "and clearly was not 'Architecture.'" Such troubling examples of the architecture of schools of architecture are not hard to find.

Standing in sharp contrast are buildings like the College of Fine Arts
(originally School of Applied Design) at Carnegie Mellon University, which
was constructed in 1912 for the departments of architecture, art, design,
drama, and music at what was initially Carnegie Institute of Technology. The
designer was New York architect Henry Hornbostel, who, in the first decade
of the twentieth century planned the campus and who, over a period of
more than 20 years, designed a number of handsome buildings there. The
School of Applied Design, completed in 1912, was, and is, gorgeous both inside and out. It has the buff brick, polychrome terracotta ornament, and
overhanging, low-pitched roofs that appear on many of Carnegie Mellon's
early buildings and that do much to make the campus a unified entity. Open
the door to the great entrance hall and you find, Edward Fenton notes in a
Carnegie Mellon centennial history, "a vaulted roof adorned with frescoes
by J. M. Hewlett—'a celestial atlas of art history,' one historian called it."
(See Figure F.1.)

Inset in the gray marble floor is a floor plan of St. Peter's Basilica in green Vermont marble. Plans for the Parthenon, Chartres Cathedral, and the Temple of Edfu in Egypt adorn the floors of a transverse hallway. At the dean's office is a reproduction of a plaster cast of the entrance to the City Hall of Toulon, France. "The entire building, which presents a variety of vistas and points of view, both classical and romantic, is a setting designed to inspire budding young artists," writes Fenton (2000, pp. 62–79).

For all its classicism, the School of Applied Design was, in its time, an innovative building. Charles Rosenblum, who teaches at Carnegie Mellon, describes it as "halfway between a Renaissance villa and a high-rise office tower," as evidenced by such elements as the high degree of fenestration and the vertical emphasis of the windows, which Hornbostel connected with terracotta ornament. "Hornbostel uses terracotta ornament in an experimental and personal kind of way," says Rosenblum. Not every student may recognize the building's ingenuity, but the inventiveness is there, just as surely as its grandeur and its highlighting of the artistic achievements of the West. Whether the building can be modified as easily as Michigan's purposely unprecious school from 1974 is doubtful, but it exudes *ambition* and *love of beauty*.

What should architectural school buildings be? How do we evaluate such buildings? Those are important questions that the editors and writers of *Designing for Designers* have pursued with seriousness and variety of approach. Ways of answering those questions differ, just as reactions to buildings such as Michigan's, SUNY-Buffalo's, and Carnegie Mellon's differ. After all the books and articles that have been written about every other type of building, from houses to museums to office towers, there is a need for more attention to the architecture of schools of architecture. These are buildings in which architects-to-be spend most of their days and a good many of their nights for three years or more. Surely these buildings leave an imprint on those who create our surroundings. Their impact can hardly be neutral or negligible.

Designers of schools of architecture need to pay closer attention to how these buildings serve and affect—and, ideally, bring the best out of—the people who study, teach, and work in them. Some designers seem not to know how serious the problems are. Some designers are pursuing too narrow or too unbalanced a set of goals. As a result, architecture schools often do not perform as well as they should. This book contributes to our knowledge of how such buildings have been designed, the roles they play, and how such buildings can be assessed. The case studies are especially useful for helping designers avoid pitfalls and realize the potential implicit in architectural schools.

Michael Mehaffy, citing the deficiencies of Berkeley's Wurster Hall, observes: "I suppose it was an, ahem, instructive building for us in that sense. But its internal disorder seemed to feed a kind of disordered professional approach to the built environment: here and there a piece of interesting art amid a general mess." He says Joseph Esherick, one of that building's designers, once explained to students, a bit apologetically, that Wurster was something of a committee design: "It would have a tower element of some kind; it would have a courtyard of some kind, and most important, the Regents would need to hate it!" Mehaffy acknowledges that Esherick's statement "was obviously a bit of tongue in cheek, but we sensed there was a level of seriousness behind it," a reflection of friction that went back to the days of the Free Speech Movement.

The aims, motives, processes, and performance of architectural school buildings need a candid and systematic airing. Frank exploration, of the kind in this book, might do the architectural profession and the public a world of good.

PHILIP LANGDON
New Haven, CT
September 1, 2006

INTRODUCTION

THE CONTEXT OF ARCHITECTURAL EDUCATION TODAY

JACK L. NASAR, WOLFGANG F. E. PREISER, AND THOMAS FISHER

This book is about the architecture of schools of architecture, or, how designers design educational environments to suit themselves. Dealing with a building type that has received little analytic attention, the book explores several questions: How has architectural education evolved, and what is its future? Are architectural schools discernable types of designs, and what are their effects on those who experience them? What lessons can be learned from evaluations of recently completed school buildings, and what guidance do they provide for the design of future ones?

CONTEXT

A significant shift of patronage and building sponsorship from the private sector to the public sector occurred in the 1980s. Government at the local, state, and federal levels became the sponsor of significant buildings, ranging from courthouses to public libraries to university facilities. As part of this wave, a number of schools of architecture and design were either renovated or newly constructed, both of which this book examines.

Architecture schools have often sought new buildings by "signature architects" as a way to build a reputation. Although some of these buildings won design awards and praise from the critics, sometimes prior to construction and occupancy, the same buildings often did not work well for the occupants. Students at Yale tried to burn their new architecture building down, and Harvard students suffered from excessive heat gain in their glass-covered studio structure. At Florida A&M, an automated heating and cooling system led to the building leaking on the students' drawings. Some new architecture buildings have features that work well: At the University of Cincinnati, the atrium/cafeteria attracts customers from all corners and levels of the college complex; and in Harvard's Gund Hall, when the cafeteria opened in the ground floor open space, it worked well as a social gathering place for students from all years and design disciplines. At the University of Minnesota, the extensive public space, while suffering from poor acoustics, provided ample space for students to see each other's work.

DESIGNING AS IF
PEOPLE MATTER

When people buy a product they expect it look good *and* work well, such as the universally designed line of kitchen utensils by OXO, called Mr. Goodgrips (Preiser and Ostroff 2001). The same philosophy should be applied in architecture. While good architecture ought to look good, appearance alone is not enough; architecture must support the needs of its occupants. Unlike works of art or sculpture, buildings must protect people from the elements and be safe, they must be functional and efficient, and they must support the psychological, social, and cultural requirements of their occupants.

If one or two people complain about a problem in a building, such as excessive noise, poor temperature control, or inadequate lighting, the complaint may reflect an idiosyncratic one. But if many people encounter a problem related to a building, it probably arises from design flaws. For example, the complexity of the University of Cincinnati's Aronoff Center for Design and Art by Peter Eisenman makes it almost impossible for most first-time visitors to find their way around, suggesting that intrinsic design problems interfere with wayfinding. The situation is even worse for people with disabilities. Often, a problem found in one building recurs in others. Feedback from occupants can build a knowledge base to prevent such problems in the future by improving the programming and design decision-making process.

At the cutting edge of knowledge, and with a history of world-class academics, American universities have become high-profile patrons of contemporary architecture. Many public and private campuses now have buildings designed by internationally known signature architects: an email survey of university architects at 25 campuses (Nasar 1996) found that most of them had built signature buildings or held design competitions in the five years prior to the survey. Of all of the new buildings on campuses, designs for architecture schools understandably receive special attention. Just as universities try to build and equip world-class science labs to attract top scientists, new buildings for schools of architecture presumably reflect the state-of-the-art in architectural education. These buildings have the potential of drawing great attention, while enhancing a school's ability to attract top students and faculty, and increased financial support from alumni and donors. They can also galvanize the academic community when alumni, faculty, and students help select the architect, and give input on the design process, the building program, and the design itself.

Historical precedents for using "signature" architects in the design of architecture schools include Walter Gropius at the Bauhaus in Dessau, Mies van der Rohe at I.I.T. in Chicago, and Frank Lloyd Wright at Taliesin West in Scottsdale. That tradition remains in place today, with Philip Johnson at the University of Houston, Peter Eisenman at the University of Cincinnati, Scogin/Elam at The Ohio State University, and Steven Holl at the University of Minnesota. Yet, in spite of the special significance of this building type, the architecture of schools of architecture has received little critical discussion (Giovannini 1996). Although some authors have written systematic reviews of architectural education, no book has focused on the architecture buildings themselves.

> **IMPROVING BUILDING PERFORMANCE**
>
> Our years of study revealed many suggestions for improving designs for designers. Some findings connect with a substantial empirical knowledge base, and others raise questions about traditional practice. We believe that clients and designers can improve building performance by following the ideas discussed in this book.
>
> **Box I.1**

Our examination of designs for designers unveiled some recurring strengths and weaknesses; and it found that some designs, such as the University of Texas, worked well, while others, such as the University of Sydney, did not. Designs by some internationally known designers had significant flaws, while the work of other designers did not.

Looking in depth at many schools, this book tried to answer the question, "What makes a good design for designers?" It also considers which lessons can be applied to other kinds of buildings.

In this book, we want to tell you what we learned. We outline the background to our work, our methods, and our key findings. Throughout the book, we have boxes for the lessons learned that give guidance on how to achieve the desired end.

OUR JOURNEY

In 1960, Kevin Lynch's *The Image of the City* showed the importance of observing and interviewing people in order to gauge their shared mental images of places. His work transformed the way many design professionals and social scientists dealt with urban form. It complemented the "art" approach to architecture with a social science approach that tried to gauge user reactions. In this book, we have used this same approach to evaluate the architecture of schools of architecture. Here's how we did it.

GETTING STARTED

Visits to architecture schools around the world and discussions with faculty showed that their designs often shared the same problems. The designs for newer buildings also seemed not to have learned from their predecessors. We saw the need for a knowledge base to guide designs for schools of design, a knowledge base that would serve practice and education in schools of design, provide guidance for other university and non-university facilities, and stand as a broader model for an evidence-based and forward-looking design process.

Having conducted many post-occupancy evaluations, Nasar and Preiser knew it would take time and resources to do the multiple evaluations needed to build such a knowledge base. Several grant applications to cover the travel and research for such a project came back rejected. Those rejections only increased our resolve. If we could not do it alone, we would do it with others. We valued collaboration and had worked with more than a hundred colleagues from around the world. With the Internet, we saw a way.

In 1999, we sent out queries on listservs saying that we planned "to initiate a project to do post-occupancy evaluations of new buildings (or additions) for schools of architecture. As many of you work and teach in such buildings, we wanted to elicit your help. We're looking for faculty or students . . . who would agree to run the survey in their school. We hope that through evaluating the performance of these new designs, we can come up with some guidelines for the future (things to avoid, things to do, etc.). Please let me know if you or a student would like to participate."

Many people responded. To each, we emailed a draft instrument (drawn from work by Preiser et al., 1988 and Nasar, 1998) for them to review. For purposes of comparisons, we wanted to have the post-occupancy evaluations based on a common survey method and procedures for analysis. After several revisions, the group agreed on shared instruments and coding. The shared method allowed for comparison across the schools to provide what we hoped would become a knowledge base to guide the design of future, new buildings, or the renovation of existing ones. As the project proceeded, and we talked about it with others at conferences, we learned that some faculty had conducted evaluations using different methods. We welcomed those evaluations to the project, believing that if independent measures found similar findings, we could have more confidence in the results.

MULTIPLE APPROACHES

This book examines architecture schools from multiple directions, including the history of architectural education and building form, typologies of schools for architecture, systematic post-occupancy evaluations (case studies) of schools of architecture, and comparisons across those evaluations.

CASE STUDIES

We eventually gathered post-occupancy evaluations of seventeen schools of architecture (eleven independent evaluations plus a set of evaluations by students of seven schools—one of which overlapped one in the eleven—by students in the eleven). These systematic user evaluations of the function, technology, and aesthetics followed Vitruvius's much quoted dictum for architecture achieving "firmness, commodity, and delight." Although each case study on its own offers a comprehensive and systematic review of the facility, we studied the evaluations for shared strengths and weaknesses, and for lessons about process to guide future designs.

STATISTICAL COMPARISONS

Prior to developing a program or selecting a designer, clients may visit other buildings for comparison. But how do they know the relative merits of what they see?

Ten post-occupancy evaluations used the same instruments and coding procedures. This included three schools not included in the case studies in the book—Guelph, University of Hawaii, and University of Michigan. For this set, we compared the responses to the exterior of the building, the responses to the features of the building, and the ratings of spaces in each building. Those analyses gave us a core set of higher-performance designs; they scored better than the other buildings in all three evaluations. The analyses also gave us a set of low-performance designs that scored lower than the other buildings on the various measures.

HISTORICAL INFORMATION

We supplemented the statistical information with invited chapters on the history and future of architectural education, the history of architecture buildings, the future of architecture buildings, and the typology of architecture buildings. All of this helped us make sense of the findings and arrive at five concepts for better buildings.

FIVE CONCEPTS

We did not approach this project with pre-conceived ideas of what we would find. We sought to uncover concepts from the data. Some concepts apply more directly to clients or users, while others offer guidance for the designer. Although we developed the guidelines in relation to schools of architecture, many of them apply to the design and design process for other kinds of facilities, on-campus and off.

Perhaps most importantly, we found one simple and intuitive finding: *The better designs tended to have a well managed process.* This involves having a good master plan, and a pre-design process that involves people and that comprehensively programs the requirements for the facility for all of the relevant aspects of the design. This does not necessarily mean a completely restrictive program; to the contrary, it may identify areas for flexibility and durability. But good programming can save money, while predicting and preventing design problems. It also involves investing the time and resources to select the right design team for the project and campus, by studying their work, checking references, conducting interviews and office visits, and finding a local architect of record. Good solutions also entail managing the design process and giving the designer feedback from the users and clients, especially early in the process before concepts get developed too far. We found it troubling that while some universities had good processes in place, they chose to

Box I.2

FIVE CONCEPTS

1. **Manage the Process**
   Developing a solid program for the design, selecting the right design team for the project, and having a strong participatory review process by all stakeholders (from users to clients and owners) can help prevent problems, identify innovative ideas, and get people to buy into the solution.

2. **Design Compatible Exteriors and Warm Interiors**
   Designs for designers are often the ugliest buildings on campus. They need not be. Good design can make a statement and still fit into its context in scale and materials, with welcoming interiors that convey warmth.

3. **Design a Gathering Space (Atrium) with Lots of Natural Light**
   Academic buildings need a heart, a well lit central gathering place where informal interaction and learning can take place.

4. **Make It Easy for People to Find Their Way Around**
   Visitors and first-time users must be able to navigate to and through the building with ease. Illegible designs create inefficiencies and stress for first-time visitors and for occupants who get interrupted to give directions.

5. **Back to Basics: Ensure Good Acoustics and HVAC**
   Most of the schools we studied had serious problems with acoustics, temperature, and lighting, hindering activities in studio and crit spaces. Most interior spaces need acoustical privacy, decent lighting, and temperature control.

relax them for the school of architecture, or for a celebrity designer. Finally, clients and architects need to evaluate the project after occupancy to fine-tune it and to learn for future projects.

We hope that in addition to offering some useful guidance for design, this book raises a broader awareness of common problems in design, and how to make architecture work better for building occupants in the future.

While some of the problems discussed in this book arise from economic and site constraints, many arise from indifference, lack of concern, or a lack of knowledge about how architectural design affects people. Many architects put their personal aesthetic priorities first, and through their involvement in the design, they can lose the perspective of the typical user or the first-time visitor. In one case, the architect told a consultant working on signage that campus parking garages should not have any signs in order "to force visitors to interact with people on campus to find their way around." Luckily, someone took the position of the typical user, and told the architect: "Most people on campus disagree . . . When I first visited the campus I arrived on a Sunday, when there was no one in the garage to give me directions" (Nasar, 2004). In summary, while designers often try to satisfy the client by focusing more on cost or maintenance than usability, usability must not take a back seat to other concerns.

In one famously flawed design, an architect told the client and his guests to move their chairs to avoid a roof leak. Instead of having the client ask users to adapt to a flaw, we would rather arm clients with the information to

---

MANAGE THE PROCESS

Guidelines

- **Program Well**
  Good designs had a better pre-design process than flawed designs. Pre-design requires real participation by the stakeholders, and a programming process that gathers relevant information on all aspects of the design. Good programming can save money as well as predict and prevent design problems.
- **Select the Right Design Team**
  Good project management involves doing the research to select the right designer, studying their work, checking references, conducting interviews and office visits, and ensuring a collaborative team.
- **Manage the Design Process**
  A strong review process with participation by users and the client to manage the design will help ensure that it satisfies client and user needs. Many universities do this well. But, to get a celebrity design, they may relax the process and give the celebrity designer more latitude. This will often result in costly and dysfunctional buildings. Good designers can work within constraints to create an innovative solution.
- **Evaluate**
  After occupancy, learn from the occupants through a post-occupancy evaluation. This can identify correctable problems to make the design work better; and it can inform future designs. It also lets users now that their opinions matter.

Box I.3

prevent the flaw. We hope this book both stimulates in you a way of thinking about architecture, and encourages you to become an advocate for an architecture in which users do not have to move their chairs to have a satisfactory experience, an architecture that is aesthetic because it works for, protects, and delights people.

TRANSFORMING
ARCHITECTURAL
EDUCATION

PART I

ROBERT GUTMAN

REDESIGNING ARCHITECTURE EDUCATION

University schools of architecture are an American invention. In Europe, architecture schools were sponsored by architectural clubs, such as the Architectural Association in London, or were located in arts and crafts schools and academies of fine arts. These latter formations were typical of many architecture programs in Germany and France, including the notable *École Des Beaux Arts* in Paris. In this country, formal architecture education began just after the end of the Civil War at the Massachusetts Institute of Technology, the University of Illinois, and Cornell University.

A major purpose behind this American movement was to upgrade the social rank and intellectual competence of architects. It was believed that university schools would advance knowledge of design and building science beyond the capability of architects who came from a background in the building trades. The schools were also intended to democraticize access to the profession for the rising middle classes. It was widely believed that to provide architects with a liberal education would enable architecture to

This is a revised and updated version of the article, "Redesigning Architectural Education" which appeared in the journal *Architecture* in August 1996.

acquire a status and level of compensation closer to the better organized professions of law and medicine.

BACKGROUND

Broadly speaking, over the last 140 years, the university schools of architecture have accomplished the goals set for them. By 2003, there were 125 accredited schools in the United States and Canada (Association of Collegiate Schools of Architecture, ACSA, 2003, p. 9). In the academic year 2002–2003, approximately 36,000 full-time and part-time students were enrolled in the accredited schools. Architects in this country enjoy a very high prestige with the general public, as is demonstrated in surveys of the status rankings of different occupations. (The National Opinion Research Center, NORC, affiliated with the University of Chicago, has been conducting surveys of occupational prestige since 1949, with the latest published version appearing in 1989. These surveys show architects ranked higher than engineers, lawyers, dentists, physicists, and authors but below Supreme Court Justices, physicians, and state governors. For the 1949 survey, see North and Hatt, and for subsequent survey results see Inter-University Consortium for Political and Social Research, www.icpsr.umich.edu). The architectural profession as a whole obviously exhibits a more comprehensive understanding of the full range of component skills required for building fabrication than any other group in the building industry. The schools also play a central role in generating new design ideas. Since the end of World War II, innovative design ideas in American architecture have been overwhelmingly the product of architects who have university appointments, on a full or part-time basis. But criticism of the schools by practitioners has escalated almost in direct proportion to their achievement. What is responsible for this curious outcome?

Architectural practice remains a troubled and beleaguered endeavor, even though some architects are now celebrities and even though there is more attention by a mass audience to architecture and design than in any previous period of American history. Some critics, and some architects too, argue that architecture focuses too much energy on winning commissions for monumental buildings and on esthetic or stylistic issues, while ignoring many environmental, housing, and urban design questions that are more closely related to the needs of the average user.

A more fundamental source of complaint among practitioners is that the architect's cultural importance does not translate into power in the economic and political realms. Despite their prestige, architects still are poorly

paid compared to lawyers, physicians, surgeons, and even unionized teachers. They do not make policy, even in the realms where they are knowledge-
able, such as preservation, land development, and housing. Their advice is
not sought by politicians as much as architects would like, or perhaps as
much as it should be. Unfortunately, this division between the cultural and
political roles of architects has been true throughout most of the profession's history.

Many clients display a personal fascination with architecture, and some
are transfixed by buildings that display the artistry of the architect. But when
it comes to hiring design services, these same clients are inclined to hire
services at lower cost from draftspersons, interior designers, engineers,
contractors, and now construction managers. To the degree that architects
have been able to acquire a certain modicum of political and economic
power, they do so as the client's representative in the building process. Corporate, government, and institutional clients have concluded, however, that
the building process often goes more smoothly by circumventing the architect and dealing directly with contractors and construction managers. Not
surprisingly, given architects' lack of control over the professional realm,
they are frequently labeled a "weak" profession, in spite of their high rank in
surveys of occupational status.

MORE IS LESS

Architecture schools have contributed
astonishingly little to the relief of their divided fate, although they are the
most robust constituency within an otherwise vulnerable profession. The
schools clearly are less buffeted by market forces and are much more secure
in their position than the typical practice. Their enrollments, budgets, and
number of faculty jobs have remained stable or have grown as the number of
students has increased. Their survival has generally been assured even during
periods when the demand for architecture services in this country has
slowed. A few university administrations have tried to diminish their architecture budgets by amalgamating them with allied disciplines, such as art,
art history, or planning, but this effort does not seem to have weakened the
schools where this move has occurred, such as UCLA or Washington University (St. Louis). To some degree architecture schools, as in schools for
other professions, have benefited from the admission of women students.
Also, there is some evidence that architecture schools actually fare better
when there are fewer jobs for architects. During the recession of the early
1990s, for example, because of the availability of tuition loans, scholarships,

and grants, many architects with first professional degrees discovered it was more advantageous to study for an advanced degree than to keep looking for jobs that did not exist.

Practitioners continue to criticize the schools because their curricula focus on training in design skills and on fields such as architectural theory. In part, the latter emphasis has developed to secure the position of the architecture schools within the university system. Many architecture teachers believe it is to their advantage to demonstrate competence in realms of learning that connect them more prominently to the humanistic disciplines. Another side of this emphasis is that most schools are unable to acquire the funds that support research in the science and engineering-based subjects that practitioners believe are more essential for the building task. Design, history, and theory, by contrast, are fields that can be investigated with the modest resources provided by architecture school budgets.

ARCHITECTURAL KNOWLEDGE: BEYOND DESIGN

As a result of the universal emphasis on design, students graduate with considerable mastery of this area, but often without much know-how in building technology and construction. This pattern reverses a situation that dominated American architectural education in the 19th century. The curriculum of many of the early university schools, for example, dealt with construction during the first two years and did not teach design until the last year (in the three-year program that was standard at that time). New graduates today covet design roles in practice and assume that "designing" is what practice will enable them to do. In many ways, the preoccupation with design is laudable and surely has been a factor in the improved design quality of American buildings. But there is a growing complaint from practitioners about the technical incompetence of new graduates. More disturbing is that this concentration on design skill leads to immense frustration among young architects. There are simply not many opportunities to do design work in the average firm. Several studies have shown that only 10 percent of the average senior architect's time is spent on this function in the building process. The amount of time devoted to design appears to diminish with seniority (cf. Gutman, 1988; Royal Institute of British Architects, 1962).

For all the criticism leveled at the schools, they still carry tremendous weight in the architectural community. With this prestige, the expectation has developed that they constitute the principal source through which the knowledge necessary for practice will be transmitted to students. This certainly was not the supposition when the university schools were inaugurated. On the contrary, it was generally assumed that formal education would elevate the position and enlarge the competence of the profession, but that a great deal of the learning would still require on-the-job training, as was also evident in the professions architecture was attempting to emulate. In fact, the education provided in the universities was regarded as supplementary, a kind of polish. It was generally assumed that the basic form of architectural training would be apprenticeship in an office. This system prevailed in almost all Western countries. There is reason to believe that the United States was alone, and in some respects still is unique, in emphasizing the academic version of architectural education. Partly, this outcome follows from the system of undergraduate collegiate education, which requires that students who intend to become architects study liberal arts subjects; and the related development for many colleges that do not have professional architecture schools to allow students to major in architecture while undergraduates.

With most architecture programs specializing in the teaching of design skills, and with all schools (some more than others) emphasizing the historical and theoretical underpinnings of design ideas, the current curriculum puts recent graduates at a disadvantage. *The schools probably now teach a smaller fraction of the totality of knowledge and skill required for practice than in any period since professional programs were established.* The reason for the situation is obvious: the scope of architecture as a discipline is expanding. The number of fields in which practitioners must be informed grows constantly, for example: the issue of sustainability; the development of new, lighter, and more flexible materials; and rapidly changing relationships between design and fabrication, often marked by an emphasis on systems of pre-fabrication. The only new technology that the schools have adopted wholesale is computerization. The use of computers seemingly enhances proficiency in design skill, and although expensive to introduce, is easily made compatible with the studio system. The results of learning appear more quickly and in more finished form. On the other hand, an increasing number of instructors are dubious about the widespread reliance on computerization. Some believe digital drawing stifles creativity.

Architectural firms themselves are now major generators of architectural knowledge. The most dramatic examples of the innovative role of practice have been in the development of software and information technology, innovations often generated in the large firms before they were developed in the schools. In devising new structures for practice, in designing new building types, and in conceiving new combinations of professional roles, the firms' expertise is frequently far ahead of the thinking in the schools.

Firms often have an advantage in introducing new ideas and technologies because they are compelled to serve clients and keep ahead of the competition. Architecture schools are shielded against the pressures of the marketplace, which has sometimes been beneficial, but in other respects, diminishes the capacity to respond to opportunities. Important research can emerge first in firms because large, corporate practices have greater financial and personnel resources than do the schools. Clients underwrite research as a project cost, and they expect a usable product to be delivered more quickly than if they were to finance research at a university.

A big question architectural education faces now is how to provide students with the more comprehensive knowledge and experience that the field as a whole is accumulating and that the profession is generating. My answer is that that there is a certain amount that the schools can do on their own, but that the real solution is to reshape the prevailing institutional relationship between the schools and practice. *Architecture firms and architecture schools must be more closely integrated.* The schools seem to be able to teach courses, seminars, and studios that reflect the new fields that have emerged, for example, on sustainability, universal design (Preiser and Ostroff, 2001), innovative fabrication, and materials. These efforts are competent, and students are responding positively. However, to make instruction in these subjects more teachable, topics are usually simplified and their applications idealized. Furthermore, although architecture has the considerable advantage of utilizing the studio method, many of the newer developments in the field are tough to handle in the studio, either because of the limited cubic footage of the space or the restricted amount of time assigned to studio.

LIFE-LONG LEARNING THROUGH CONTINUING EDUCATION

When I say that the only genuine solution is to transform the current institutional relationship between the schools and practice, and integrate the two more closely, I mean that the schools must assume a more active and influential role in the continuing education of the students after they get their degrees. At the present time, this responsibility is put almost exclusively in the hands of the American Institute of Architects (AIA) and the National Council of Architectural Registration Boards (NCARB), through the agency of the Intern Development Program (IDP). IDP now includes some very comprehensive and well written monographs on various critical issues in contemporary practice. Among the topics covered in the monograph series are ethics, sustainability, and improving building performance. However, so far as I can tell, the schools have no authority in this operation, which is completely controlled by NCARB and the firms in which the novice is employed. Why couldn't schools or the Association of Collegiate Schools of Architecture (ACSA) and the organizations representing practitioners set up collaborative endeavors, in which schools and practices would operate together? Such endeavors should be especially easy to achieve for firms and employees who are situated in cities where schools exist. Even if there are no schools nearby, I believe cooperative arrangements are feasible.

The lack of connection between a school and a practice is one of the principal reasons why IDP has not been more effective, and why many young architects regard the fulfillment of the program's requirements as a joke. Except in unusual cases, the staff members in the firm responsible for running these programs are not experienced educators, and are unlikely to have much knowledge of the relationship between what the novice is studying in the IDP program and the knowledge acquired in his or her academic education. Neither NCARB nor the AIA member firms are to blame for the current situation. The schools are equally if not more culpable.

This is not a radical proposal, even though it departs from the current situation. We already have examples of schools that have made office experience an essential part of their curriculum. There is a case for expanding the number of schools that make available to their students a version of the cooperative education program, for which the School of Architecture and Interior Design at the University of Cincinnati has long been famous. It will celebrate its centenary this year. Rice University sponsors a similar program for its undergraduate architecture students in their final year. We also can regard as models the many community design workshops attached to schools, which remain the most common form of work experience through which students receive academic credit for office experience. Any one of these three types of programs has the great advantage that students have a chance to work in offices, and while they are doing so, the school maintains a relationship and exercises some control over the work experience. I am advocating that some version of this relationship between school and practice become more widespread and be maintained after students have received their degrees.

CONCLUSION

We live in a world of continuing education. All professions insist on it as a condition of their members maintaining the qualification to practice. Even nonprofessional organizations regard continuing education as mandatory training for workers at all levels.

Architects have joined this world by complying with state registration board and AIA requirements to acquire continuing education credits. Several large firms conduct in-house training programs for employees at all levels to acquaint them with new developments in the field, even after the architect has achieved registration. It is to the credit of the AIA and NCARB that they inaugurated the IDP program, and that they continue to advocate its use. The delinquents in the mix, I regret to say, have mainly been the schools. With rare exceptions, they have focused their attention on the education of their students while they are in the student role, but have not paid much attention to enhancing the competence of their graduates once they enter the world of practice. Architects don't have the good fortune of physicians who receive their practical training in a hospital setting *before* they sit for their board exams; nor are they as lucky as lawyers whose schools have inaugurated larger and more frequent programs of clinical legal education. But the fact that the institutional arrangements are missing in architecture is all the more reason to invent them. The profession needs these liaisons between schools and practice. The schools have the administrators, the teachers, and the budgets to help launch the effort. Many firms have supported the Cincinnati and Rice programs, or have employed students during the summer. They surely will be happy to collaborate with the schools of architecture to integrate academic education and education in practice.

DANIEL S. FRIEDMAN

2

ARCHITECTURAL EDUCATION ON THE VERGE

> A philosophy is never a house; it is a construction site.
> — G. BATAILLE

> If the people who are currently building nanotechnology and virtual reality have their way . . . what we think of today as architecture will be considered as something like classical music . . .
> — W. GIBSON

> Computers are only the tip of the iceberg.
> — A. PICON

The aim of this essay is to sketch briefly three related developments that suggest fundamental changes in the ways we might soon teach and build: first, the widening influence of contemporary theory on building composition; second, the proliferation of pedagogies that dissolve professional or disciplinary distinctions based on scale; and third, the shift from linear perspective to virtual modeling and its impact on the relation between the logic of representation and the logic of construction.

The first development involves a shift in emphasis from static to dynamic form. Deeper, more precise understandings of time and movement suggest the radical transition from plane and solid geometry to morphogenesis. Complex systems have effectively displaced classical proportion and order as the basis of formal experimentation. In this new compositional vocabulary, *field* supersedes *figure, event* supersedes *object,* and *vector* supersedes *axis.* Such terms derive in part from the analysis of ecology and landscape, intricate systems that "escape definitive control or closure" and "address the complexity of loosely structured organizations that grow and change with time" (Allen and Corner 2003). Design pedagogies that use animation software to stimulate the exploration of dynamic form are increasingly commonplace.

Most of these pedagogies stage formal exploration within a theoretical framework heavily influenced by the contemporary avant-garde, trailed closely by the popular press, which regularly showcases heterodox (or eccentric) digital composition.

The second development results from the confluence of these new theories of form with the ever-widening discourse on sustainability. Energy conservation and sustainable technologies now influence policy in both the marketplace and the university; more and more, commercial manufacturers market "green" design. Related research extends sustainable principles through the transfer and adaptation of manufacturing technologies from the automotive and aerospace industries to building construction (Kieran and Timberlake 2004). One characteristic of the overlapping pedagogies that exercise these discourses is increasing sensitivity to the behavior and interdependency of dynamic networks across multiple scales of production. Distinctions between small, medium, and large are therefore increasingly difficult to maintain or enforce, both within and outside the academy.

The third development relates to new digital technologies that can precisely model and specify the three-dimensional construction of a building in virtual space and time. Commonly known as building information modeling, this technology heralds an epistemic shift in the relationship between representation and construction; further compounding its consequences are time-annihilating global markets and increasing demand for digital interoperability. Building information modeling is an established practice in the aviation and automotive industries; Boeing built its new 777 aircraft first in a computer. Once Building Information Modeling (BIM) takes hold in the construction industry, it will accord unprecedented authority and advantage to anyone who can command it, which is why it bears so vividly on the future of the professional curriculum. Whereas the first two developments present promising opportunities for new ways of thinking about form and design, building information modeling presents new ways of thinking about business and construction, with seismic consequences for architecture.

In themselves, advanced digital media and sustainability do not suggest a dramatic break with mainstream practices, but rather the continuous adjustment of methodologies and techniques in response to stimuli within and beyond the university. However, in confluence with the novel capabilities of building information modeling, these trends begin to suggest a radically different educational mission than those that inadvertently perpetuate both social and intellectual distance between architects and builders. Unlike advanced digital animation programs that allow designers to explore the formal and topological effects of dynamic forces, building information modeling allows users to manipulate data points that embody parameters such as dimensions, specifications, material properties, structural behavior, and cost. In principle, building information models connect all the data points in an assembly, such that a change to any part registers throughout the whole. Building information modeling transforms the conventional relationship between representation and construction: "Drawings" embody all the properties of "reality"; thus, the more operators know about how real things behave, the more they can optimize both compositional and economic benefits.

As Phillip Bernstein, Vice President of Building Solutions at Autodesk and adjunct professor at Yale University School of Architecture, and other industry leaders note, new modeling technology itself is not our biggest challenge. The challenge is institutional, more a matter of how we reorganize business practices and legal relationships to fully exploit the value of this form of documentation (Bernstein and Pittman 2004). Building information modeling transforms the fundamental roles and responsibilities of the owner, architect, and contractor in the production of a building. And, although comprehensive interoperability among the various trade-specific software applications is still on the horizon, the true potential of this technology in practice (for architects) presupposes deeper collaboration among parties to the contract. That means dynamic hierarchies, joint authorship, and shared risks, responsibilities, and rewards—and we can expect subsequent changes in the contract language to reflect these new relationships.

This fact warrants serious consideration. If the architect is no longer the sole line of liability—no longer the single individual in the building delivery and life cycle process who understands and controls the relation between part and whole—then what becomes of one's fundamental privileges, claims, and responsibilities? The Latin prefix *archi-* means "chief or principal, first in authority of order" (also, significantly, "primitive, or first in order of time); *-tect,* of course, means "builder" or "carpenter" (although most of us would recoil at being called mere *technicians*). The name *architect* therefore suggests twin responsibilities—authority on the one hand, and origins on the other—which indissolubly couple access to first things with the power of final say.

The traditional authority of the architect issues in part from command over the relationship between the divisions of construction and the work as a whole, especially in respect to its symbolic meanings and ornamentation; and in part from the privileged familiarity with the circumstances under which acts of construction begin, and with the root principles and antecedents that connect present work with history and past traditions. At stake therefore is the name *architect* itself. Who exactly comes first in the order of authority—who ultimately takes responsibility for the work as a whole (including and especially its abstract, unquantifiable, historical, and poetic significance)—is increasingly problematic. Current industry pundits express two minds on this point: some argue that building information modeling marks the return of the master builder; some think it signals the evolution of the architect into a kind of chief information manager.

These new representational technologies clear a space for teachers and practitioners to reexamine the underlying principles of professional education. Chief among these principles is the idea that architecture schools form a community based on their shared fidelity to practice. Many schools situate this principle in larger ideas about public health, well-being, and environmental integrity. Notwithstanding the autonomy of architectural criticism, how effectively we realize these ideas in practice depends largely on our influence in the construction industry.

The clearest expression of a general core mission is the list of student performance criteria produced by the National Architectural Accrediting Board (NAAB). The current list of student performance criteria suggests a weakening commitment to content that addresses the concrete realities of building. For example, only eight of the 34 current NAAB student performance criteria deal expressly and directly with construction technology or building science. Of these eight criteria, only two—building systems integration and technical documentation—require *ability*, defined by NAAB as "the skill in using specific information to accomplish a task, in correctly selecting the appropriate information, and in applying it to the solution of a specific problem." The other six—construction cost control, building materials and assembly, building service systems, building envelope systems, environmental systems, and structural systems—require only *understanding*, defined as "the assimilation and comprehension of information without necessarily being able to see its full implication" (NAAB 2005).

The location of American schools of architecture in the university system has steadily increased pressure on full-time career faculty to adopt university standards of achievement, which in all but a few rare cases preclude full-time practice (Gutman, 2006); typically, public universities limit full-time tenured or tenure-track faculty to about a day of external consulting per week. What began as an effort to augment technical know-how with broad knowledge of the humanities (an educational standard espoused since antiquity), increasingly subordinates direct knowledge of construction to the great humanistic narratives. For decades we have argued that theoretical investments in the humanities repay the profession in the form of moral leadership, yet the social and organizational realities of building production increasingly place the future role of the architect in doubt. Nonetheless, the hunger for solid research in the profession has never been greater, and a long tradition of social scientific, behavioral, technical, and evidence-based scholarship may finally enjoy its proper audience.

What's at stake? According to industry analyst James Cramer, total billings by architecture firms represent less than 3 percent of the annual combined economy for architecture, construction, and engineering (Cramer, 2005). Among the strongest arguments for industry-wide adoption of building information modeling is cost savings: the Construction Users Round Table estimates that as much as 20 percent of the total cost of construction —some figures suggest $100 billion annually—represent errors and their remedies, and that these errors usually stem from the quality of construction documents and other forms of communication (Tibbit 2005; Thorne and Ballard 2005). Developers and contractors have already seized on the economic benefits of building information modeling; most owners care less about who actually operates the software and what the building composition looks like than how much the building costs. One of the earliest and most broadly touted building information modeling case studies, for example, is the construction of the new Mt. Everest ride at Disneyworld in Orlando.

If owners, contractors, and developers see a way to reduce costs dramatically by substituting software for expertise ordinarily supplied by architects during the design development and construction documentation phases of the project, they may very likely conclude that many traditional architectural services are unaffordable, if not obsolete. Our profession will lose its regulatory status; schools will focus on building design, in the same sense adjacent programs focus on graphic, product, interior, and urban design; "architects" will provide building design services for developers and owners, who will assume the risks and responsibilities for the details of construction, and likewise enjoy the rewards.

So the question is: How might we reformulate the curriculum in view of emerging technologies that allow owners, architects, contractors, and subcontractors to virtually manipulate construction in real time, with exacting precision, earlier in the process—during schematic design—such that all parties to the contract enjoy equal access to the model; and such that any change in the assembly of the building or its structure or enclosure or mechanical systems registers instantly and uniformly throughout the composition, adjusting for price, size, and performance, among other parameters? In other words, if this technology stimulates the reformation of architectural services around emerging diagrams of integrative practice, what would a correspondingly integrative curriculum look like? How would preparation for integrative practice be different from current curricular models?

What would happen if schools dismantled not just their current curricula, but also the entire educational apparatus and its resources, and recombined the elements of instruction based on an integrative model, driven by shifting topics, repertoires, vocabulary, skills, and sequence, in dialogue with changing requirements and conditions for practice, including the need for new critical methodologies commensurate with emerging technology? What would happen if schools acknowledged design as an epistemology more than as a skill; reoriented the development of individual expertise to the ethos of the team; expanded the studio as the laboratory for *all* academic activity in architecture; renounced the jury in favor of rounds (on the medical school model); elevated building technology, engineering, construction economics, and professional practice to exactly the same status in its curricular mission as composition; and sponsored legislation that would permit faculty members and students to dissect derelict buildings unhindered by excess liability? What would happen, within this pan-studio model, if programs elected to concentrate certain areas of instruction in all-day workshops that last one week, instead of two ninety-minute lectures per week for fifteen weeks? What would a program look like if the same logic were applied to the delivery of instruction as to the analysis of complex systems—i.e., less a "core" than a flow or fold?

What would a program look like if faculty reorganized their intellectual resources around radically different models of learning and production, based on the need for collaboration, transdisciplinary expertise, improvisational management, and a nonhierarchical distribution of administrative responsibilities? VISA credit card founder Dee Hock, for example, based his highly collaborative management philosophy on a "radically decentralized" organization, "where tolerance of chaos generates order as in nature" (Hargrove 1997). Jazz—"rigorous collective improvisation" (Ratliff 2005)—provides additional models (Brown 2005). These and other alternative organizational schema may obviate certain increasingly questionable nineteenth and early twentieth century pedagogical habits, vestiges of the Beaux Arts and Bauhaus curricula. Moreover, they may help stimulate a more inclusive environment for research, study, and practice—one more hospitable to genuine diversity.

An all-studio curriculum of the future might hybridize integrated instruction in building science and economics with intensified critical methodologies and theoretical analyses. One such promising pedagogy is the case method (for a helpful example of a case narrative specifically developed for use by architecture students and practitioners, see "Casey, Kovacs and Associates: The Broyton Graduate School of Business" (O'Mara 1986). Like studio, 'case method' refers to a *process*. Case method instruction employs a highly disciplined and rigorous classroom exercise, characterized by Socratic dialogue that incorporates stories of events, conflicts, and persons relevant to particular professional practices. In the case method pedagogy perfected by the Harvard schools of business and law, trained instructors use incomplete, open-ended narratives to stimulate the exchange of alternative conclusions, interpretations, and judgments. In the traditional production of case method narratives, trained observers record developments in real time, as events unfold, without predisposition as to outcome. The value of a good case derives from the vitality of the problem, not the solution. Case method interprets, questions, and multiplies alternative outcomes, which students examine and evaluate on the merits, in live discussion; it cultivates agents, not spectators (Rorty 1998).

"The outstanding virtue of the case method," wrote Charles Gragg, "is that it inspires activity under realistic conditions" (Gragg 1954). Case method is above all action teaching, both in the sense that it sparks lively dialogue, and in the sense that it teaches students how to act. In an article about case method, author David Garvin quotes a business school alumnus: " 'The case system,' [he] observed, 'puts the student in the habit of making decisions.' Day after day classes revolve around protagonists who face critical choices. Delay is seldom an option. Both faculty and students cite [a] 'bias for action'—the 'courage to act [in the face of] uncertainty' " (Garvin 2003, Friedman, 2004). The great pragmatist philosopher John Dewey, spiritual father of the case method, warns us, "failure to take the moving force of an experience into account—so as to judge and direct it [based on] what [it's] moving into—means disloyalty to the principle of experience itself" (Dewey 1997).

In 1996, the Carnegie Foundation for the Advancement of Teaching released a long-awaited report entitled *Building Community: A New Future for Architectural Education and Practice* (Boyer and Mitgang). Eight years later, leaders of the Congress of New Urbanism released their own prescription, entitled *The Windsor Forum on Design Education,* which, incidentally, employs nearly identical cover color, typography, and dimensions as the Boyer report. (Bothwell et al., 2004). The Boyer report argued for a more liberal, flexible, and integrated curriculum, but it failed to excite much change. More significantly, the report failed to anticipate the magnitude and intellectual consequence of digital technology. The Windsor Forum advocates for the canon law of New Urbanism, which essentially rejects contemporary theories of form and their application, relying instead on compositional rules and codes that derive from nineteenth- and early-twentieth-century town planning and design.

The Boyer report and the Windsor Forum base their curricula on strikingly similar presuppositions about the modern community. Beside these two, allow me to juxtapose an alternative view, best expressed perhaps in

Bill Readings' critique of American higher education, *The University in Ruins*. Readings argues that the contemporary American university has lost its traditional cultural function. He envisions a new scene of teaching that "opens up a space [where it's] possible to think the notion of community otherwise, without recourse to notions of unity, consensus, and communication. At this point," Readings argues, "the University becomes no longer a model of the ideal society but rather a place where the impossibility of such models can be thought—practically thought, rather than thought under ideal conditions. Here the University loses its privileged status as the model of society and does not regain it by becoming the model of the absence of models. Rather, the University becomes one site among others where the question of being-together is raised. . . ." (Readings 1998).

Schools of architecture are well positioned to reconsider the generative energies of community formation. However, if architecture seeks to lead the complex community of people who build, we have little to lose and much to gain by asking whether the current curriculum is adequate to equip students for changing conditions of practice. Do today's curricula supply sufficient practical knowledge to sustain our authority over the relationship between composition and construction? Do our curricula sufficiently integrate the lessons of design with corresponding lessons in business, engineering, and management? A new, integrated curriculum might have to adjust some of its traditional assumptions in support of new priorities, including the need to produce and disseminate research and knowledge at the intersection of architecture, construction, planning, law, manufacturing, and real estate, among other vocabularies. By intensifying their commitment to the growing challenges of a changing Architecture/Engineering/Construction (A/E/C) market, schools may strengthen strategies for practice that sharpen critical discourse, further stimulate professional innovation, and create new opportunities for both artistic and economic leadership.

3

HISTORICAL DEVELOPMENT OF ARCHITECTURE SCHOOLS

The discipline of architecture can be traced to the seventeenth century when it was given official recognition by the French government. Louis XIV established the Académie Royale d'Architecture, a school for training architects. In 1692, the Académie moved to the Louvre, remaining there, in one location or another, until the Revolution. Although the Académie was closed during the French Revolution it was revived in 1795 with the founding of the Institut de France that soon became known as the École des Beaux Arts (Egbert 1980).

The limited number of students at the Académie indicates that the great majority of French architects were still being trained under the apprentice system. To understand such things as the design of ornament, mathematics, surveying, and all the details related to the construction of buildings, it was necessary to go to different masters to be instructed in each area, which prolonged the time to complete all the studies. As a result, Francois Blondel formed a School of the Arts, in which several professors proficient in each subject would teach in the same place in order to instruct the student in architecture. This private instruction typically consisted of one instructor with one to six students conducting classes in a single room or office, sometimes with the student residing in a room made available in the building or a house nearby. Figure 3.1 shows examples of some work.

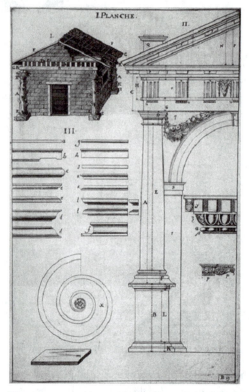

Fig. 3.1.
Example
of student
work from
the École des
Beaux Arts in
Paris, 1816.

German architectural education in the nineteenth century took a somewhat different form. In Berlin, Schinkel designed a building for the Bauakademie that would unite the school that was "scattered in makeshift quarters" into one monumental building (Bergdoll 1994). The four-story building (Figure 3.2) was organized around a central cubic courtyard. By late 1831, the uncompleted building was redesigned to accommodate ground-floor shops on three sides. The main entry had two grand doors—one for the Bauakademie and one for the Oberbaudeputation. With the innovative use of masonry and vaulted construction, the building was heralded by Friedrich Adler in 1869 as a building that "had remained the very model of modern architecture for over thirty years" (Bergdoll 1994). United in the building were the architectural classrooms, administration, library, the building administration (Oberbaudeputation), and map room.

By the early twentieth century, the focus of education at the Bauhaus in Weimar, Germany, had shifted to the integration of form, craft, and technology, with workshops headed by two masters to ensure the students' practical and theoretical development. The Bauhaus did not have a department of architecture, but students formed an architecture seminar to focus development of a program. Government intervention blocked further development at the Weimar institute, and so the Bauhaus moved to Dessau, where instruction was given in the main building, formerly the Grand-Ducal Academy of Art, and with workshops being located across the avenue in the former Arts and Crafts School. The faculty of the former Academy of Art conducted classes in the right wing of the main building, and competed for dominance with the Bauhaus, which had administrative, classroom, and studio space in the building.

Changes in the organizational structure of the Bauhaus manifested themselves in the division of functions into different departments and the integration of instruction in crafts and architecture. The Dessau Bauhaus's first large building characterized the Modern Movement's new conception of form, space, and use of modern materials (Figure 3.3). Primarily designed by the school's founder, Walter Gropius, the building arose out of collaboration among the instructors and students at the Bauhaus, with some of the preliminary design and interior work carried out by students (Sharp 1993). Participation in the design and construction by the users of the building enhanced their appreciation and knowledge of the resulting facility.

Fig. 3.2. Bauakademie Berlin by Karl Friedrich Schinkel, 1836.

Fig. 3.3. Dessau Bauhaus building by Walter Gropius, 1926.

The building has loosely connected functional zones organized into three wings. Service and workshop functions are on one side, separated by a road, and joined by a bridge. Administrative services along with residential and educational functions are on the other. The building's three separate sections are connected by a hub containing an auditorium and food service, located to focus informal exposition and display of work and to create a large communal space. After the building was constructed, critics complained that the flat roofs were inappropriate for the climate, and that the use of large expanses of glazing in areas such as the workshop created well lit interiors, but also overheating problems.

Architectural education took yet another form in England. In 1660, Charles II granted his patronage to the Royal Society, which had a discussion group about architecture, but no responsibility for instruction (Crinson and Lubbock 1994). Meanwhile, the Royal Works served as an informal training ground for the field of architecture as young men progressed through the skills of producing buildings. During the eighteenth century, practicing architects commonly adopted apprenticeship as a means of instruction, although after 1768, pupils could supplement training by attending lectures at the Royal Academy in the evenings, instructing students about theory, graphic skills, and composition. Eventually, King's College, University College, and the Government School of Design established architecture programs.

In America, throughout the mid-nineteenth century, architects received most of their training as apprentices in the offices of self-taught, established architects. According to Henry Cobb (1985), the university-based school of architecture is an American invention. "Although the pedagogical methods employed in the training of architects have evolved principally from European models, the idea that such training should be located in a university, rather than within the profession or in specialized academies, originated not in the Old World but in the New."

Architecture schools had their origin in the United States after the Civil War with the establishment of the Tenth Street Atelier in New York. Its founder, Richard Morris Hunt, modeled the education program on his École des Beaux Arts training. The standard for American architectural education was, however, set by William Robert Ware when in 1868 he organized the architecture program at MIT, the oldest college of architecture in the United States. Ware spent two years surveying architectural programs in Europe and launched an American program similar to the German system of classroom training in engineering and history, in contrast to the French beaux arts emphasis in design and graphic presentation.

The University of Pennsylvania began a program in architecture in 1890,

emphasizing fine arts; in 1903, Phi-
lippe Cret, as head of the department,
brought the strong tradition of the
beaux arts to Penn (Crosbie 1985a).
The Penn department of architecture
was first located in the second floor
of College Hall, designed by Thomas
Richards. The building combined separate divisions, or school wings linked
by shared space, with a library and
chapel in the center. The student population grew to thirty or more students, each requiring space and a desk.
One large room was made available
for the architecture program, and this
served as drafting space. Shared by sev-

Fig. 3.4. The
open studio
in the United
States may
have its
origins at
MIT design
studio at the
start of the
twentieth
century.

eral classes, the resulting cross-level interaction allowed the newer students
to learn from the more experienced ones (Strong and Thomas 1990). Figure
3.4 shows one of the first open-studio designs.

The early years of the architecture school as a building type have evolved
from that of a private atelier to a public institution. In the post–World War
II years, most schools seemed to favor a functional articulation as exemplified by the Bauhaus at Dessau. Buildings such as the Architecture Building at
Georgia Tech and Wurster Hall at Berkeley were composed of wings, towers, and slabs, which articulated the various components of the building.
Alan Plattus (1990) explained the different theoretical approaches to buildings that house schools of architecture with the example provided by Harvard. The role of beaux arts monumentality was expressed by Robinson Hall
designed by McKim, Mead, and White in 1904 for the School of Architecture, while the role of architectural program and function was expressed by
Gund Hall, designed by John Andrews Architects in 1972. The twentieth
century reveals how the architecture of schools of architecture has oscillated
between institutional monumentality and functional expression.

Buildings designed specifically for architecture in a university setting are
a recent phenomenon. The past two decades have yielded more than 20 new
and renovated university architecture buildings constructed in America
alone, many of which have been documented in the architecture press. In
very few instances have there been any systematic evaluation of responses to
the new facility by the buildings' occupants. There have, however, been anecdotal reactions from critics, students, and faculty. For example, in 1969
students purportedly set afire the Yale School of Architecture, housed in the

1963 Art and Architecture Building (Figure 3.5), designed by Paul Rudolph. By the late 1980s, the building was "in bad shape, butchered by renovations, dirty, leaky, bombed daily by pigeons who roost in its towers, cold in winter, hot in summer, unbelievably cramped for space" (Crosbie 1988a). Too little daylight reached the internal areas of the workspace since remodeling divided two-story spaces into separate single stories. The original concept was for the drafting rooms to be multi-level affairs, "so you couldn't help but see and be quite aware of what other people were doing" (Crosbie 1988a). According to Rudolph, the division of major spaces and resulting change in light levels was most damaging to the original design intent. The library was "overstuffed" and there was "too little classroom and administration space" (Crosbie 1988a). The building was designed to grow to the north, and was not large enough the day it opened.

In a similar vein, the College of Environmental Design at Berkeley was established in 1959 under the guidance of William Wurster, for whom Wurster Hall is named. Designed by a collaborative group including Joseph Esherick, Vernon DeMars, Donald Hardison, and Donald Olsen, the building was intended to meet Wurster's goal of having a building that looked "Like a ruin that no regent would like. . . . unfinished, uncouth, and brilliantly strong" (Crosbie 1985b). In keeping with this goal, the building is described by students with the statement "there's good, bad, worse, and Wurster." Built out of rough concrete with the internal workings all exposed, the building presents a rough and aggressive appearance.

At Philadelphia, expansion in the late 1950s meant a new building for the Penn School of Architecture. The building was not well received by many of the students and instructors. "For all the building's shortcomings, Penn's experience was not unique. . . . protest also occurred at Yale, Harvard, and Berkeley, each of which built new buildings for the design schools, and each of which found these buildings attacked by their users" (Strong and Thomas 1990).

A building for the teaching of architects should engage, not distract the inhabitants of such a building. However, the lack of any systematic documentation of user responses to architecture buildings clearly suggests a repeat of previous malfunctions and unnecessary dissatisfaction. Post-occupancy evaluations of architecture schools, such as those in this book, have the purpose not of establishing universal solutions, but rather of allowing designers to predict consequences resulting from their design decisions.

THOMAS FISHER

THE ARCHITECTURE SCHOOL
AS A TYPE

While architecture school buildings differ depending on their context and chronology, they all fall into four categories, reflecting the origins of the profession in the nineteenth and early twentieth centuries. These four types, with buildings that range from pure examples to combinations of more than one type, have proved remarkably durable. They have weathered changing theories of architecture and technologies of construction, reflecting the profoundly conservative nature of architectural education, whose studio-based pedagogy has remained largely unchanged over the last century and a half. At the same time, these archetypal forms each reflect a different approach to architectural education, all of which remain influential today, to varying degrees. Finally, these types say a lot about the self-images of architects, revealing some of the sources of our attitudes toward cities and people, as well as toward other disciplines and ourselves.

BACKGROUND

As a building type, architecture schools remain relatively rare, with perhaps no more than 150 structures dedicated to this use in North America. Examining this type, however, results in lessons that apply to more than just this particular kind of building. It helps us understand how architects think, what we aspire to, and how our ideas about our field have changed over time.

THE COURTYARD TYPE

Karl Friedrich Schinkel's 1836 Bauakademie in Berlin established the first of these architectural types (Figure 4.1). A palazzo-like building, the Bauakademie had a ground floor of shops, above which stood two floors of offices, classrooms, and studios arranged around an inner corridor and central, open-air court, with exposed brick walls and repetitive windows around the perimeter. Like the mix of artistic and practical education in the Bauakademie's curriculum, this courtyard form mixed academic and commercial activities, standing in the middle of the city, while creating a place apart from the city with its own courtyard.

The courtyard type established a pattern that architecture schools— whether rural or urban—have repeated. The flexibility of the courtyard plan, as well as the sense of community its central focus can create, has probably contributed to its popularity. However, the stand-alone courtyard building may perpetuate the public perception of architects as introverted and standoffish within the academy, as well as to reinforce the view of architectural education as isolated and atypical within the academy.

One of the purest modern examples of this type is the 1960 school at the University of Minnesota, designed by John Rauma of Cerney Associates, with its repetitive narrow windows and studios, classrooms, and offices ringing a square, clerestoried court (Figures 4.2a, b, and c). What this type loses in efficiency (usable space, with single loaded corridors being less

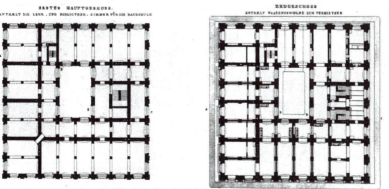

Fig. 4.1. Bauakademie, upper floor left, ground floor right.

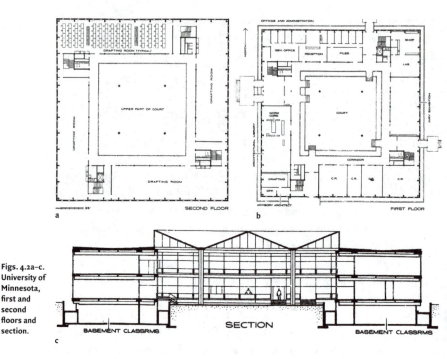

Figs. 4.2a–c.
University of
Minnesota,
first and
second
floors and
section.

compact than double loaded ones), it gains in community, offering a layout that allows students, faculty, and visitors to visually sense the whole.

Variations of this type include the 1959 architecture building at the University of Manitoba, designed by Smith Carter Searle Architects, with both an enclosed space and open courtyard at the center of a rectangular, curtain-walled structure (Figures 4.3a and b). The more recent 1989 addition to the College of Design at Arizona State University, designed by Alan Chimacoff of the Hillier Group, has stacked center spaces wrapped on three or four sides by classrooms, offices, a library, and cellular studios not unlike those in the Bauakademie (Figures 4.4a and b). The latter two buildings modify the courtyard type by providing a greater range and variety of central spaces, suited to the growing diversity of needs within schools.

In other projects of this type, the courtyard gets extruded either upward or outward, with varying effects. Schools such as McCarty, Bullock, Holsaple's design at the University of Tennessee (Figures 4.5a and b) and Philip Johnson's design at the University of Houston (Figures 4.6a and b) have tall atriums, with balcony corridors overlooking their expansive central spaces, creating visual drama and greater efficiency with the stacking of floors, but probably reducing the social interaction and intimacy of the lower-scaled examples of this type. The 1995 building at Illinois Urbana-Champaign, designed by Ralph Johnson of Perkins & Will, modifies the type further

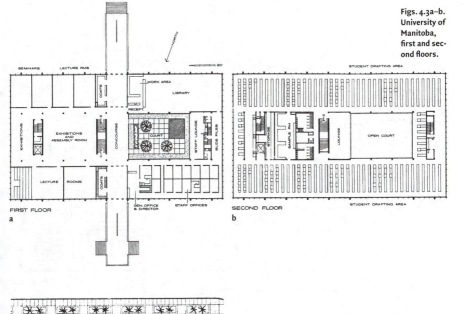

Figs. 4.3a–b. University of Manitoba, first and second floors.

FIRST FLOOR
a

SECOND FLOOR
b

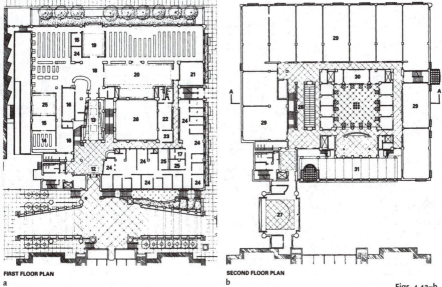

FIRST FLOOR PLAN
a

SECOND FLOOR PLAN
b

Figs. 4.4a–b. Arizona State University, first and second floors.

37

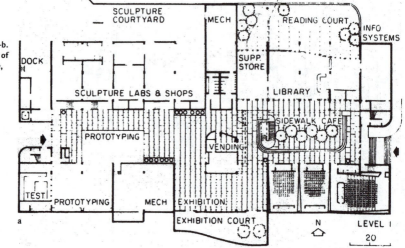

Figs. 4.5a–b.
University of
Tennessee,
first and
fourth
floors.

SCULPTURE COURTYARD

MECH

READING COURT

INFO SYSTEMS

DOCK

SUPP. STORE

SCULPTURE LABS & SHOPS

LIBRARY

PROTOTYPING

SIDEWALK CAFE

VENDING

TEST

PROTOTYPING

MECH

EXHIBITION

a

EXHIBITION COURT

N

LEVEL I

20

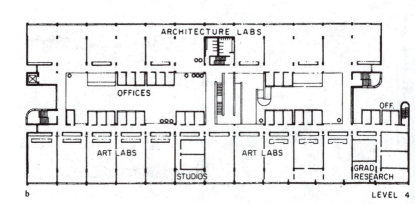

ARCHITECTURE LABS

OFFICES

OFF.

ART LABS

ART LABS

STUDIOS

GRAD RESEARCH

b

LEVEL 4

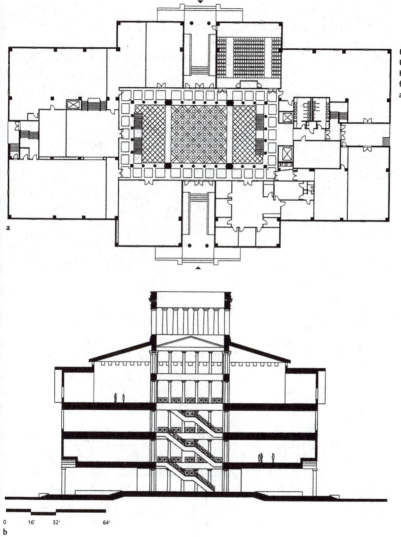

a

0   16'   32'   64'

b

39

(Figures 4.7a and b). It has an L-shaped, multi-story form, with a tall, sky-lit atrium separating rows of faculty offices from the studio and review spaces. The L-shape opens the court out to the campus, while maintaining the efficiency of stacking functions, but with it come noise problems from the mix of activities overlooking the space.

Examples of horizontally extruded central courts also abound. Gwathmey Siegel & Associates' 1991 College of Architecture at the University of North Carolina, Charlotte (Figures 4.8a and b), has a long, two-story, sky-lit court, lined with faculty offices and meeting rooms. Lecture halls and a

Figs. 4.7a–b. University of Illinois, first floor and upper floor.

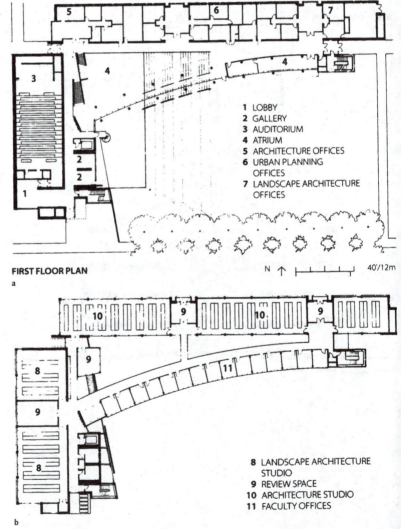

1 LOBBY
2 GALLERY
3 AUDITORIUM
4 ATRIUM
5 ARCHITECTURE OFFICES
6 URBAN PLANNING OFFICES
7 LANDSCAPE ARCHITECTURE OFFICES

FIRST FLOOR PLAN

N ↑   40'/12m

a

8 LANDSCAPE ARCHITECTURE STUDIO
9 REVIEW SPACE
10 ARCHITECTURE STUDIO
11 FACULTY OFFICES

b

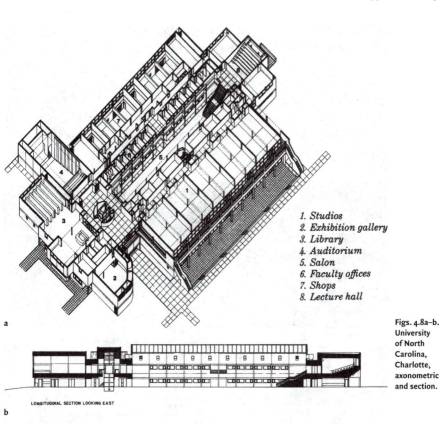

1. *Studios*
2. *Exhibition gallery*
3. *Library*
4. *Auditorium*
5. *Salon*
6. *Faculty offices*
7. *Shops*
8. *Lecture hall*

a

LONGITUDINAL SECTION LOOKING EAST

b

Figs. 4.8a–b. University of North Carolina, Charlotte, axonometric and section.

gallery cap either end of the court, while studios and shops encircle the perimeter. The building has a clear diagram, making way-finding relatively easy, but the court decreases the privacy of the offices that overlook it, with a ratio of length to width that makes the court feel more like a street than a yard. The two double-loaded corridors along either side of the building also reduce the visibility of activities in the court.

The 1988 architecture building at Roger Williams University, designed by Kite Palmer Associates (Figures 4.9a and b) has another variation of the courtyard type. Its extruded court serves as a large circulation space, with classrooms, offices, and library along it, and a large studio space off the back. The building's layout recalls the familiar form of a mall, with a big box attached to one side, placing all of the studios in one large space, with the attendant noise and privacy problems that can come with that.

A 2003 courtyard design for the Florida International University School of Architecture by Bernard Tschumi responds to the local context (Figures 4.10a and b). Suiting the tropical climate, it has an open-air central courtyard, and, reflecting the local Latin culture and South Beach area, it uses brightly colored forms that contain lecture halls, exhibit space, and the like. The building, however, stacks the studios behind a row of review rooms that face away from the courtyard, the main outdoor space.

In all of these courtyard schemes, the central space may provide a sense of identity and community, and, if faculty and students spend time in these common areas, may enhance the learning experience. Over time, though, this type has moved from well proportioned, low-scale courtyards to taller

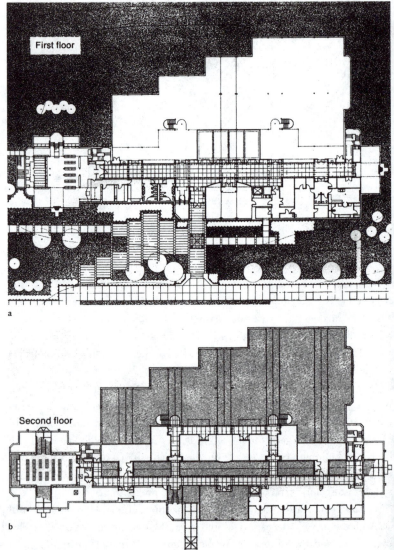

Figs. 4.9a–b. Roger Williams University, first and second floor.

First floor

a

Second floor

b

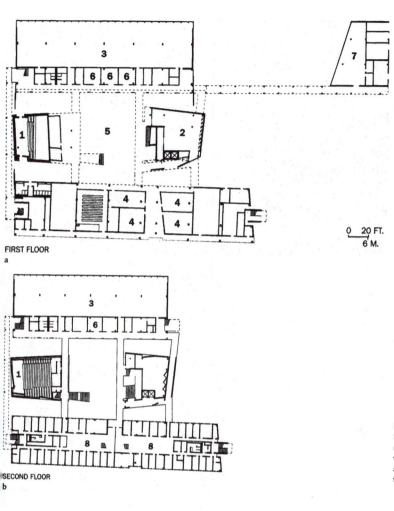

FIRST FLOOR
a

0   20 FT.
6 M.

SECOND FLOOR
b

Figs. 4.10a–b.
Florida Inter-
national Uni-
versity, first
and second
floor.

atriums or longer, mall-like spaces, with an attendant change in reference from that of a traditional academic building to either an office building or a shopping mall. While that change in reference may align more with what students know and understand, it also echoes the growing pressure on universities to move away from traditional academics toward a more vocational or consumer model of education.

THE COMPOUND TYPE

If the atrium or mall now provides a model for courtyard projects, the city remains the point of reference for compound schemes, evident in the first architecture school to fit this type:

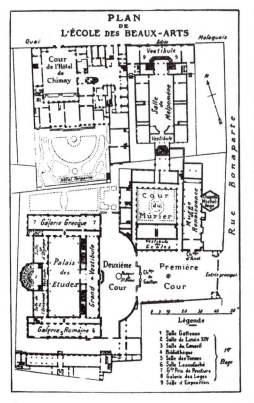

Fig. 4.11.
École des
Beaux-Arts,
site plan.

Felix Duban's École des Beaux Arts. Although the school dates back to 1648, in 1816 it moved into a group of historic buildings in Paris's university district, with an entry court behind a high wall and gate, leading to several buildings clustered around an open-air plaza (Figure 4.11). With so many aspects of modern architectural education, good and bad, deriving from this school—the charrette process, the schematic design focus in studio, the relative lack of contact with real clients, even the all-nighter—it seems fitting that the Ecole's compound of buildings wedged within the city serves as a type that other schools have emulated.

Alvaro Siza's school of architecture at the Universidade do Porto stands as one of the clearest recent examples of the building-as-compound (Figures 4.12a and b.). Occupying a sloping, triangular site, the school consists of a series of studio buildings linked by a below-grade gallery that face an inner yard, and are situated across from the library, exhibition space, auditorium, and administration building. Although it stands somewhat apart from the city, the density—a series of school buildings squeezed together on a small sliver-like triangle site—make it feel like a city unto itself. In that sense, the school serves as an urban model for the students to emulate in their designs, even as the somewhat fragmented layout forces them into more isolated quarters in separate buildings.

The University of Miami has had two schemes by two different architects for an addition, both of which create a compound of the school. Aldo Rossi's design called for a series of linked barrel-vaulted library, office, and support buildings, with a separate auditorium and rotunda, on axis with a meeting/jury room tower (Figure 4.13). Leon Krier's recently completed design, with an octagonal lecture hall and an adjoining, rectangular exhibition gallery and classroom, would have the architectural school stand among the existing complex of the school's buildings, creating a campus of its own. Both schemes have well defined outdoor spaces and a strong formal order in the buildings themselves, although Rossi's scheme, the closely spaced buildings have almost a barracks quality to them, evocative of the way architecture school can sometimes seem like a boot-camp experience, with relatively little time to spend outside its walls.

If the military camp serves as one model of compound type, the medieval cloister serves as another. An example of the latter is Barton Meyer's design for the school of architecture at the University of Nevada, Las Vegas (Figure 4.14). Its cloistered quality recalls the medieval origins of modern universities. A set of sculptured structures—a library, set of lecture rooms, gallery, and administrative offices—sit within a court defined on four sides by studios and classrooms, with a colonnade connecting the complex. While the open desert of Las Vegas allows for such an expansive compound of buildings, so too does the nature of architectural education, which

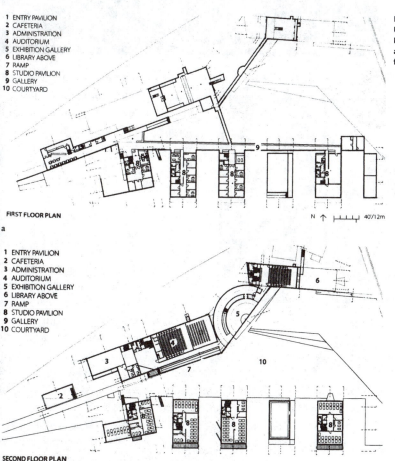

1 ENTRY PAVILION
2 CAFETERIA
3 ADMINISTRATION
4 AUDITORIUM
5 EXHIBITION GALLERY
6 LIBRARY ABOVE
7 RAMP
8 STUDIO PAVILION
9 GALLERY
10 COURTYARD

FIRST FLOOR PLAN

N ↑ 40'/12m

a

1 ENTRY PAVILION
2 CAFETERIA
3 ADMINISTRATION
4 AUDITORIUM
5 EXHIBITION GALLERY
6 LIBRARY ABOVE
7 RAMP
8 STUDIO PAVILION
9 GALLERY
10 COURTYARD

SECOND FLOOR PLAN

b

Figs. 4.12a–b. University of Porto, first and second floor.

Fig. 4.13.
(right)
University
of Miami,
site plan.

Fig. 4.14.
(below)
University
of Nevada,
Las Vegas,
first floor.

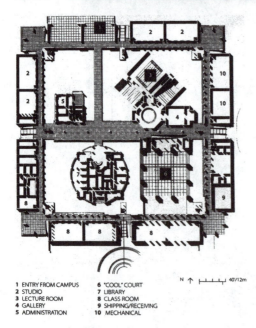

1 ENTRY FROM CAMPUS   6 "COOL" COURT
2 STUDIO   7 LIBRARY
3 LECTURE ROOM   8 CLASS ROOM
4 GALLERY   9 SHIPPING/RECEIVING
5 ADMINISTRATION   10 MECHANICAL

N ↑ ├─┴─┴─┴─┤ 40/12m

needs a smaller amount of specialized spaces and a lot of open and relatively generic studios. The low, spread-out quality of the plan, though, echoes the sprawl of the surrounding city, with considerable distance among its parts.

The idea of a school becoming a city or campus unto itself leads to schools that treat the larger campuses in which they sit as their urban context. At places such as the University of Texas, Cornell, and Columbia, the schools occupy several buildings, many of them historic, at the centers of their campuses, integrating architectural education into the larger university. Their integration shows how architecture can be about background buildings, about fitting in to contexts, even if it sometimes means a physical fragmentation of the schools themselves into more than one building.

New buildings can also serve a campus in this way. Stirling Wilford Associates' Rice school of architecture (Figures 4.15a and, b) stands as an addition to an existing set of buildings, and yet the architects so carefully knit it into the university's fabric that it hardly looks like an addition, extending the materials, proportions, and form of the University's original quadrangle. Stirling continued the compound that is the campus itself, with a central, two-story jury-review space between the old and new wings that echo the central quadrangle outside. If there is a drawback, it lies in the double-loaded corridors having to serve as social space as well as circulation, something that works fine in most disciplines, but that tends to work against the 24-hour community of architecture schools.

MIT offers another version of the compound concept. Part of the campus's "endless corridor," the architecture school occupies a section of the

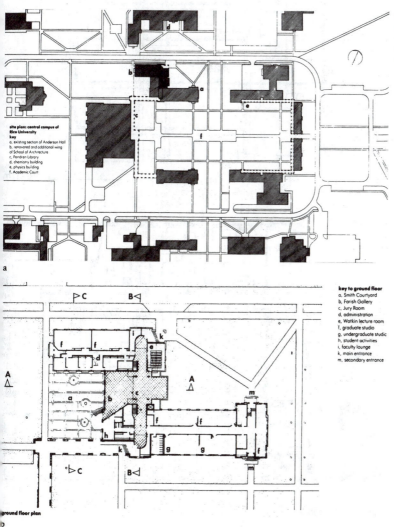

Figs. 4.15a–b. Rice University, site plan and first floor.

site plan: central campus of Rice University
key
a, existing section of Anderson Hall
b, renovated and additional wing of School of Architecture
c, Fondren Library
d, chemistry building
e, physics building
f, Academic Court

key to ground floor
a, Smith Courtyard
b, Farish Gallery
c, Jury Room
d, administration
e, Watkin lecture room
f, graduate studio
g, undergraduate studio
h, student activities
i, faculty lounge
k, main entrance
m, secondary entrance

ground floor plan
b

original campus's single large building, identifying itself with a distinctive interior renovation in 1997 by Leers, Weinzapel Associates and with selective insertions, such as the Rotch Library addition along one side of an inner court, by Schwartz Silver Architects (Figures 4.16a and, b). Here, the architecture school takes its place among an accretion of additions and alterations, evolving over time, inseparable from the compound that is the campus.

Figs. 4.16a–b.
MIT Rotch
Library addition, section
and second
floor plan.

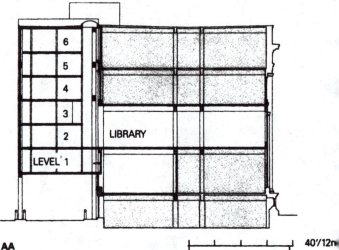

SECTION AA
a

40'/12m

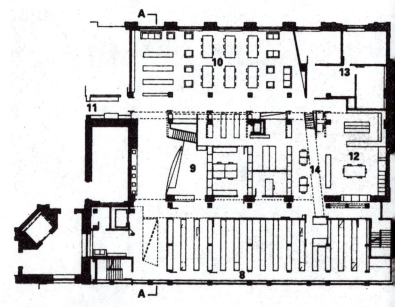

SECOND FLOOR PLAN
b

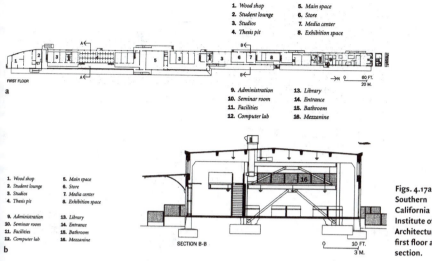

1. Wood shop
2. Student lounge
3. Studios
4. Thesis pit
5. Main space
6. Store
7. Media center
8. Exhibition space

9. Administration
10. Seminar room
11. Facilities
12. Computer lab
13. Library
14. Entrance
15. Bathroom
16. Mezzanine

**Figs. 4.17a–b.
Southern
California
Institute of
Architecture,
first floor and
section.**

Pedagogically, it signals an integration of the architecture program into the intellectual life of the larger university, although it has the effect of working against the separate identity that is also part of a professional program.

The compound type can also occur entirely inside a building, as in the Southern California Institute of Architecture, which occupies a former freight depot whose length has led to the creation of diverse parts, with a number of architects involved—Gary Paige, Kappe Architects Planners, and Studio Works (Figures 4.17a and b). Like all extruded plans, this one allows for a broad range of activities along its length, although that also works to widen the proximity of related activities. The long bar of a building, with its several structures inside its former industrial shell, leads us to the next type: the architecture school as workshop.

THE WORKSHOP TYPE

The first two types of architecture buildings express the often opposite ways in which our profession sees itself in relationship to others: as apart from or a part of our context, creators of isolated objects or contributors to the urban fabric, with a single point of reference or multiple perspectives. The next two types embody a different set of issues, having to do with how we see our own disciplines: as a craft or a fine art, focused on making or thinking.

Walter Gropius's 1926 Bauhaus school in Dessau, Germany, represents one end of this spectrum. Comprising a set of overlapping and interpenetrating bars of buildings, Gropius's design gave form to the interdisciplinary

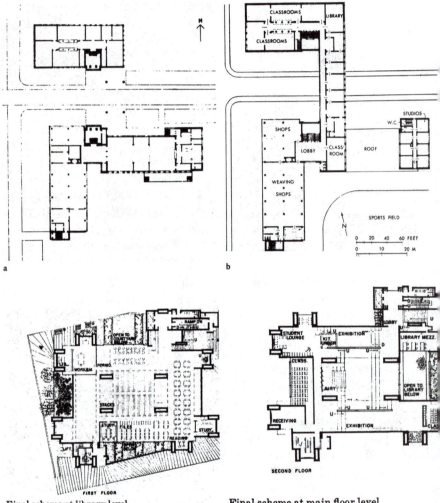

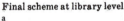

Final scheme at library level
a

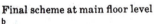

Final scheme at main floor level
b

Figs. 4.18a–b. (top) Bauhaus, first and second floors.

Figs. 4.19a–b. (bottom) Yale University, first and second floors.

nature of the school, where architects, designers, and craftspeople lived an worked together or in close proximity (Figures 4.18a and b). The schoc seemed more like a medieval craft guild, even though the nature of what it students and faculty produced, and the environment in which they worked had a decidedly modern aesthetic, with its walls of glass and open, almos industrial interiors. The pinwheel form of the building, bridging a road, als expressed a different attitude toward context: neither an internalized objec nor an integrated piece of urban fabric, it reaches outward in a way that cor veys a sense of optimism and activism. The Bauhaus curriculum, with it foundation courses in abstract form and space and its dedicated pursuit of Modernism, remains an influence in architectural education today, as does the factory-like building it occupied.

The workshop type has found various expressions in architecture schools. Paul Rudolph's 1963 art and architecture building at Yale stacks the bars of offices, classrooms, and studios vertically around central review and exhibition areas, with multiple levels on each floor, allowing for ample visibility (Figures 4.19a and b). While the interpenetrating floor plates express the interdisciplinary ideal of this type, the fact that the art studios originally stood at the very top and bottom of the building, with architecture in between, suggests the limits of collaboration among fields, even when located in the same structure. Also, despite the pinwheel form of the studios, the building has the character of a fortress as much as a workshop, a place in which people seek privacy as much as sociability.

The 1965 Wurster Hall at Berkeley, designed by Joseph Esherick, Vernon DeMars and Donald Olsen, has more of the expansiveness of the Bauhaus, albeit rendered in a much heavier way, with its exposed concrete walls and sun screens (Figures 4.20a and b). A tall tower containing offices and studios intersects a lower building that forms an outdoor court at its base. Like the Bauhaus, Berkeley has stood by the idea of interdisciplinarity, in the latter case through the broad notion of environmental design, although the verticality of buildings such as Yale's and Berkeley's, with their dependence on elevators to connect people and floors, tends to work against interaction. Nor have their exposed concrete surfaces weathered very well over the years, with both buildings undergoing recent renovations.

Another version of the expansive, workshop type is Steven Holl's industrial-like addition to the University of Minnesota's building, with its concrete-framed, copper-clad wings that extend outward in a rough cruciform, with end-walls of channel glass that

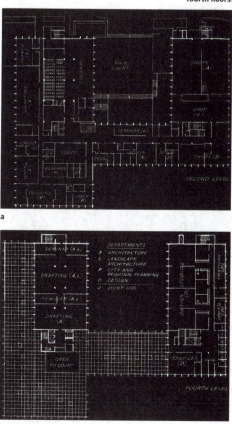

terminate axes on campus and glow like lanterns at night (Figures 4.21a and b). The school's embrace of both architecture and landscape architecture takes the form of alternating buildings and gardens, with constant views from one to the other, and interlocking interior spaces, visually linking studios, offices, and the library. While low enough to encourage interaction, this addition also shows the limits of that goal because of the physical separation of spaces, vertically, required by fire codes. What architects aspire to and what we're allowed to do can differ greatly.

The University of Cincinnati's addition by Peter Eisenman shows how far we can test the design limits for the sake of openness and visibility (Figures 4.22a and b). Consisting of rotated and twisted bars of space, snaking its way up a hill next to the existing building, the Aronoff Center for Design and Art defines a complex interior street along which students from various design disciplines walk, sit, converse, and present their work. Acoustical conflicts occur because of the interpenetrating space, working against the

Figs. 4.21a–b. University of Minnesota addition, second and third floors.

a

b

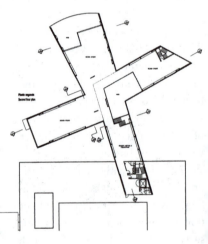
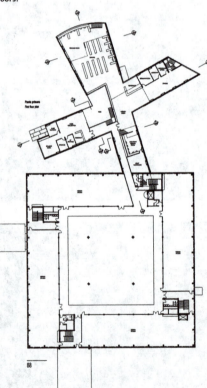

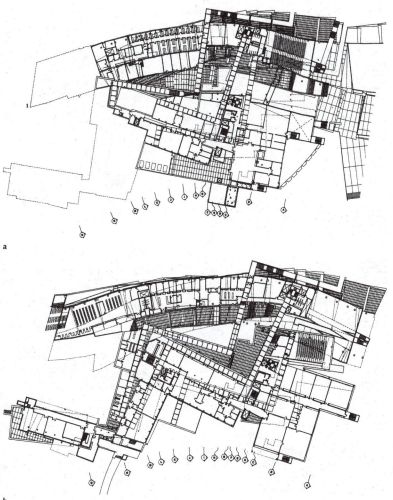

a

b

Figs. 4.22a–b.
University of
Cincinnati,
main and
upper floors.

goal of bringing students and faculty together. And, in the case of Cincinnati, the complexity of the space can disorient and impede access, even as it tries to connect people and activities.

THE ATELIER TYPE

If the workshop-like Bauhaus envisioned a school in which various disciplines would interact, breaking down the boundaries and the egos among them, Frank Lloyd Wright's Taliesin

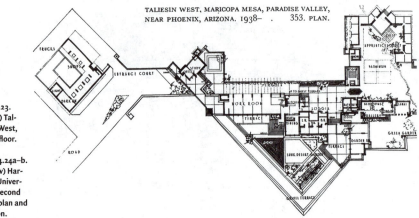

TALIESIN WEST, MARICOPA MESA, PARADISE VALLEY, NEAR PHOENIX, ARIZONA. 1938– . 353. PLAN.

Fig. 4.23. (right) Taliesin West, main floor.

Figs. 4.24a–b. (below) Harvard University, second floor plan and section.

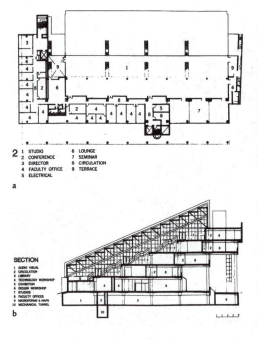

2
1 STUDIO
2 CONFERENCE
3 DIRECTOR
4 FACULTY OFFICE
5 ELECTRICAL
6 LOUNGE
7 SEMINAR
8 CIRCULATION
9 TERRACE

a

SECTION
1 AUDIO VISUAL
2 CIRCULATION
3 LIBRARY
4 TECHNOLOGY WORKSHOP
5 EXHIBITION
6 DESIGN WORKSHOP
7 STUDIOS
8 FACULTY OFFICES
9 MICROFORMS & MAPS
10 MECHANICAL TUNNEL

b

East and West took a different path. They stand in the tradition of the atelier studio, in which architects and their students and staff work in one large room, often on the top floor of a building (Figure 4.23). While the two Taliesins sit out in the countryside in low-slung structures, they echo the tradition of the garret studio in the city, with heavy timber roof framing in Taliesin East and a top-lit roof in Taliesin West. These big rooms eliminate distinctions, but also limit the diversity of activities that can occur there. This type also suggests a blurring between school and practice, which has both advantages and disadvantages pedagogically.

John Andrews's 1972 design of Harvard's Gund Hall offered an influential variation on the single room, with trays of studios stepping down the back of the building under a sloping, clerestoried roof (Figures 4.24a and b). The ability of students to interact and to see each other's work as they traverse the trays gives this form its educational power, although students have also complained about the noise and lack of privacy, something less of an issue in Taliesin's more controlled, office-like environment. The difficulty in accommodating tight urban sites also makes this type of limited value in some contexts.

The new architecture school at Ohio State shows one solution to that dilemma. Occupying a long narrow site, the 2005 Mack Scogin & Merrill Elam designed building has a curving perimeter wall and central ramp, recalling Le Corbusier's Carpenter Center, that distributes people to a staggered series of studio floors, as in Gund Hall (Figures 4.25a and b). Below the studios are offices, classrooms, and public spaces and at the top of the building, a library. This vertical packing of the program along ramps avoids the elevator connections that detract from high-rise projects such as Berkeley and Yale, and it provides a spatial variety and accessibility that can enhance student learning. But, unlike the clear diagram of Harvard, Ohio State's complexity can make it seem labyrinthine.

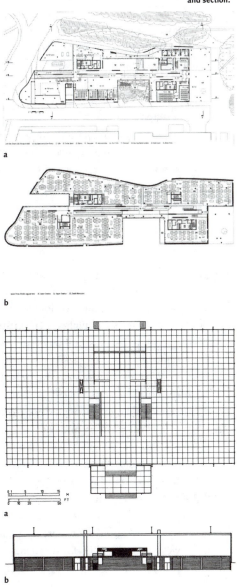

Figs. 4.25a–b. (top) The Ohio State University, first and third floors.

Figs. 4.26a–b. (bottom) Illinois Institute of Technology, plan and section.

On more open sites, the big room can take a more pure form. Perhaps the most famous example of this is Mies van der Rohe's 1956 Crown Hall at the Illinois Institute of Technology, whose main studio space consists of a high-ceilinged, glass-walled room with a few partitions within it (Figures 4.26a and b). While Wright and Mies differed on almost everything architectural, they envisioned a remarkably similar environment for architectural education—a single, large space, with desks neatly aligned. Crown Hall maximizes flexibility and emphasizes openness, two values important in any educational environment, but it also minimizes individual personalization. Mies may not have valued the latter, however many students do.

The University of Michigan's 1974 building boasts the world's largest academic studio, at 30,000 square feet, sprawling across the entire third floor. Here, the traditional daylit garret that has served architects for more than a century gets reinterpreted as a modernist open space, with walls of glass. The advantage of this solution lies in the accessibility of other student work and students' proximity to classrooms, offices, and other support spaces immediately below, although visual and acoustic privacy suffer.

Putting everyone in one large space like this may seem as if the architects had simply given up on creating the diverse spaces that characterize most of what we do, but that kind of "non-architecture" may work well for architecture schools. Another example appears in the "temporary" buildings that schools sometime occupy for extended periods of time, including literal barracks that once stood at the University of Hawaii at Manoa, and Quonset huts formerly at North Dakota State University. These temporary quarters can also be designed with architecture in mind, as happened with the College of Environmental Design at Berkeley, during the major upgrading of its building. While these schools have moved or returned to more permanent quarters, the temporary quarters may have worked surprisingly well. It's a paradox of architectural education that students may thrive in the most casual and even slightly decrepit quarters, perhaps because such facilities may allow a certain freedom and accommodate the intense use—designing, eating, and sleeping—of the studio.

CONCLUSIONS

Although almost every architect over the last century has spent a lot of time in architecture schools, there remains surprisingly little written in the architectural press about them. Whether this stems from our overlooking the obvious or from our wanting to forget the long days and nights spent in studio, architecture schools remain a relatively unexamined building type, something that this book hopes to begin to remedy.

What conclusions can we draw from the above four types? They seem to span time periods and cultures fairly easily, perhaps because studio-based architectural education itself has changed rather little in structure over the last couple of centuries and has also grown into a global subculture that crosses national boundaries. One reason to look at the typology of architecture school buildings now is the distinct possibility that the technological and intellectual transformation going on in architectural education may lead to major changes in some aspects of these schools.

As students almost universally use portable computers and mobile technology in wireless settings, the question arises: do they still need or want to work at assigned desks in often noisy, messy studios? Clearly some, perhaps many, will. But a growing number of students at universities have begun to learn that they can work almost anywhere, putting a premium on spaces that offer comfort or quiet. Schools will undoubtedly still have studios in decades to come, but we doubt they will need as many or have the same characteristics of studios today.

The same could be said for support spaces such as libraries and lecture halls. In a digital age, the library as an institution will not end, but its size and character will change. Likewise, the lecture hall, in which students listen to professors talk with slides projected on screens, may become automated. Lecturing seems destined to split between the online conveyance of information and face-to-face discussion of ideas in seminar settings. Add distance learning to demands for universal access for wheelchair users and the sight-impaired, and the fixed-seat auditoriums of the past may evolve even more in the future.

All that said, the four types of architectural school buildings—courtyard, compound, workshop, and atelier—will probably remain. These cases represent the ways architecture has adapted to pedagogy, and they model higher education itself. Is the university a focused, unified community or a loose confederation of units? Is it a place of uninhibited, interdisciplinary production or one of controlled, disciplined attention? Should it stand apart from the city and campus or become an integral part of it? And should it open itself to its surroundings or create a world of contemplation unto itself? Universities have all answered those questions in different ways and will no doubt continue to do so. In that light, architecture offers not just the means of achieving the visions of a campus, but also a way to demonstrate the range of options a university might pursue. And as we've seen here, the possible variations on those options seem almost endless.

ASSESSING ARCHITECTURE SCHOOL DESIGNS

PART II

WOLFGANG F. E. PREISER AND
JACK L. NASAR

ASSESSING DESIGNS OF
SCHOOLS OF ARCHITECTURE

INTRODUCTION

Based on more than 35 years of design
and behavior research, the editors believe that people can carry out credible
and consistent assessments of building and interior designs, and that those
assessments have value in the understanding of the design professions, their
role in society, and their output. Signature design has stressed aesthetic
statements above all else and the notoriety it can generate for the client and
the designer. As case studies in this book demonstrate, however, some signature designs fall short of satisfying health, safety, and security standards, not
to mention the aesthetic values of those who experience the design.

A new paradigm for design has evolved based on the field of cybernetics,
advocating feedback on the quality of building design and applying the lessons learned in future, similar projects. The system as envisioned by the editors is dynamic, evolving, self-regulating, and resilient and allows a project
to adjust its course as it moves toward a pre-programmed target, such as
high quality design. Along these lines of thought, the famed cyberneticist
Heinz von Foerster showed that there are no absolutes in the world of environmental design, only conventions and standards for the performance
of buildings, standards shared by regions, cultures, as well as code and

standard-making organizations (von Foerster, 1973; von Foerster & Poerksen, 1997).

Ultimately, the issue of design evaluations comes to a fundamental question of values. Whose values and what criteria should architects subscribe to in design? Much of architectural design—and that includes signature design—can be characterized by values that are positioned on bipolar scales, with opposite descriptors, for example: idealistic versus pragmatic; artistic versus functional; formal versus informal; exclusive versus inclusive; top-down versus bottom-up; organic versus artificial; and so on. As noted above, architects, even the most extreme, have to think also about function, cost, materials, and details. Thus the entire argument revolves around which values one emphasizes. According to that view, good design transcends the banality of a building as a box, or simply a container of activities.

We advocate democratic values: bottom-up, inclusive, human-oriented, and user and client involvement concerned with meaning and context (Preiser and Vischer, 1991). From this perspective, successful design must work for and please a majority of users. The democratic principle of equality and inclusiveness also holds true for universal design (Preiser and Ostroff, 2001). It strives for the design of artifacts and environments that are accessible to and usable by most people, regardless of gender, ethnicity, disability, health, or cultural background.

Judgments of performance need to factor in the functional performance of a design, as well as its compositional and aesthetic appeal and quality. Those who hold the authoritarian view argue society should let the architect decide on aesthetics, as well as the mundane tasks of making the building structurally and technically sound, and keeping the rain out. But in the real world of architectural practice, most architects try to meet their clients' needs, the budget, and the schedule, even if they don't always succeed.

Scientific research cannot answer questions of values, but it can inform them. Two sets of findings argue for the importance of popular assessments of buildings. First, research indicates major differences between what architects like and what the public likes regarding high versus popular style design, and it shows that architects do not lead popular taste. To the contrary, public preferences show remarkable stability over time (Nasar, 1999). Second, research on the wisdom of the crowd suggests that one gets more accurate information from a large number of independent, autonomous observers than from a few experts (Surowiecki, 2004). Again, this points to the value of tapping the opinions of many users, in addition to trusting the judgment of one designer. What about the client's responsibility to respect and incorporate building users' needs and preferences? Most school buildings presented in this book probably had multiple architects and multiple layers of approval checkpoints to overcome: the state architect (in case of a public school); the university architect; the university's architectural review committee; the project architects, who were often from out of town (especially if they were signature architects); and, the architect of record, usually local. This high level of complexity probably contributes greatly to problems in the quality of resulting buildings.

But how do you get popular assessment of visual quality and meaning if "beauty lies in the eye of the beholder"? Using psychometric techniques, we can quantify and evaluate the perceived qualities of buildings; and research confirms remarkable agreement across individuals on these assessments (Nasar, 1998).

AN INTEGRATIVE FRAMEWORK FOR BUILDING PERFORMANCE EVALUATION

Returning to the argument of environmental design cybernetics and control in the context of design: Researchers since the 1960s have put forth well documented techniques and conceptual frameworks for the assessment of building performance (Preiser, 2005). Large client organizations, such as governments and corporations, have been actively involved in post-occupancy evaluation to learn from buildings (cf. Federal Facilities Council, 2001). Over the years, ever larger, more sophisticated, and system-wide evaluations have been carried out and the methodology refined (Preiser and Vischer, 2005). The introduction of the "Performance Concept" (Preiser, Vischer, and White, 1991) advocates the monitoring of building performance from the perspective of the client's vision, mission, and goals, continuing all the way through the building delivery and life cycle of a building. This allows for infusing future designs with the lessons learned from successes and failures. Conceptualizing environmental design as a system with feedback loops leads to the next step in the evolution of a comprehensive evaluation process model—the integrative framework for building performance evaluation. It was first published in a set of essays on timely topics in the 7th Edition of *Time-Saver Standards* (Preiser and Schramm, 1997), and since then, has been adopted by the National Council of Architectural Registration Boards (NCARB) in its Professional Development Monograph series entitled, *Improving Building Performance*.

As illustrated in Figure 5.1, the framework has six phases in the delivery and life cycle of a building: planning; programming; design; construction; occupancy and recycling. Designs for design schools should go beyond satisfying the standard expectations and criteria for performance—health;

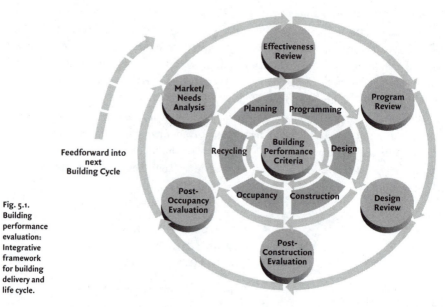

Fig. 5.1.
Building
performance
evaluation:
Integrative
framework
for building
delivery and
life cycle.

safety; security; functionality; workflow; efficiency; as well as social, psychological, and cultural performance—to serve as role models for the students aspiring to become design professionals, and the community at large. As such, the designer's creativity can become value added after the design has satisfied the listed standard criteria. The comparative analyses and case studies in this book report on both positive and negative evaluations. The lessons learned should help programmers and building clients create better architectural programs for future design schools, and they can help designers of those schools make better decisions.

ASSESSMENT APPROACH AND DATA GATHERING METHODOLOGY

To assess the design of design schools, this book focuses on the process of post-occupancy evaluation. The diagram in Figure 5.2 illustrates the phases and steps in post-occupancy evaluation as described in *Improving Building Performance* (NCARB, 2003). The comparative analyses and case studies reported here represent review outcomes. The findings and recommendations can serve as the beginning of a future database on the performance of design schools, which might be a national, nonprofit clearinghouse type of organization, created for the purpose of sharing the positive and negative lessons learned from evaluations of recently completed architecture schools. This might pertain not just to their designs, but also to the performance of particular building components and features, such as offices, computer labs, classroom spaces, appearance and wayfinding, applicable to many other building types.

In 1998–99, Nasar and Preiser planned the study. On May 6, 1999, Nasar posted a request on various planning, architecture, and planning list servers for people "willing to participate in a national project to do post-occupancy evaluations of recent (1979 to present) schools of architecture." The posting drew more than 40 responses from around the world, from faculty who worked in buildings that had additions or remodeling, and from faculty in landscape architecture buildings, all of which broadened the project. The posting also drew in an already completed set of post-occupancy evaluations (POEs) by Henry Sanoff (Part III, Ch. 15) who obtained student evaluations of six schools of architecture. Nasar and Preiser adapted Preiser's POE form (Preiser, Rabinowitz, and White, 1988) and Nasar's exterior appearance rating form (Nasar, 1999) as preliminary drafts of the POE instruments. They e-mailed them to all potential participants for comment, and the subsequent exchanges led to a standardized set of instruments to assess: a building's appearance including its interior; background information; observations, and photographs; and procedures for compiling, coding, and analyzing the data. Of the 40 volunteers—several of whom came from the same schools—11

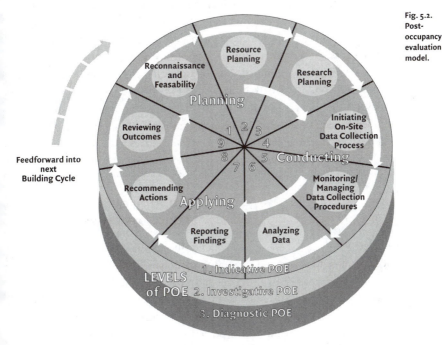

Fig. 5.2. Post-occupancy evaluation model.

completed and wrote up POEs (included as case studies in Parts III and IV). Three—Texas A&M, University of California, Berkeley, and University of Minnesota—had developed and used their own methods. Three—University of Hawaii, Guelph, and Michigan—submitted data that we analyzed in the comparison across schools (Part II, Chapter 6). Most participants completed their evaluations by the end of 2001. However, the evaluation studies continued from 1999 through 2005, as two buildings came on line in 2004. Nasar ran comparative analyses on data from all of the schools (Part II, Chapter 6). The case studies from the United States and elsewhere appear in Parts III and IV.

The Appendices display all of the data gathering instruments (i.e., background information, exterior survey and interior survey, and procedures), selected statistics, and figures. We hope others will use or adapt this tool kit for evaluations of their facilities. In the following pages, we outline the procedures in greater detail.

BACKGROUND INFORMATION

For background information, we requested that participants try to get: the name of the designer(s) and other consultants; dates (start and completion of construction); type of construction; kind of project (new, addition, renovation); total square footage of school facilities; net to gross square footage; net usable space grouped into categories for studios, all classrooms, crit space, library; degree of university oversight/control/design review from program to final construction; total project cost; information on operating costs; maintenance costs; heating and cooling costs; typical cost and square footage of other campus buildings; the process for selecting the designer; enrollment by discipline; number of faculty and staff and number in each category; photographs of building exterior; and photographs of selected spaces in the building (particularly photos of most admired and most undesirable features).

EVALUATION OF THE
EXTERIOR APPEARANCE

For the survey on the exterior, people used a systematic sampling procedure to obtain completed questionnaires from at least 30 passersby, 15 males and 15 females. Interviewers set up at a location with a view of the building. They used a random number table to pick a number, and then counted passersby until that number to select someone for an interview. If that person was the same gender as the previous respondent, they stopped the first person after that number of the opposite gender. Note unlike the interior survey, which gauged reactions of building inhabitants, this survey sought impressions of the building on passersby. The interviewer told each person we wanted to get their opinions of the building exterior, that their identities would be kept anonymous, and that they could withdraw at any time.

Those who said they agreed, i.e., usually more than 90% of those approached, received the questionnaire. It had three parts. First, it had the respondents rate their agreement with 13 statements about the exterior appearance on a 7-point scale (ranging from strongly disagree to strongly agree). The scales included three that represent salient dimensions of people's response to the environment (Russell, 1988): pleasant, calming, and exciting. People sometimes get into response set, meaning that without reading the question, they check the same value they checked for other questions. When given several rating scales, people tend to check the same point on each item, without reading the items. To avoid this response set bias (Judd, Smith, and Kidder, 2005), we reversed the pole on four items (selected at random): 1) calming; 2) fit the overall campus image; 3) felt safe after dark; and 4) is one of the most attractive buildings on campus. For these, the questionnaire asked, 1) whether the building looked distressing; 2) whether it did NOT fit the overall campus image; 3) whether it felt unsafe after dark, and 4) whether it was one of the most ugly buildings on campus. The survey then had the respondents write down what features they liked most about the exterior and what features they liked least. Finally, it asked for some background information, including position, gender, and years on campus.

EVALUATION OF THE INTERIOR

For the interior evaluation, we tried to get responses from each of the groups using the building, such as faculty, students in various majors and at various levels, and staff. This evaluation had eight parts. It started with two open-ended questions asking what features the respondents liked most about the facility, and what features they liked least. Then, it had them rate their satisfaction (again on a 7-point scale from very dissatisfied to very satisfied) with 15 aspects of the design, such as: the amount of space; wayfinding; security; and relationship between spaces/layout. Third, for a list of spaces in the facility, the survey had them rate their satisfaction with each one. Fourth, it had them indicate the amount of time they spent in each space, i.e., from 0–5 hours up to more than 40 hours per week. Fifth, it had them select two of the spaces that they found

least satisfying, and for each one write down what features led to their dissatisfaction. Furthermore, respondents were asked to rate their satisfaction
with those two spaces with regard to nine items, including: adequacy of
space, acoustics, and flexibility of use. Sixth, it had them select two spaces
they found most satisfying. They were asked to describe the satisfying features, and then rate them on the nine items used for the least satisfying
spaces. Seventh, it had them list amenities and facilities currently lacking and
make suggestions for improving the facility; and finally, eighth, the survey
requested background information, including the respondents' positions,
discipline / major, and gender.

In conclusion, the case has been made for getting user input during the
typical phases in the building delivery and life cycle of buildings. This should
include design schools, considering that the learning environment can have
an important impact and influence on aspiring design professionals.

ANALYSES

Most of the case studies (Chapters 7
through 18) contain post-occupancy evaluations based on the data gathering
process described above. The case studies report the results of those evaluations. However, three chapters (Chapter 9, University of California, Berkeley; Chapter 12, University of Minnesota; and Chapter 15, Architecture
Schools from Student Perspectives) used different data gathering strategies, and thus, report slightly different kinds of results. That said, most case
studies herein report the results in three parts, which describe: 1) the background and history of the project; 2) the evaluation of the exterior appearance of the facility; and 3) the evaluation of the interior of the facility.

The exterior ratings generally had responses to 11 scales. The analyses reported the mean score on each scale and the grand mean across the scales. In
interpreting the means for the exteriors and interiors, the reports took into
account acquiescence and Pollyanna biases. In acquiescence bias, respondents tend to agree with statements, and in Pollyanna bias, they tend to respond favorably (Boucher and Osgood, 1969; Francescato, 2002; Marans,
1976). Thus, the case studies treated mean scores of 4 or below on 7-point
scales as negative evaluations, scores between 4 and 5 as neutral, and scores
above 5 as positive evaluations.

The analyses for the interiors factored in several kinds of data on how
well various built features worked, how well various spaces worked, and
why. For building features, the analyses report the mean scores for the rated
satisfaction with various features of the building (such as amount of space,
ease of finding your way around, and quality of materials); and as with the

Box 5.1

HOW TO DO AN INVESTIGATIVE POE

Of the six phases in building performance evaluations (BPE) perhaps the most familiar one is post-occupancy evaluation (POE), as described in detail by Preiser, Rabinowitz, and White (1988) and NCARB (2003). POEs vary in the amount of effort and cost required, the degree of sophistication in data collection and analysis, and the kind of results they generate. *Indicative* POEs, which take a few hours, document major successes and failures through archival and document evaluation, review, pre-visit evaluation questions, and a walk-through evaluation. *Investigative* POEs like the ones described in this book may take several weeks, and they explicitly state and evaluate according to performance criteria across a range of building performance categories. *Diagnostic* POEs are not unlike traditional scientific research, which may take several months or longer, and which use multiple methods to understand causes related to specific building-related variables. Below we outline the steps for conducting an *Investigative* POE.

- **Plan the POE.** With the client organization, develop the level of effort, scope of project, key liaisons, workplan, schedule and budget, and research plan.
- **Conduct the POE.** With the client organization, coordinate the timing, and location of POE activities, pre-test data collection procedures.
- **Who.** Select relevant sample, i.e., representatives of various groups of occupants for evaluation of interior performance, as well as passersby for exterior appearance survey. We recommend a census (interviewing everyone), random or systematic sampling from the relevant groups, and confidential and anonymous response formats. For small groups, try to interview all group members. For larger groups, use a random sample. For passersby, set up a systematic procedure to select people, such as stopping every fourth person. That way, one avoids biasing the sample with an unintentional selection bias.
- **What.** For exterior appearance, surveys should at least ask about preference, excitement, calming, and compatibility, and in addition other questions could ask about particular meanings of qualities, such as high status, welcoming, or stable, that the client believes the facility should communicate for effectiveness. For the interior, the survey should ask about:
  - Overall evaluation
  - Most liked and least liked features
  - Most liked and least liked spaces
  - Perceived facility performance on dimensions of interior and exterior aesthetics, such as amount of space, quality of lighting, acoustics, temperature, security, accessibility, adjacencies, and other relevant concerns for the specific facility (see Appendix for sample instruments).
  - Amount of time spent in various spaces
  - Evaluations of those spaces where the individual spends most of his or her time
  - Respondent characteristics, such as gender, age, unit, years in the facility, to allow an assessment of the representativeness of the sample

(continued)

Box 5.1
(continued)

- **How.** On-line survey sites, such as Survey Monkey, allow you to gather data on-line and have it transferred into a data file. You can also give each respondent a hard copy to complete and return by a certain date.

  □ Start with general questions, such as asking about most liked and least liked features of the building or its exterior, and most liked and least liked spaces. Then move to specifics.

  □ For ratings of exterior appearance, ask for the general reactions of passersby first, and then use bipolar adjective scales, such as, exciting/boring, calming/distressing, compatible/incompatible, friendly/unfriendly, and, like/dislike. Passersby can check these on a 7-point scale, such as very exciting, exciting, fairly exciting, neither, fairly boring, boring, very boring. Alter the positive and negative ends of the scales to avoid having people simply always checking one and the same answer.

  □ For various interior features and spaces, have respondents rate their satisfaction with each on a 7-point satisfaction scale (very dissatisfied to very satisfied). They can also rate qualities of the building or spaces on a "very poor" to "very good" scale.

  □ For time spent in spaces, ask the respondent to specify up to five spaces, and give the amount of time spent in each one in the previous week in either an open-ended format, such as ____ hours (fractions acceptable), or fixed format (less than 1 hours, 1 to 5 hours, 6–10 hours, etc.).

  □ Obtain ratings of the quality of those spaces, using a "very poor" to "very good" scale for items such as space, lighting, acoustics, aesthetics, security, accessibility, and legibility.

  □ Give respondents the Other (please specify) ____ option to capture concerns you may have missed.

- **Analysis.** Calculate means skewness and standard deviations for scaled responses, and organize them in descending order to clearly show the best and worst aspects of the design. Use medians if data is skewed. For open-ended questions, list the spaces or features mentioned, count the frequency of mention for each, and organize those frequencies in descending order. If relevant, look at between-group comparisons.

- **Report.** Summarize the results, describe what works, what does not work, and offer suggestions for improvements: short-term solutions at no cost, low cost, and easy to do; medium-term solutions, which are more costly and harder to do; and long-term solutions, which are most likely handled in major renovation or future buildings. Describe the method. Present preliminary oral and text report to client for feedback, before submitting final report.

- **For the Future.** Keep and monitor results for general trends in evaluations. Do the same kinds of problems appear over and over? If so, how can design prevent their recurrence?

exterior, they report a grand mean for all of the features. For spaces, they report the mean scores and statistical comparisons for rated satisfaction with various spaces in the buildings. In addition, they report the frequency with which respondents cited various spaces as either most liked or most disliked. The two analyses provide an understanding of the most liked and least liked spaces in the building. For each of those spaces, the post-occupancy evaluation had two kinds of data to help understand a building's success or failure. The evaluation had ratings of satisfaction with features of those spaces and open-ended responses to what people liked or disliked about the particular spaces. The case studies used the mean scores of the satisfaction ratings and the frequency with which people cited various features to describe why the good spaces worked well and the poor spaces did not.

Finally, each case study provides a summary of lessons learned from the evaluation of the new facility. Case studies from the United States appear in Chapters 7 through 14; and international case studies appear in Chapters 16 through 18.

Beyond the evaluations reported in each case study, the book has two composite evaluations, each of which gives a broader summary of the findings. Chapter 15 offers a summary of student evaluations of six schools of architecture. Those evaluations used different data and instruments than those described above, because they took place prior to the design of the present project.

Chapter 6 offers lessons learned from all of the evaluations. It identifies the common areas of success and failure in the case studies to suggest things to avoid, processes to use, and future directions to improve the designs. One part of that chapter contains a composite analysis of the evaluation data from all of the schools with similar data. Data from three schools—Guelph, University of Hawaii, Manoa, and for the exterior evaluation, University of Michigan—are not included in the case studies, because participants from those schools provided the data only. That analysis identifies successes and failures among the set of designs and discusses the lessons learned about process and design.

JACK L. NASAR, WOLFGANG F. E. PREISER,
AND THOMAS FISHER

LESSONS LEARNED ANI
THE FUTURE OF SCHOOLS O
ARCHITECTURE BUILDING.

Our review of the sixteen post occupancy evaluations (Chapters 7 through 18) of sixteen architectur school buildings identified common strengths and weaknesses. Passersby, fo example, often saw the buildings as among the ugliest on campus, dislikin their appearance and seeing the designs as not fitting the surroundings or th campus. Occupants often gave the building interiors high scores for ope space and lighting, but low scores for efficiency, wayfinding, HVAC, an acoustics. Some schools had special support spaces that occupants likee such as atriums/public gathering spaces (Figures 6.1a, b, and c show thre from the set that includes University of California at Berkeley, the Univer sity of Cincinnati, Texas A&M, University of Illinois at Urbana/Champaig (UIUC), Minnesota, Nebraska, Texas, Dokuz Eylul, and the Swedish Un versity of Agricultural Sciences), libraries (Figures 6.2a, b, and c show thre from the set that includes Cincinnati; Minnesota; Nebraska; Ohio State; an the University of Sydney, Australia), and cafés (Cincinnati, Ohio State), bu spaces more central to their mission—the computer laboratories, circula tion, and studio/crit spaces—often drew criticism. Student evaluations c six schools of architecture (Chapter 15) found similar problems to thos identified in our post-occupancy evaluations. Student complained abou

Figs. 6.1a–c.
Well-liked
public areas:
a. Texas,
b. Nebraska,
c. Illinois.

c

a

Figs. 6.2a–c.
Well-liked
libraries:
a. Nebraska,
b. Ohio State,
c. Cincinnati.

b

problems with wayfinding, location of stairs, physical comfort, lighting and acoustics in studios, and the exposed building structure.

How did these designs fare relative to one another? Of the 16 designs 10 used the same instruments to obtain responses from passersby, faculty staff and students: Dokuz Eylul University, The Ohio State University, and Universities of Cincinnati, Guelph, Hawaii, Illinois, Michigan, Nebraska Sydney, and Texas. Appendix B has additional background information and statistics for the comparisons in this chapter. Comparisons of the 10 design found three which consistently received better ratings than the others for exterior appearance, interior features and spaces: Texas, Illinois, and Ne braska. Texas had the best scores, but Illinois and Nebraska also had high ratings. In each case, university personnel chose a designer who valued func tion as much as form, and who respected the context and evolving nature of a campus and its buildings. In addition, university personnel managed the process, exercising strong control over the design. Texas and Nebraska rep resent renovations and additions, designed to fit the earlier structures.

How to explain the differences in ratings? One can conceptualize a con tinuum with a four-part division (Tesor, 1989): form is relative (functional ism); form is absolute (form follows form or formalism); form is persona (form follows person or individualism); and, form is evolutionary (form fol lows precedent, traditionalism). Different kinds of designs may embody or require different values. However, a public design for a complex facility such as a state university, land grant, and even a private university, should a least respond to function and form as evolutionary. The best projects em body a combination of "form is relative" and "form is evolutionary," while the worst ones combine, to different degrees, "form is absolute" and "form is personal." Just as designers should use their knowledge of history, percep tion, materials, and craft as a base on which to build innovative solutions designers should use knowledge about such things as sustainability and user needs as a base onto which they can superimpose their creativity.

The Ohio State University has a strong review process, from program ming, through selecting the design team, through managing the design and construction process. The university architect reported that Ohio State es tablished this review process in part due to the failure to reign in the high costs and dysfunctions of a previous high-profile building on campus: Peter Eisenman's Wexner Center design (Nasar, 1999). The university has typically had a building committee from the academic unit, staff from the architect's office and budget office, and a design review committee. It is intended to help select the designer and to critique designs from the perspective of the users the university, the master plan, and other criteria. This process has produced many successful designs, according to post-occupancy evaluations by Nasar.

Why didn't the review process lead to a success for the new architecture building? For it, the Director of the Architecture School bypassed that process. While he posted the design drawings in the school, he did so more for display than input. He did not forward written critiques from faculty on the design to the university architect or the designers. The critiques covered potential problems with the building's appearance, ramps, wayfinding, acoustics, open studios, sustainability, and restroom locations. This resulted in lost opportunities to integrate knowledge about sustainability, occupant behavior, landscape architecture, as well as practice and technology, into the program and building design. Real participation and user input could have led to a more successful design.

EXTERIOR

Let's look at each rating separately, starting with the meanings conveyed by the exterior appearance. Passersby liked Texas the best, followed by Nebraska and Illinois (shown in Figures 6.3a, b, and c). The rest of the buildings received below average scores, with

Figs. 6.3a–c. Well-liked exteriors: a. Texas, Goldsmith Hall; b. Nebraska, Link; c. Illinois.

Sydney anchoring the ratings. The evaluations of the building exteriors had 549 observations across nine schools (See Appendix B: Building Exterior Evaluations for details). While each passerby rated the exterior appearance on 13 scales, factor analysis condensed those into three factors:

1. Preference
2. Compatibility
3. Safety

For the first factor (Preference), passersby gave the most favorable scores to Texas, followed by Nebraska and Illinois. The scores represent moderate but not high level preference. Next came Ohio State and Cincinnati with neutral to negative ratings. Hawaii, Michigan, Guelph, and Sydney had scores below the average (4.30), with Sydney receiving the lowest score. For Compatibility, Texas again received the most favorable score; and Cincinnati, Ohio State, and Sydney received the lowest scores. Figures 6.4a, b, and c show their exteriors. The other five exteriors received neutral to negative ratings. For Safety, passersby gave the most favorable scores to Nebraska, Illinois, and Texas. Next came Michigan and Hawaii. The lowest scores went to Ohio State, Cincinnati, Guelph, and anchoring the ratings, Sydney (for statistics see Appendix B: Comparisons between Exteriors). Combining the three factors, we can rank the buildings in descending order (best to worst) as

Figs. 6.4a–c.
Disliked and
incompatible
exteriors:
a. Sydney,
b. Cincinnati,
c. Ohio State.

a

b

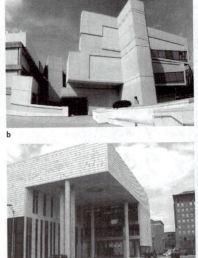

c

follows: Texas, Nebraska, Illinois, Ohio State, Cincinnati, Guelph, Hawaii, Michigan (neutral to negative scores), and Sydney (for statistics, see Appendix B: Comparisons between Exteriors). Because each school had different people doing the ratings, the different scores may partly result from the raters, but studies have consistently shown much smaller effects from differences among individuals than buildings (Stamps, 1999). Thus, it seems likely that the ratings accurately reflect the perceived character of the exteriors. Furthermore, ratings of the exterior aesthetics by occupants in each building yielded a similar order of preferences: Texas first, followed by Nebraska, Illinois (with favorable ratings), Cincinnati, and Ohio State (neutral to low scores), Hawaii, Guelph (lower scores), and Sydney (lowest score).

INTERIORS

The analyses of the interiors centered on user satisfaction with *building features* and *spaces* in each building. The comparisons involved 1,445 users across nine architecture buildings. We received data for two schools (Universities of Guelph and Hawaii) which are not represented in the case studies. As with the exteriors, we used factor analysis to condense the data. For *building features*, the analysis looked at three factors: *Quality of Materials*, which included floors, ceilings, walls, and building materials; *Accessibility*, which involved accessibility, security, maintenance, and wayfinding; and *Appearance / Functionality* which pertained to proximity to views, interior aesthetics, exterior aesthetics, adaptability, relationship between spaces, amount of space, and quality of lighting, acoustics, and temperature.

For *Quality of Materials*, Texas, Illinois, and Nebraska had higher scores, while Guelph, Ohio State, Sydney, and Cincinnati scored below the average (4.68). For *Accessibility*, Illinois, Hawaii, Texas, and Nebraska had the best scores. Dokuz Eylul, Guelph, Cincinnati, and Sydney scored below the average (4.66). For *Appearance / Functionality*, Texas, Nebraska, and Illinois had the best scores. Dokuz Eylul, Guelph, Sydney, Hawaii, and Ohio State scored below the average (4.66) (for statistics see Appendix B: Interiors). Combining the three factors, we can rank the interiors of these buildings in descending order (best to worst) as follows: Texas, Illinois, Nebraska (shown in Figures 6.5a, b, and c), Hawaii, Cincinnati, Ohio State, Sydney, Dokuz Eylul, and Guelph. Figures 6.6a, b, and c show views of the disliked interiors of Sydney, Ohio State, and Cincinnati.

Now consider the ratings of spaces. Factor analysis identified three groupings of spaces (see Appendix B: Interior Spaces) *Classrooms*, which included large classroom, medium classroom, large lecture space, and seminar

a

b

**Figs. 6.5a–c.
Good interior
quality, ac-
cessibility,
appearance,
and func-
tionality:
a. Texas,
b. Illinois,
c. Nebraska.**

c

a

**Figs. 6.6a–c.
Poor interior
quality, ac-
cessibility,
appearance,
and func-
tionality:
a. Sydney,
b. Ohio State,
c. Cincinnati.**

b

c

rooms; *Offices,* which encompassed the library, administrative offices, faculty offices, and exhibition gallery; and *Studio / Crit and Public spaces,* which involved jury / crit space, circulation, studio, and public areas (entrance, atrium, connecting spaces). For each factor, Texas, Nebraska, and Illinois received the highest satisfaction scores (for details, see Appendix B: Interior Spaces). Occupants gave low scores to Guelph, Dokuz Eylul, Sydney, and Ohio State. *Classrooms* in five buildings received good satisfaction scores, but four—Guelph, Dokuz Eylul, Sydney, and Ohio State—received scores below the average (4.77). *Offices* and administrative spaces, such as those at Texas, Nebraska, and Illiniois (Figures 6.7a, b, and c) generally received high satisfaction scores, with one exception—Guelph. Occupants gave Hawaii, Dokuz Eylul, and Sydney (shown in Figure 6.8) acceptable but below the

Figs. 6.7a–c. Liked administrative office spaces:
a. Texas,
b. Illinois,
c. Nebraska.

Fig. 6.8. Disliked administrative/ office spaces (Sydney).

Figs. 6.9a–b. People liked private studio/crit spaces: a. Texas, b. Nebraska.

Figs. 6.10a–b. Disliked open, noisy, poorly lit studio/crit spaces: a. Sydney, b. Ohio State.

average (5.07) scores. As for *Studio / Crit* and *Public* spaces, the well-liked examples at Texas, Nebraska (Figures 6.9a and b), and Illinois contrast with lower scoring spaces at Dokuz Eylul, Guelph, Sydney (Figure 6.10a), and Ohio State (Figure 6.10b), Hawaii, and Cincinnati joined them with scores below the average (4.62). The combined scores on the three space factors allowed us to rank the buildings from best to worst as follows: Texas, Nebraska, Illinois, Cincinnati, Hawaii, Ohio State, Sydney, Guelph, and Dokuz Eylul. Ohio State, Sydney, Guelph, and Dokuz Eylul all scored below the composite average (4.62).

GOOD AND FLAWED DESIGN FEATURES

PROVIDE A HEARTH

Occupants liked the large open public spaces (atriums and other gathering spaces in the buildings), and future designs would do well to have such spaces, particularly at points of convergence. As noted in chapter 17, the building needs a hearth. These gathering places can become that hearth. The design should furnish these spaces with features that will attract use—lots of seating, a variety of seating options including movable seats, connection and views to heavily used circulation routes, food service facilities, greenery, and moving water (Project for Public Spaces, 1984, 2000; Whyte, 1980, 1988; Zacharias, Stathopoulos, & Hanqing, 2004). In warm climates, these places can become outdoor courtyards; and even in colder climates, the design should create outdoor gathering places near the major entrance, as a way to enliven the entrance plaza. If the building has a restaurant or coffee shop, it makes sense to locate it near the plaza, to both provide extra seating for the food service and to enliven the plaza with users from it.

> ### ACTIONS FOR CLIENTS INVOLVED IN PLANNING NEW FACILITIES
>
> - University staff planning new design facilities could benefit from visiting and observing the features of the successful buildings—Texas, Nebraska, and Illinois.
> - They can learn what to avoid through visits to some less successful buildings—Cincinnati, Ohio State, Guelph, Dokuz Eylul, Sydney.
> - They might do well to note the differences in the planning and design process that led to the successful and flawed designs.
> - Their buildings can add to the knowledge base through post-occupancy evaluations, which use measures of the exterior appearance and interior features and space items used here.

Box 6.1

STUDIOS AND CRIT SPACES NEED ACOUSTICAL PRIVACY

Many, in fact most, designs for designers have open-plan studios. The post-occupancy evaluations in this book revealed consistent problems with such designs. The choice of open-plan for studios may arise from assumptions about informal learning and interactions across studios in such plans. Most architectural offices also have open offices, in large part because of the fluid way they work, with shifting teams depending on each project, and because of the extensive amount of communication among members of a team doing a project. The open plan studio, then, seeks to simulate the anticipated work environment once students enter the workforce.

However, several streams of research provide information relevant to the open design, which questions the appropriateness, because of negative performance aspects. Research on open or landscaped offices has found that while the open design may aid communication and work flow (due to lack of barriers), and make for easier supervision, it also has many disadvantages. It can produce tension, irritability, a disliked sense of supervision, and desire for visual and auditory privacy (Becker, 1986; Brill, 1984; Marans and Spreckelmeyer, 1981; Sundstrom, 1986). Although open studios can offer visual privacy by pin-up partitions among studios or over every desk, that still leaves the problem of noise and distraction.

Do the problems found in offices apply to design studios? Research on open plans in schools suggests that it may. Studies found the same problems observed in open offices: noise distractions and inadequate privacy (Ahrentzen, Jue, Skorpanich, & Evans, 1982; Bennet, Andres, Hegarty, & Wade, 1980). In response, many schools have erected walls and makeshift partitions. While one could argue that open school classrooms are significantly different from university studios, some analogies may be valid. However, broader research on noise and privacy suggests that the problems would apply to the college-level design studio as well. Noise is a stressor. In particular, its negative effects increase with its volume, unpredictability and perceived lack of control. Although the open studio may not have high volume noise, it does have unpredictable noise, which students and faculty cannot control. In addition, the noise may block performance of a task—the shared review. Noise has damaging physiological effects (Evans and Cohen, 1987; Glass and Singer, 1972). It has negative effects on learning (Glass, Singer, et al., 1973; Bronzaft and McCarthy, 1975) for young children, negative effects on task performance (although people may adapt), and negative after effects, such as reduced frustration tolerance (Wohlwill, Nasar, & DeJoy, 1976), and reduced helping behavior (Mathews and Canon, 1975). For a variety of tasks, noise, particularly speech and high reverberation, distracts people and hurts learning and performance (Beauman, 2005). All of this can lead to physical and social withdrawal, the opposite of the ideal informal learning space desired in the open studio plan.

Research on privacy (cf. Altman and Chemers, 1980) points to additional problems with open plans. People value their privacy; and loss of control of privacy (access to one's self) has negative effects. For example, one study found higher drop-out rates from college for nonacademic reasons related to inability to get adequate privacy in the dorm rooms (Vinsel, Brown, et al., 1980). Loss of auditory privacy, particularly through the sound of other voices, appears to have strongest effects (Sundstrum, 1986).

Taken together the findings suggest that noisy open studios interfere with learning and likely have other negative effects on the students who spend hours in them. While this may require an empirical test specific to the studio environment, for now the results suggest that the design of the studio should provide acoustical privacy and controls, so students can hear and participate in the crits.

MAKE THE BUILDING LEGIBLE AND ACCESSIBLE

Most of the designs have problems with circulation and wayfinding, which creates ongoing problems for visitors, regular users, and the design. The visitor experiences stress at feeling lost, and may miss or arrive late to classes or meetings. The regular user suffers regular work interruption from lost visitors asking directions. The building gets littered with improvised paper directional signs to help visitors find key destinations. As many schools have large lecture spaces for university-wide and public lectures, ease of wayfinding becomes more important. Disorientation can create stress, anxiety, and frustration (Carpman and Grant, 2002; Evans, 1980; Lawton, 1994) all of which may threaten well being, and the desire to visit a place (Lynch, 1960). What Lynch (1960) said about cities applies to buildings. They need to be legible to help occupants have a clear mental map and find their way around.

The wayfinding problems arise from complex and disrupted plans that lack differentiation at decision points, lack adequate you-are-here maps, and sometimes have numbering systems that contribute to the problem. Research on legibility suggests several ways to make places easier for users to navigate. Some key recommendations are highlighted below:

Simplify Route Choices and Add Differentiation at Decision Points

Spatial complexity, or amount of information to process, affects wayfinding. Studies in a variety of contexts and with various populations have found that people have more difficulty finding their way around in places with complex route networks than those with simpler ones (Cubukcu and Nasar, 2005; Abu-Obeid, 1998; O'Neill 1991a; O'Neill, 1991b; Weisman, 1981). Complexity involves both the amount of information and its ease of processing. At decision points, fewer route choices offer less complexity than more route choices. Right angle turns are easier to process than turns at other angles. Although not tested in the vertical direction, the results probably apply to the vertical as well as the horizontal system.

Differentiation at decision points also affects ease of wayfinding (Abu-Ghazzeh, 1996; Abu-Obeid, 1998; Cubukcu and Nasar, 2005; Passini, Pigot, Rainville, & Tetreault, 2000). Differentiation refers to the degree to which an element looks different from its context. Research suggests at least two kinds of cues of particular importance for differentiation (Lynch, 1960), paths and landmarks. Consider a study that manipulated both kinds of cues (Cubkcu and Nasar, 2005). In virtual reality, it created decision points where paths stood out from other paths (in width or surface texture and color), or where vertical elements stood out from others. Tests of navigation in the environments found better spatial knowledge for either kind of differentiation than for more uniform ones (i.e. those lacking differentiation).

Provide Visual Access

People judge destinations that are visible as closer than hidden ones; and if they see a desired destination they will take the route toward it (Nasar, 1983; Nasar and Cubukcu, 2005), even if signs accurately direct them in another direction (Seidel, 1983). Thus, key destinations should be made visible from various places. In addition, visual access to the outside can help provide a frame of reference for orientation and wayfinding. Visual access also emerged as a well liked feature in most of the POEs.

Think Before You Number

Americans are accustomed to streets having odd numbers on one side and even numbers on the other; and we are accustomed to those numbers increasing in parallel to one another as we move along the street, possibly jumping by a hundred at intersections. These conventions inform our expectations, and they become expectations for the numbering systems in buildings. We do not expect to find room 190 across a hall from room 10. Instead, we expect to find room 9 or 11, odd numbers close to 10. We also expect numbers on the same floor to follow sequentially, and thus, we do not expect to move from say 9, 10, 11 to 103 within a single hallway. However, in building additions, this kind of numbering change sometimes takes place.

In the Aronoff Center at the University of Cincinnati (Chapter 10), the building and room numbering system is anything but intuitive: it refers to the four phases of construction as the building complex evolved over the years. No outsider or first time visitor can make any sense out of that!

An intuitive numbering system would keep orientation and wayfinding simple and in accord with the user group expectations. To give an example of what not to do, consider Ohio State. The building has a front entrance on the east, and a split between its north and south sides, the longer dimension. It also has spaces at the west end between the north and south. An intuitive numbering system would have odd numbers along one side, and even ones along the other, each increasing as one moved east from the entrance. Instead, the numbering system follows a circle, increasing odd–even–odd along the north side of the building, increasing toward the west end, and, increasing further while moving back toward the front entrance to the east. People looking for room 190 (near the front entrance) will follow numbers to the opposite end of the building, before they discover they are lost (they hit a dead end), or if they do not see numbers on the first floor, or take a ramp, they may follow numbers on the second floor to the far end, until they realize they are lost. Had the numbering system moved up sequentially, odd on one side, even on the other, possibly with an east or west label (W 100, E 101), building users would have had an easier time. Users familiar with the building would learn the retrofitted system; and new visitors would not need to adjust to it, since they would not know about the change. Regrettably, staff in the university architect's office, on hearing the problem and proposed solution in the POE report, said it was too late to change; room numbers had gone into administrative files throughout the university.

Universal Design

Finally, equal access for all building users is a must, and integration of inclusive design concepts from the outset is recommended (Preiser and Ostroff, 2001). This pertains to physical access through the same means (ramps, doorways, etc.), to orientation and wayfinding systems, accessible bathrooms, crit spaces, and other functional areas and amenities, such as automatic door openers. As role models for aspiring design professionals, schools of architecture should not be handicapping environments, but in the spirit of universal design, they should be uplifting and truly exemplary in their accessibility.

HEATING, VENTILATION, AND AIR CONDITIONING (HVAC)

HVAC seems to be the Achilles heel of most buildings, even brand new ones. Ignoring solar directions and time of exposure can have disastrous consequences. As pointed out earlier, excessive glass expanses (e.g., at the Harvard School of Design) can lead to overheating and very uncomfortable conditions. Expensive retrofits, such as solar screening of an open, sunexposed space or repositioning poorly located air diffusers, do not always solve such problems, given the inadequacy of the initial design concept. In such cases, the very common attempts to "balance the system" are exercises in futility, and the building occupants suffer. Furthermore, quite often makeshift solutions like taping up air supply registers are a sign of too much air in the wrong places, and whenever one sees individual desk fans in action, that is a sign of inadequate air flow. On the opposite end of the spectrum, spaces that are too cold make it impossible for building occupants to function. In such cases, not much can be done, and people will use personal space heaters to compensate for lack of warm air.

SUMMARY

In sum, designs should provide a hearth with features to attract activity in the building and be an activity generator at the front entrance. They should provide acoustical privacy for the studio and crit spaces, and adequate HVAC throughout the facility. To improve legibility, wayfinding, and accessibility, designs should simplify the layout configuration, add differentiation and possibly direction signs at key decision points, provide visual access to key destinations and to the outdoors, use a numbering system that fits expectations, have correctly designed you-are-here maps at entrances, and insure equal access for all.

TIPS FOR CLIENTS

A design for a private individual on private property that no one can see, might not require any controls. However, design on public property, using public money, which is experienced by many people, and visible from public spaces, should have some controls. Depending on the complexity and goals of the project, those controls might put different weights on different kinds of requirements (such as technical, economic, human, site). However, a good client should not treat the management of an architectural project differently from other kinds of project management. First, clients should spend time in the careful selection of the right architect to satisfy the needs of the project. They should study the works of designers, check references, and interview the architect and the collaborative team. Then clients should pick the designer who seems most likely to satisfy the needs of the project. Because the process returns control to the client, it should yield a better building.

We recommend three additional actions to get a more democratic solution that works for the public, the users, and the client:

- Prepare a detailed program.
- Manage the design (have a structure for in depth and open evaluation of the designer and the design as it develops) throughout the process.
- Monitor the results through construction and after occupancy.

THE PROGRAM

The design needs a detailed program (or brief) evaluating the feasibility of the site, the space-planning needs, and the fit between the two. Interviews with 73 architects found that they felt programming produced "successful projects and happy clients" (White, 1972, p. 37) and that it facilitated "the design process, marketing, project management, client confidence in the project and firm, and (it saved) the client and firm time and money" (p. 52).

A good program involves more than general statements about the number of needed rooms and their sizes. The client should hire a programming architect or develop the in-house expertise to create the program for the facility. Many people have written useful guides to programming that give overviews of programming, step-by-step descriptions of programming activities, and case studies. (See Appendix B: The Program, for some of these guides.)

Programmers face two questions about how to proceed: What programming steps should they follow, and what concerns should the program address? A summary of the steps of various programming models (Sanoff, 1989) points to eight steps:

1. Plan the program.
2. Understand client's organization and philosophy.
3. Establish project goals.
4. Organize the information search.
5. Analyze the information.
6. Develop the concept.
7. Identify budget-related problems and needs.
8. Consider the project impact.
9. Undertake program review and revision.

Each step may have several actions.

Box 6.2

DETAILS OF PROGRAMMING PROCESS
(adapted from Sanoff, 1989)

1. Plan the program. Identify:
   a. Participants and organize programming team
   b. Programming objectives
   c. Program context
   d. Information needed
   e. Process, sequence, task, schedules, rules, responsibilities
   f. Primary information sources
2. Understand the client's organization and philosophy. Learn about the:
   a. Nature of organization, image, and philosophy
   b. Organizational function and communication process
   c. Satisfaction and dissatisfaction with present facility
   d. User objectives
3. Establish project goals, including:
   a. Functional goals
   b. Form related goals
   c. Time related goals
4. Organize the information search.
   a. Collect and organize project related facts.
   b. Conduct surveys and interviews.
   c. Do a relevant literature search.
   d. Observe use of existing operations and facilities.
   e. Get background information from client.
   f. Review similar building types and operations.

(continued)

Box 6.2
(continued)

g. Collect facts related to building function, form, economy, and time (historical, present, future).

5. Analyze information.
   a. Analyze collected facts.
   b. Analyze functional space standards.
   c. Tabulate space requirements.
   d. Develop spatial diagrams.
   e. Develop interaction patterns among activities.
   f. Create written description of functional units.

6. Develop the concept.
   a. Uncover, test, and develop conceptual alternatives.
   b. Develop functional concepts.
   c. Develop form, economy, and time related concepts.

7. Identify budget related problems and needs, including:
   a. Functional needs
   b. Form needs
   c. Economic needs

8. Consider project impacts, such as those on the:
   a. Client's organization and operation
   b. Community
   c. Ecological systems

9. Program review and revision
   a. Revisit the various issues

Though the actions and steps appear linear, they are iterative. Information can feed forward to subsequent steps and feed back to earlier ones.

The contents of a program should offer criteria for concerns of relevance to the particular project. In broad terms, the concerns include commodity (function), firmness (structurally sound and durable), and delight (aesthetically pleasing) (Vitruvius, 1960). In more detail, the program might address some of the following concerns or performance criteria: pleasing appearance, function, durability, and technique. Pleasing appearance covers connotative meaning, emotional quality, and identity (denotative meaning). Function covers fitness to purpose, activities of users to be supported, circulation, comfort, convenience, environmental characteristics to support needed activities, flexibility, goals of the facility, legibility, personalization, privacy, safety from accidents and hazards, security from crime, social interaction, territoriality, and visibility. Firmness covers structural soundness, energy systems, acoustics, heating, ventilation, air conditioning, lighting, olfactory environment, radioactivity, environmental impact, site design and foundation. Technique involves assembly, economy, construction cost, maintenance costs, operating costs, life cycle costs, project phasing, quality of materials, and finishes.

A more comprehensive set of concerns includes human, environmental, cultural, technological, temporal, economic, aesthetic, and safety (Hershberger, 1999). Human concerns deal with functional, social, physical, physiological, and psychological aspects; environmental concerns include the site, climate, context, resources, and waste; cultural concerns deal with historical, institutional, political, and legal issues; technological concerns deal with materials, systems, and processes; temporal concerns deal with growth, change, and permanence; economic concerns deal with finance, construction, operations, maintenance, and energy; aesthetic concerns deal with form, space, color, and meaning; and safety concerns deal with structure, fire, chemical, personal, and criminal safety. The programmer would work with the client to establish the hierarchy of priorities of these concerns for the desired performance of the new facility.

Each concern would have associated with it guidelines or performance criteria for the completed facility. Different building purposes may require different sets of criteria, and some buildings may require additional criteria not listed. Here, in addition to formulating the criteria, the program should make clear how to interpret and weigh them. Successful programming will involve a variety of individuals related to the delivery and occupancy of the facility.

Although programming may cost some money up front, research suggests that it saves money by eliminating unnecessary features and improving the efficiency of the solution for the client and occupants. The POE/Programming process for plazas in New York City, the Marriott Hotel, the Federal Bureau of Prisons, hospitals, and public housing (Nasar, 1999) all saved the client money. Failure to develop or adhere to the program can create significant cost and functional problems (cf. Nasar, 1999, Chapter 6).

DESIGN REVIEW

First, the client should research and talk with various firms to select the ones to participate. If inviting nonlocal firms, the client should set up a procedure for pairing them with local firms (familiar with local codes and construction practices) and for evaluating the full team. With a clear program for the facility, this approach should improve the fit of the designer to the building purpose. It should also allow an in-depth evaluation of each team. To get at the whole picture, the review team should include experts in a variety of aspects relating to the design (master planner, programmer, specialists in mechanical systems, structures, and construction, as well as representatives of various user groups.

To make the results accountable, the client might consider having deliberations open and available to the public. Courts of law and public hearings have public records of the proceedings. The design selection process could also use open proceedings with a written or taped record. Although many communities have public hearings on development projects, they tend to occur after the architect has been selected and a design developed. For a public building, the public should have the right to monitor the process. This means open proceedings. As in courtrooms, the observers can follow rules that maintain order and prevent biasing influences on the jury. The taped or written records (as in court proceedings) would allow people to refer to the record. The record should go beyond the deliberations.

MONITORING THE DESIGN

The selection of a design team is not the end of the process. It starts a new process. After selecting the architect, the client must work closely with the architect to shape the design so that it works as intended. This means holding the design to the program, master plan, desired appearance characteristics, budget, and timeline unless a change in needs creates a change in these requirements. After completion and occupancy, the client should evaluate the building to see how well it performs relative to the program, and any unexpected parameters. Earlier, we discussed the ways in which a post-occupancy evaluation systematically evaluates buildings after construction and occupancy: to identify successes and failures in the facility for users; to provide systematic and objective information about the functioning of a completed and occupied building; to identify and solve correctable problems in the facility; and to create a knowledge base to improve the performance of future buildings, to improve space utilization; and last but not least, to improve occupant attitudes. It can also make the architect more accountable. Public information about performance, from consumer surveys such as those in *Consumer Reports,* have had some success in leading producers to improve their products for consumers. Perhaps the same can occur in architecture.

DESIGN INNOVATION AND THE CHALLENGE OF CHANGE

Finally, we wish to quote from the book *Design Intervention: Toward a More Humane Architecture* (Preiser, Vischer, and White, 1991). "In order to innovate, architecture has to reconcile three different mandates or roles, in education and practice. These correspond to the three basic goals of architecture as articulated by Vitruvius, that is, commodity, firmness, and delight. They are:

- Architecture as problem solving (commodity)
- Architecture as a service to the building industry (firmness)
- Architecture as the artistic expression of social and cultural ambitions (delight)

Design innovation can occur in terms of any of these three definitions. We are in danger of overlooking the importance of balancing these three aspects in creating good architecture. The purpose of architecture is to generate something new, to solve a problem in a way that is unique to that problem, whether it is art, social action, or something else. Innovation implies change, and change implies improvement."

EVALUATION
CASE STUDIES
(UNITED STATES)

PART III

JACK L. NASAR

7

AUSTIN E. KNOWLTON HALL

THE OHIO STATE UNIVERSITY

SUMMARY

The post-occupancy evaluation of Knowlton Hall at the Ohio State University included analysis of archives about the building, interviews with members of the university architect's office, a short evaluation from 62 faculty, students, and staff members two months after occupancy, and nine months later, more comprehensive surveys of 272 passersby and building occupants (students, faculty, and staff), as well as observations of use in the building and surrounding landscape. Results revealed mixed responses. In the short evaluation, occupants complained about a top-down, closed process that excluded meaningful input; and they gave the design neutral ratings. The later survey on the exterior appearance, completed by 79 passersby outside Knowlton Hall and 58 passersby outside a new Physics Research building, found that respondents disliked the exterior. They gave Knowlton lower scores than those for the Physics building, and lower than those obtained for 15 campus buildings. In particular, they rated it as a poor fit to the campus and surroundings, unfriendly and ugly. Observations of use of the site found low use, and a lack of basic amenities to attract people to sit or linger. The comprehensive interior survey, completed by 135 occupants, yielded more mixed results. Occupants gave the interior negative to neutral evaluations. They gave low ratings to the environmental quality, ability to find your way around, quality of materials (wall, floors, ceilings), and interior aesthetics. Only one feature received a favorable evaluation—the amount of space. As for individual space categories, occupants liked the library and computer labs, but disliked circulation and the studio spaces. In response to this, a member of the university architect's office who worked on the project commented that the building failed on its two major purposes: People could not find their way around, and the design studios did not work.

BACKGROUND

By its opening in 2004, The Austin E. Knowlton School of Architecture building had a 20-year history. For years, Jerry Voss, Director of the School of Architecture sought funding from Austin E. "Dutch" Knowlton. A 1931 Ohio State University (OSU) graduate in civil engineering, Knowlton owned and ran his father's construction company, which built hundreds of public buildings throughout the country. In 1994 Knowlton pledged $10 million for a new architecture building. He also presented the university with a scale model of what the building should look like. He wanted a marble exterior.

The State of Ohio had higher construction priorities. Each year the university's list of projects for state funding included Knowlton Hall, and each year it failed to make the cut for state money. Brown Hall, the 100-year-old home to architecture, continued to fall apart. After three years of this, Knowlton had four post-tensioned concrete columns delivered to the campus. It cost $1 million from the project budget to store and erect the columns. Shortly afterward, the state allocated funds for the project.

For site selection, OSU gave other units, such as physics, higher priority. The donor and school eventually settled on a site on the northwest edge of campus, where a former dairy barn housed architectural studios.

The project was delivered under the University's standard contractor system, in which OSU managed the process and held all contracts. However, the School of Architecture followed a procedure at odds with what occurs elsewhere on campus. Usually, the academic unit has a committee to represent it, along with the university architect. That committee would report to the faculty, students, and staff and seek input from them. In contrast, the Director of the School of Architecture ran the process as a closed, top-down process. Although he reported to school faculty about some steps and decisions, he seldom sought or listened to input from most faculty members.

To select the architect, the university architect's office and the director assembled a list of 10 "signature" architects, all of whom had experience designing on university campuses. When the director presented various versions of the list at faculty meetings and faculty suggested designers to add or remove, he disregarded the suggestions. Through interviews, office visits, project reviews, and references, the team narrowed the list to one: Mack Scogin, Merrill Elam Architects. The design team also included Wandel and Schnell, Architects Inc. (local partners), Michael Van Valkenburgh Associates (landscape architect), and HAWA of Columbus, engineers.

In 1998–99, the architects developed two schemes, one for an addition to Ives Hall, and the other to replace it. By December 1999, a revised replacement scheme was accepted. The architects spent two months exploring non-marble exteriors, but the donor rejected them, insisting on marble. The building has a marble rain screen "shingle" system, in which marble sheets cover the waterproofing material, Tyvek. Elsewhere, the marble is attached to concrete walls as is dark glass over metal studs.

The architects completed the schematic design in March 2000, construction documents in June 2000, and design development in October 2000. The designs were posted in the school, and the school had meetings with the architects. Unfortunately, the director of the School did not forward suggestions on the design from experts on the faculty to the university architect or the designers. When asked about this at a faculty meeting, he said, "I do not have to represent you." In public meetings with the architects, he also cut off discussion. OSU awarded the construction contract in February 2002. Construction started June, 2002 and was officially completed on August 2, 2004. The building was dedicated in October 2004.

In 2004, Austin E. Knowlton Hall housed 982 people (615 students in architecture, 180 in landscape architecture, 96 in city and regional planning, 74 faculty members, adjuncts, and visitors, and 17 staff and administration personnel). Funding included $33 million in state and private funds, $26 million of which went to the construction budget. The building has 175,386 gross square feet (GSF), with an estimated cost of $165/square foot in 2004 dollars, according to the project manager). Although it was built at a low cost, it has relatively little usable space, with efficiency (assignable square feet to GSF ratio) of 0.55.

PRELIMINARY EVALUATION

How did this building perform for the users? A preliminary evaluation was conducted in October, shortly after occupancy but too early for a full post-occupancy evaluation. The evaluation gathered responses from a small (N = 62) but diverse sample of occupants,

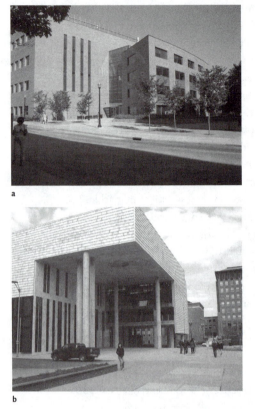

a

b

Figs. 7.1a–b.
Respondents
liked the
appearance
of the Phys-
ics Research
building
(top) more
than Archi-
tecture
(bottom).

with 16.5 percent faculty, 10.6 percent staff, 72.9 percent students, and with representatives from all three sections in the school: 33.8 percent from architecture, 40.3 percent from city and regional planning, 26.0 percent from landscape architecture. They gave neutral ratings to the overall building, interior aesthetics, and exterior aesthetics (4.71, 4.11, and 4.87, respectively), and a low rating for the ease of finding your way around (3.25). Recall from Chapter 5 on "Assessing Design," that due to acquiescence and Pollyanna bias, scores of between 4 and 5 on the 7-point scales represent neutral ratings. The survey also asked about the process. Although the architects met several times with building users to discuss the design, respondents who participated in those meetings described them as closed to user input. The architects might have wanted feedback, but the school director said he did not want "a design by committee." He ran the meetings to exclude meaningful participation and feedback. As a result, the respondents described the meetings as "opaque" with "no meaningful public discussions," "dictatorial and closed to user input," and "designed to appear inclusive but . . . not" where "after expressing opinions," one got "facetious answers."

POST-OCCUPANCY EVALUATION

A more comprehensive evaluation took place nine months after occupancy. It obtained responses to the exterior and the interior of the building, using the instruments described in Chapter 5 and shown in the Appendix.

EXTERIOR PERFORMANCE

The master plan called for preservation of open space, various circulation routes and vegetation around the building, and a landmark building at the site. As the exterior POE revealed, the building does stand out from its surroundings, making it a kind of landmark, but it stands out in an undesirable way. People dislike its appearance. For exterior appearance, the POE obtained ratings from passersby of both Knowlton Hall and the Physics Research Building. Both completed in autumn of 2004 and less than a block apart, these two buildings look nothing alike (see Figures 7.1a and b). Figure 7.2 shows the mean scores for ratings of each building. As you can see, Knowlton received lower ratings on every scale, and a lower overall mean. Passersby gave Knowlton's exterior appearance unfavorable ratings. The overall mean for Knowlton represents a negative evaluation. The ratings show that respondents did not see it as friendly, a good fit to the campus image, or a good fit to the buildings around it. They gave more favorable scores to it for impressive, exciting, like its overall appearance, and not distressing, but in light of the acquiescence bias, these probably represent neutral to negative ratings; and they are significantly lower than the scores given to the Physics Research Building.

The scores also represent the lowest ratings of 15 buildings evaluated on campus with similar methods. Up until Knowlton Hall, the Wexner Center (Peter Eisenman, Architect; Laurie Olin, Landscape Architect) held that distinction (Nasar, 1999).

Research has shown the desirability of sittable space facing pedestrian activity, activity generators, water, and sun with deciduous trees to enliven spaces (Project for Public Spaces, 1984, 2000; Whyte, 1980, 1988; Zacharias, Stathopoulos, and Hanqing, 2004). And although the front plaza faces a major pedestrian path, the design created a dead space — barren, concrete, no tables, no focal point, undesirable seating, and no water or trees. Hundreds of observations reveal that pedestrians seldom use the concrete seats planted in gravel. The rear entrance has activity generators (concrete ping pong tables), but they seldom get used, because pedestrians are elsewhere.

In sum, while the exterior meets some of the standards of the master plan, it fails on many other accounts. Part of this may have to do with the

Fig. 7.2. For exterior, the Knowlton School of Architecture building received consistently lower ratings than did the Physics Research Building (combined means: Knowlton = 4.23, SD 0.09; Physics = 5.28, SD 0.06).

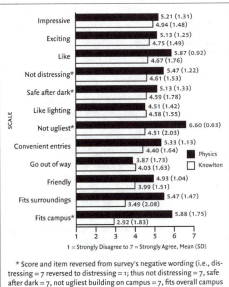

1 = Strongly Disagree to 7 = Strongly Agree, Mean (SD)

* Score and item reversed from survey's negative wording (i.e., distressing = 7 reversed to distressing = 1; thus not distressing = 7, safe after dark = 7, not ugliest building on campus = 7, fits overall campus image = 7).

marble cladding. When asked what features accounted for their evaluations, people most often cited the tiles (15.5 percent), marble (15.5 percent), and the dull gray color (14.8 percent). They also complained about its fit with the campus, walls of glass, concrete, and lack of landscaping. Yet some people liked the marble and glass. When asked what features they liked about the exterior, respondents most often cited the marble (18.2 percent), windows (27.3 percent) and shape (12.1 percent).

INTERIOR PERFORMANCE

One hundred twenty-nine respondents answering the question about the most liked features mentioned the openness (23.3 percent), windows (23.3 percent), the library (20.2 percent), and presence of the café in the building (10.9 percent) most often. Respondents answering the question about disliked features cited 32 different problems. They most frequently complained about the unfinished concrete (38.8 percent), acoustics (31.8 percent, often in relation to crits and studios), ramps (26.4 percent), inoperable windows and dark spaces (16.3 percent), circulation (15.5 percent), stairs (14.7 percent), inaccessible restroom locations (15.5 percent), temperature (9.3 percent), studios (10.1 percent), the design of the roof garden (7.8 percent), and the marble shingles (7.8 percent).

The interior also received neutral to negative evaluations (Figure 7.3). As with the exterior, the composite rating of the interior represents a negative evaluation. While respondents liked the amount of space, they gave low ratings to the environmental quality, ability to find your way around, wall, floors, ceilings, and interior aesthetics; and they gave neutral to negative ratings to the exterior aesthetics, adaptability, accessibility, proximity to views, security, maintenance, and relationships. I subsequently learned that a blind student refused to take a class in the large lecture space, because the corridor outside the space led directly to a down stairway, with no cues to the stair. He had fallen down the stairs.

Though not rated by users, the design lacked basic elements for energy efficiency. When asked about using green design principles in the design, during an early crit, Mack Scogin said that it would "have operable

Fig. 7.3. Ratings of the Knowlton facility (grand mean, 4.33) revealed favorable ratings of the amount of space but unfavorable ratings of the interior aesthetics (including materials and environmental quality) and ease of finding your way around.

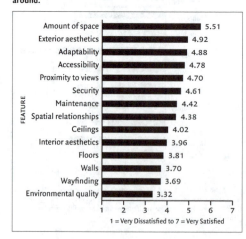

windows." While the building has operable windows in faculty offices, a
3-foot work surface blocks access to
them. To open or close the windows,
one must climb on the work surface,
operate the lower latch, and stand on
the work surface to operate the upper
latch 8 feet up.

Key findings from the second post-
occupancy evaluation are reported below.

People Liked the Library and Computer Labs

Two sets of questions measured satisfaction. One had respondents rate their
satisfaction with each space. The other had them mention up to two spaces
they found most satisfying and two they found least satisfying. The ratings
(Figure 7.4) yielded high satisfaction scores for the library; and fairly high
satisfaction scores for the computer labs and faculty and administrative offices. City and Regional Planning students gave the labs negative ratings and
lower scores than did the other students. The open-ended responses about
the most satisfying features echoed the ratings. Of the 204 responses, the library appeared most often (28 percent), followed by the computer labs
(13.2 percent) again with few City and Regional Planning students giving
the labs favorable ratings. Fewer users selected the public areas and studios
(10.3 percent each) and offices (9.3 percent) as most satisfying places. Ratings of most other spaces did not exceed 5 percent.

Part of the desirability of the library may have to do with its move from a
location outside the building to one inside the building, but the design also
has a light and airy feel. The library (see Figure 7.5) has windows behind and
above most bookshelves, a view outside, and a variety of seating and study
options. The designer thought the natural light would not damage the books.
However, shortly after the building opened, the windows required a retro-
fit to filter the light. The 53 respondents who rated qualities of the library
gave it high ratings for its lighting, aesthetics, amount of space, acoustics,
and security (means above 5.5); they gave neutral scores for temperature
and flexibility (around 5.0), and lower scores for odor and accessibility (4.6
and below). When asked directly what they liked about it, 55.8 percent of
the respondents cited glass, windows, or lighting. Smaller percentages pertained to comfortable chairs, and convenience, views, quiet, and openness.
Fewer users mentioned the library's design, comfort, collection of designer

Fig. 7.4.
Ratings of
spaces in
Knowlton
showed that
users are
satisfied
with the
library,
computer
labs, and
administra-
tive offices;
and dissatis-
fied with the
jury space,
restrooms,
storage, and
circulation.

Fig. 7.5.
Respondents
liked the
library for its
presence in
the Knowl-
ton building,
its open-
ness, and
variety of
comfortable
seating
options.

furniture, colors, privacy, and carpet. Some people reported dislikes including leaks, uneven heating/cooling, and lack of cubicles or private study
places. The respondents represented a good mix of people from architecture, landscape architecture, and planning.

As for the computer labs, the 23 respondents who rated qualities of the
labs gave them high scores for the lighting, space, and security (above 5.5),
lower but favorable scores to acoustics and access (above 4.5), and neutral to
negative scores for aesthetics, odor, flexibility, and temperature. Counts of
liked features revealed that users most often cited the number of computers
(40.1 percent), and light (29.7 percent). Fewer people cited quiet, privacy,
windows, security, amount of space, temperature, and accessibility. The
computer labs also drew some complaints. Everyone who complained mentioned temperature, but they also complained about its sterile impersonal
materials, noise from those materials, and a slamming door.

People Disliked Circulation and Studios

The satisfaction ratings (Figure 7.4) show lower scores for circulation, storage, restrooms, jury space, and studios. Responses to the question about
least satisfying spaces echoed the negative evaluation of circulation, studios,
and restrooms. Of the 211 mentions of least satisfying spaces, circulation accounted for 20.4 percent. Adding mentions of ramps (2.4 percent), stairs
(2.8 percent), elevators (0.5 percent), and public areas (7.1 percent) raises

dissatisfaction with circulation to roughly a third of the respondents. Fewer people cited the studios (17.1 percent) and restrooms (15.2 percent). No other space category had a score above 5 percent.

The circulation system has a set of ramps that force people to walk out of their way, it has enclosed fire stairs often disconnected from the ramps (Figures 7.6 and 7.7), and two elevators roughly 300 feet apart. It also has glass-edged, narrow corridors that were found scary by some females. Circulation received lowest ratings for acoustics and aesthetics (less than 3.0), followed by lighting and flexibility (less than 3.5), space, temperature, and odor (less than 4.0) and security and access (less than 4.3). Frequency counts of disliked aspects of circulation revealed that most people complained about the ugly, narrow, and scary stairs (39.3 percent), ramps that led nowhere (37.8 percent) and indirect disconnected routes in general (35.7 percent). They also complained about the difficulty in finding your way around (17.9 percent), the inadequate speed and number of elevators (16.1 percent), and to a lesser extent the concrete and noise.

The studios (such as the one shown in Figure 7.8) received low ratings on just about every design quality, with lowest scores for acoustics (1.6) and lighting (2.6), followed by aesthetics, security, temperature, and accessibility (all less than 3.4), followed by flexibility and odor (less than 3.9) and space (4.5). (Flexibility refers to the ease of adapting the space for various uses). Frequency counts of disliked features revealed that users most often

Fig. 7.6. People disliked the long ramps that lead nowhere forcing people out of their way and causing confusion.

Fig. 7.7. Users felt forced to use the dark, enclosed fire stairs, which they disliked.

Fig. 7.8. The open-design studios suffered from problems with acoustics, cramped space, security, and inadequate lighting.

complained about the acoustics (56.4 percent) and inadequate lighting (43.6 percent). Fewer people complained about dysfunctional chairs, desks, and furniture (23.1 percent), concrete (20.5 percent), and layout (20.5 percent). Additional complaints concerned temperature, inadequate views, theft, and uncomfortable environments. A minority of respondents, most of whom were architecture students, liked some aspects of the studios, often citing the amount of space. Perhaps this resulted from their move from cramped, makeshift studio spaces in a 54-year-old food sciences building.

METHOD

One hundred thirty-seven people completed surveys on the exterior appearance of two buildings (79 for Knowlton Hall and 58 for the Physics Research Building). Interviewers contacted passersby at various sites around each building. While not a random sample, this kind of sample (called an opportunity sample, because it samples available people) does represent passersby and it resulted in diverse samples for each building. For Knowlton, the sample had 53.2 percent males, 46.8 percent females, with an average reported age of 24 years (ranging from 18 to 41 years) and time on campus at 2.8 years (ranging from months to 15 years). The sample included undergraduates from every year, graduate students, doctoral students, faculty, and staff. For the Physics Research Building, the sample included 62.1 percent males, 37.9 percent females, with an average age of 25 years (ranged from 19 to 60 years) and time spent on campus at 3.3 years (ranging from months to 30 years). Each sample included undergraduates from every year, graduate students, doctoral students, faculty, and staff, and more than 16 different majors.

The survey on interior performance had 135 respondents (54 graduate students, 31 undergraduate students in architecture, 27 undergraduate students in landscape architecture, and 23 members of faculty and staff) with an average age of 29 years old (ranging from 19 to 63 years old) and an average of 4.3 years at school (ranging from 1 to 33 years). By year, the sample had 14.8 percent second-year undergrads, 21.3 percent third year, 16.7 percent fourth year, 38.9 percent masters level, and 6.5 percent doctoral students. Participants entered their responses via an online survey site—Survey Monkey. Survey Monkey captures the respondents' email addresses, allows them to stop answering and return to complete or edit their responses, and prevents individuals from completing more than one survey. Students in my graduate-level City and Regional Planning class (Programming Facilities for Human Use) solicited participation from various groups in the online survey; and school list servers for each group announced the survey and gave the web address for participants to complete it.

CONCLUSIONS

The POE revealed a fairly flawed building. The exterior evaluation found Knowlton Hall as the ugliest building of 15 buildings so far assessed on campus, and a poor fit with the surroundings and campus. The landscape design failed to take advantage of the site and to provide basic amenities for a lively entrance plaza, where people would sit, linger, and engage in informal interactions. The interior drew neutral to negative ratings. While users like the library and open space, they dislike the interior aesthetics, quality of materials, difficulties in wayfinding, and noise that interferes with studio and crits. The corridor outside the main large lecture space, which is used for classes and public lectures, presents a danger to blind users: a stairway without any cue for a blind person; and for a building which will likely serve the school for 100 years, and which requires the school to pay operating costs, it neglects basic design principles of energy conservation. Most of the problems could have been avoided or diminished through use of well established research findings on human use and a more open participatory process. Faculty members had mentioned most of these potential problems during the planning and design process, but their suggestions were ignored.

LESSONS LEARNED

- Use research and a participatory process throughout the planning and design process to gain the benefit of the wisdom of the crowd (Surowiecki, 2004).
- Seek better compatibility, less novelty, and warmer materials. People dislike the extreme novelty and incompatibility of the design with surrounding buildings.
- Enliven the front entrance with amenities such as seating, deciduous trees, water elements, and views to pedestrians.
- Simplify wayfinding. Use a simpler layout, distinguishing features at decision points, and an intuitive room numbering system: odds on one side, evens on the other, progressing forward, like most American street systems; and use well designed you-are-here maps (Levine, 1982; Levine, Marchon and Hanley, 1984) to make the building's massing and layout legible and easy for users to navigate.
- Enclose each studio and crit space for acoustic privacy. Multiple studios or classroom spaces opening onto one another create acoustical problems and interferences with the educational process.

Box 7.1

MARDELLE MCCUSKEY SHEPLEY
AND HILAL OZCAN

8

THE LANGFORD ARCHITECTURE CENTER

TEXAS A&M UNIVERSITY

SUMMARY

The Langford Architecture Center at Texas A&M housed approximately 1,700 students and 210 faculty and staff in three buildings—A, B, and C. In 1999, the College formulated a proposal to expand and remodel the existing complex. We did a POE to inform that process. The POE had an exterior and two interior evaluations. The exterior survey paralleled the protocol established by the multi-university POE study and involved 30 participants. One part of the interior evaluation surveyed 145 users about the best liked and the least liked physical properties of Langford Architecture Center. The other part used Sanoff's Six Factor Architecture Building Assessment tool (see Part III, Chapter 15) to have 43 users evaluate the technical, functional, and behavioral elements of the newest addition, Building A (completed in 1977).

The results indicated the importance of creating unifying exterior spaces, more comfortable and energy-efficient buildings, and more sensitive fit with context. The assessments also revealed a need for nature focused, naturally lit, and socially supportive space. Some spaces and attributes (e.g., atrium and façade recession) received both high and low ratings, perhaps due to the boldness of their design expression.

BACKGROUND

In 1999, the College of Architecture at Texas A&M formulated a proposal to expand and remodel its existing complex. At that time, the Ernest Langford Architecture Center had three buildings—A, B, and C. The main building, Building A (1973–1977), was an addition to the existing College of Architecture, Buildings B and C (1963). Building A is a four-story building with 109,000 gross square feet. It contains studios, classrooms, and faculty and administrative offices. At the

Figs. 8.1a–d. (left and overleaf) Floor plans of Building A, B, and C.

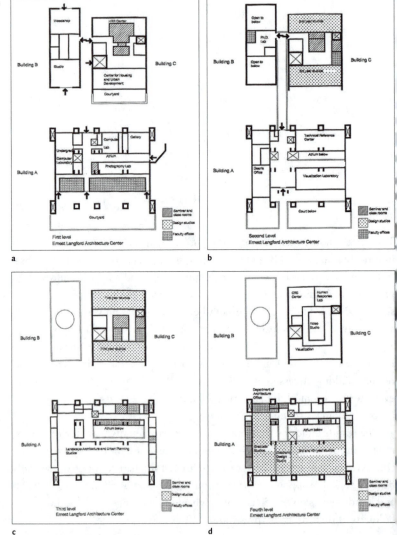

time of the POE, Building B was a two-story research/workshop building of about 12,000 gross square feet; and Building C was a three-story classroom/studio building of about 48,000 gross square feet, to which a 16,000-square-foot floor was added in 1990. The total square footage of architectural facilities (for floor plans of the first, second, third, and fourth levels, see Figure 8.1) was 185,000 gross square feet (Office of Institutional Studies and Planning, 2001). The facility accommodated 1,709 students and 210 faculty and staff.

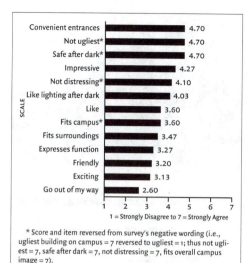

1 = Strongly Disagree to 7 = Strongly Agree

* Score and item reversed from survey's negative wording (i.e., ugliest building on campus = 7 reversed to ugliest = 1; thus not ugliest = 7, safe after dark = 7, not distressing = 7, fits overall campus image = 7).

Fig. 8.2. Passersby gave the Langford exterior neutral ratings, with favorable ratings for convenience of entrances, safety, and not among the ugliest buildings on campus, and unfavorable ratings for like it, fit to surroundings, friendliness, excitement, and would walk out of my way to see it.

The architect for Building A was Harwood K. Smith & Partners Architects in Dallas (Harwood K. Smith & Partners, 1973). Datum (structural engineers) and Gaynor & Sirmen (mechanical) were the consulting engineers. Dean Raymond Reed's 1973 statement of purpose for Building A called for a design that would: 1) illustrate knowledge and excellence in architecture, 2) express the building's functions without pretense, 3) avoid isolating departments from one another, 4) have flexible studios and laboratory spaces to accommodate changes in student enrollment and/or teaching methodology, 5) harmonize with the Texas climate and minimize energy consumption through appropriate orientation, insulation, and shading of glass areas, and 6) have high quality lighting and ventilation in all spaces to permit maximum use of natural light and ventilation. In addition, it would: 1) function as an effective teaching aid; 2) avoid high-rise concepts requiring elevator staff for other than those with disabilities, or for service use; and 3) provide continuity between the existing and new facilities.

RESULTS

Results were grouped into two categories, those pertaining to the building exterior, and those pertaining to the interior.

BUILDING EXTERIOR

Figure 8.2 shows the ratings of the exterior. As you can see, passersby gave it neutral ratings (grand mean = 3.80). They judged it as safe, as having

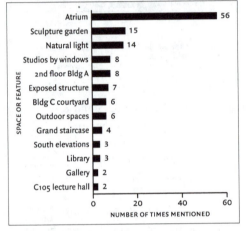

convenient entrances, and as not among the "ugliest buildings" on campus, but they judged it as a poor fit, unfriendly, unexciting, and not worth walking out of their way to see.

Examination of responses by three groups in the sample revealed that faculty, staff, and students gave it slightly below average ratings, with faculty giving it the lowest scores (all thirteen means below 3.33), followed by staff, and then students. All three groups agreed that the exterior looked distressing, and that the exterior did not clearly indicate the interior functions.

In response to the question about physical features they disliked, faculty cited materials, scale, finishes, detailing, and style relative to the rest of the campus. They described it as having no personality, feeling inhumane, cold, inaccessible, and having entrances that were not compelling. Staff members complained about the amount and appearance of the concrete, which they described as "gray," "heavy," and "dark," and they described the exterior as "ugly," or an "ugly modern building," "cold," lacking in "personality" and "uninteresting." Some saw the exterior as dirty (see Figure 8.3), and they disliked the staircase. Additionally, they judged the building as not matching surrounding buildings. Students said they disliked the lack of color, the plain, flat surfaces, its lack of match to other buildings, its awkward entrances, its failure to convey the interior function and symbolism of an architecture building. It was described as "ordinary," "more like a Computer Science Building," or a "square box." They also complained about its orientation showing ignorance of the sun's path, natural ventilation, accessibility of entrances, poor design of the green spaces, unused front porch by the south entrance, and the steep staircase at the east entrance.

Staff reported some features they liked, including the multiple windows and good lighting compared to other buildings, welcoming entrance with ramp, bold features such as "huge concrete," and the garden area. Students liked the south façade (how it recessed back, the terraced and layered look,

Fig. 8.3. (top) View of Langford's main elevation from southwest.

Fig. 8.4. (bottom) Positive features. Respondents most often mentioned the atrium and its grand staircase as the most positive attributes of the Langford Complex (43 percent of respondents).

different levels and the distinction of floors, and the relationship between mass and void), the extensive number of windows, the green areas in general, and especially the courtyard in the west and the sunken garden in the south, finish, and materials (exposed concrete, and the functionality of the expansion joints).

INTERIOR SPACES

Figure 8.4 shows the frequency with which respondents cited various features or spaces as best liked. The atrium emerged as the best liked space. Of the 145 respondents, all but 11 mentioned more than one space. Forty-one percent mentioned the atrium or the grand staircase contained within it as positive attributes. One hundred thirty-four responses referred to positive attributes. In addition to the atrium (see Figure 8.5), respondents said they liked: the garden with sculpture and benches, natural light, the layout of the second floor, the organization of studio space (particularly those spaces by windows), the exposed concrete structure, the courtyard adjacent to Building C, general green spaces, the grand staircase, south elevations and overhangs, the Technical Reference Center (TRC), the gallery, and the lecture hall in Building C. Approximately 24 percent mentioned outdoor space or natural light as being positive, in spite of the solar radiation and normally warm temperatures in College Station.

Fig. 8.5. The atrium showing the grand staircase.

One hundred forty-two responses mentioned *negative* attributes of Langford (Figure 8.6). These included the HVAC system (21 percent), followed by the studios (12 percent) shown in Figure 8.7, windowless classrooms and computer lab (11 percent), and to a lesser extent, the general organization of space, inadequate lighting, acoustics, main entrances, second floor atrium, elevator, lack of proper review spaces, loading/bridge area, restrooms (especially ventilation), first floor "garden" (adjacent to loading area) and water leaks. Interestingly, while people said they liked the atrium, its second floor received criticism, because its tile surface created acoustical problems for crits.

Fixed ratings for six factors of use (shown in Figure 8.8) revealed neutral to positive scores for context and wayfinding, neutral scores for interface (the place where the building interior and exterior meet) and massing, and negative ratings for socio-spatial factors and comfort. While socio-spatial factors have a great impact on "studio culture," teamwork and interaction among students, the low comfort scores confirm the open-ended complaints about design features, in particular the HVAC systems. These findings do not fully agree with the exterior ratings. They suggest higher scores for context and appropriateness of massing than the ratings obtained from passersby about fit. The difference probably results from differences in respondents (more architects judging the factors) and questions (with multiple questions for each factor).

The neutral score for interface, as defined above, perhaps reflects a mix of the positive rating for the convenience of the entrances, but the open-ended complaints describing the entrances as among the worst aspects of the buildings. The college has multiple doors leading to it, and the small size of the vestibule at the main entrance makes it difficult to navigate. Additionally, one entrance, although conveniently located, is so steep that people refer to it as the "suicide stairs."

The faculty evaluations of Building A judged the design as less successful on the six components (*context, massing, interface, wayfinding, socio-spatial,* and *comfort*) and put them in a different order. For each component, respondents received a list of items which they rated for appropriateness (from 1 = highly inappropriate, to 7 = highly appropriate). In this context, the term *appropriateness* means "satisfactory" or "successful." While faculty gave context and wayfinding the highest scores (4.43 and 4.04, respectively), interface and massing middle scores, and socio-spatial factors and comfort the lowest scores, the order of two pairs switched. At the bottom, socio-spatial dropped below comfort (3.24 and 3.58, respectively). In the middle, interface and massing received lower scores, and interface dropped below massing (3.59 and 3.99, respectively). In sum, they judged most factors as

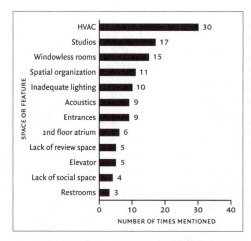

Fig. 8.6. Negative features. Respondents most frequently cited as the most negative attribute of the Langford facility the poor HVAC system, inadequate studios, and windowless computer labs and classrooms.

Fig. 8.7. Fourth-floor design studios in Langford. Some respondents described the studios (located throughout the complex) as negative features.

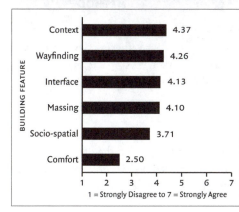

Fig. 8.8. Respondents agreed that the Langford Complex fit its setting, but performed poorly for socio-spatial factors and comfort.

unsatisfactory. Students and staff evaluated two factors as unsatisfactory: comfort (students 2.91; staff, 3.17), and socio-spatial factors (students 3.77; staff 3.90). They gave somewhat higher ratings to massing (students 4.12; staff 4.06), interface (students 4.15; staff 4.60), wayfinding (students 4.22; staff 4.78), and context (students 4.32; staff 4.62).

Faculty and students often had similar evaluations, which sometimes differed from those of the staff. This may result from the architectural background of the student and faculty participants. These individuals typically rated the same specific properties of the assessment criteria as the most or the least satisfactory features of the building. For instance, both groups evaluated the relationship of building parts as the most successful aspect of massing, while staff thought pleasing appearance was the most successful. Likewise, faculty and staff rated the appearance of the building in relation to surrounding buildings more negatively than did staff. All groups complained most often about the inability to adjust temperature individually, but students and staff gave significantly lower scores to comfort overall (2.91 and 3.17 respectively) than did faculty (3.58).

Although the building design intentions included a goal of energy efficiency and good ventilation, it received criticism for comfort and energy issues, and especially ventilation, thermal comfort, and lighting. It succeeded in providing a light space in the Atrium, but also had disliked windowless areas.

Both the exterior and interior studies revealed dissatisfaction. Variation across the groups showed the faculty in both studies as less positive than students, who were less positive, in turn, than staff. For the interior, faculty gave the lowest total score (22.87) followed by students (23.49) and staff (24.13).

METHOD

The approach to this study generally mirrors the methodology of data gathering devised for all project participants, although variations in surveys and interviews occur in some. See Chapter 5 for a more detailed explanation of the methodological approach.

EXTERIOR STUDY

The POE of Langford Architecture Building took place in 1999. The exterior survey used the same questions and procedures of the multi-university POE study (Chapter 5), with one exception: The interviewers conducted the survey orally. Interviewers stopped passersby in front of the main (south) entrance of Langford Architecture Center, until they had 30 respondents, half male and half female. This yielded a diverse sample. The ages of respondents ranged between 20 and 60, with the mean age being approximately 35 years. Interviewees had 1 to 30 years of experience on the campus. While the sample had 12 people from the College of Architecture, it also included people from many other areas, including Plant Pathology, Office of Graduate Studies, College of Agriculture and Life Sciences, and International Agriculture. It also included students at all levels from first year undergraduate to Ph.D. students.

INTERIOR STUDY

The interiors POE used Sanoff's (2000) framework (also covered in Chapter 15). It had two surveys. One, with a sample of 145 respondents, asked users to report the best liked and the least liked physical properties of Langford Architecture Center for all three buildings. Another, with a sample of 43 respondents, used Sanoff's "Six Factor Architecture Building Assessment" tool to obtain ratings of the *technical, functional, and behavioral* elements of Building A.

The sample for best liked and least liked properties were recruited by 14 students in an architectural programming class, each of whom were asked to solicit responses from a minimum of 10 students, faculty, or staff. That sample included 108 students, 20 faculty, and 17 staff members. Although gender was not specified, it is assumed that the results reflected the overall approximate distribution for the college, which was as follows: students, 30% female and 70% male; faculty, 25% female and 75% male; and staff, 67% female and 33% male.

The sample for the six-factor assessment of Building A included 19 students, 16 faculty, and 8 staff members. Faculty and staff received the questionnaire in their mailboxes. Students in graduate programming and undergraduate seminar classes received the questionnaire in class. This questionnaire measured six key components of building performance: *context, massing, interface, wayfinding, socio-spatial* (ability of the building to support social interaction), and *comfort*. Chapter 15 discusses the components and the items that make up the component. For example, for context, respondents rated the appropriateness of the building scale matching the site. The mean score of the items on a component represented the component score. The average of those means represented an overall score for the building of 3.89.

CONCLUSION

The post-occupancy evaluation (initiated in 1999) sought to provide data to inform the design process for facilities slated for construction in 2004–2005. The results raised multiple issues including the importance of creating unifying exterior spaces, more comfortable and energy-efficient buildings, and more sensitive context-awareness. It also suggested the need to provide nature focused, naturally lit, and socially supportive spaces.

After completion of the POE, the Langford complex underwent a major remodeling. It has a new auditorium, a covered link between the three buildings, remodeled space for Ph.D. students, and new offices. The new construction addressed several problems identified in the POE. For example, it replaced tile finishes in the second-floor atrium with carpet to improve acoustics, added a social gathering space (Internet café), and fixed roof leaks. Unfortunately, multiple efforts to correct problems associated with the HVAC system have not yet fully rectified the problem.

Future work should consider some broader questions about the degree to which the university process encourages good design and building performance, and the degree to which design intention and application can become more closely aligned.

LESSONS LEARNED

- The exterior should have some contextual compatibility.
- Though difficult, try for a design that meets the professional standards of an architecturally sophisticated population as well as those of the lay population.
- The interior should have an atrium or other large-scale social gathering feature in the design. Most Texas A&M users enjoyed the atrium, which also served as the spatial organizer.
- Make sure the design has an excellent HVAC system to insure a comfortable environment.
- To the extent possible, adhere to LEED standards for an energy efficient building.
- Provide access to nature through windows, gardens, and courtyards.
- To enhance the academic experience, provide naturally lit, socially supportive spaces.

Box 8.1

GALEN CRANZ, WITH JESS WENDOVER,
IRIS TIEN, MARK GILLEM, AND JON NORMAN

COLLEGE OF ENVIRONMENTAL DESIGN

UC BERKELEY TEMPORARY HOME

SUMMARY

The Hearst Field Annex (HFA) is a complex of four new, prefabricated steel buildings at the University of California at Berkeley intended to accommodate academic departments while their regular quarters undergo seismic upgrading. First designed to meet the needs of the College of Environmental Design (CED) and its three departments—Architecture, City and Regional Planning, and Landscape Architecture, the complex is intended to serve as a surge building for many different departments over the upcoming decades. The College occupied the buildings from 1998 to 2003. We conducted the POE in 2001.

The results indicate satisfaction among faculty and students in the College of Environmental Design with HFA as a temporary facility. Most users judged it as "effective" and "well organized," but also saw the need for many improvements. We observed a tension between the desire for community, and the (usually frustrated) desire for privacy and territory. As a social space, the courtyard stood out as one of the most successful features of the complex. In contrast, wayfinding and climate control stood out as problems. These findings lead to recommendations for retrofitting HFA, improving Wurster Hall, and enhancing architecture departments elsewhere.

117

BACKGROUND

In late 1997 the CED had to plan to relocate for the upcoming fall semester of 1998. Desperate for a place to move within eight months, and with no time for the luxury of an architectural selection process, Harrison Fraker, Professor of Architecture and Dean of the College, took on the responsibility of designing a new temporary headquarters for the College.

The site, previously a playing field, was chosen because locating new buildings there would not interfere with existing public space patterns. Moreover, it would displace relatively few users, because of the nonregulation size of the field and its infrequent use for sports.

The overall site plan called for four demountable Butler buildings (steel building systems) arranged around a courtyard. Building A contained the au-

Fig. 9.1a. University of California at Berkeley Campus plan with Hearst Field Annex (HFA) circled.

Fig. 9.1b. HFA plan with Buildings A, B, C, & D surrounding the courtyard.

ditorium for classroom instruction and film screening by the Pacific Film Archive (PFA); Building B accommodated the administration of the three departments within the College; Building C held computer labs, studio space, and a half dozen small faculty offices, and Building D had design studios exclusively. Two buildings lay parallel to the street and city grid, and the other two parallel to the campus grid (see Figures 9.1a and b for the siting and HFA plan). As the buildings had a prefabricated wall structure, only the utilities, slab, and foundation required on-site construction. This allowed construction to take place in nine months (at a low cost of about $100/square foot), and occupancy by the following fall. The project cost $4 million plus $800,000 for the landscaping, the arcade around the edge of the courtyard, special features in the theater, and air conditioning. Given the financial pressures and timeline of the project, the University administration and the CED were satisfied. Later our study looked at the satisfaction of the 400 users. In siting and detailing these buildings Fraker focused on three issues—community, wayfinding, and sustainability—and these three issues became the focus of our evaluation.

METHODOLOGY

Nearly 30 four-person teams of architecture students within a class "Social and Cultural Factors in Architecture and Urban Design" in UC Berkeley's Department of Architecture collected the data in the spring of 2001. To answer the research questions, we used five different data collection techniques: observation, direct observation, interview, questionnaire, and content analysis of archival documents that included architectural documents, planning memos, and newspaper coverage. Recurrent patterns across the techniques would increase the confidence in their reliability. The strength of this study lies in multiple measures pointing to the same conclusions.

RESULTS

The study revealed information with regard to community and privacy, the successful courtyard, wayfinding, and sustainability. We will consider each one separately.

COMMUNITY AND PRIVACY

Since the early twentieth century, architects have aspired to use the design of buildings as a way to forge and support community. HFA brought the graduate and administrative groups for all three departments closer together than before in the three separate wings of Wurster Hall, but it dispersed the undergraduates, a significant blow to the formation of community. Undergraduate students reported spending one to five hours at HFA per week for lectures, conventional classes, administrative activities, or toilets; for studios, they had to go to three other buildings on campus. In contrast, graduate students, who had their studios in HFA, reported spending 20 to 60 hours per week at HFA. (Some graduate students may have enjoyed the exclusivity of their separation into a little town of their own.) Most undergraduates saw HFA as "mostly for grad students" and therefore many felt uncomfortable in HFA. Despite alienation from HFA, when asked how they would tell someone else where CED is, most undergraduates (66.7 percent) said "HFA," 40 percent said "Wurster," and only 4 percent said "Giannini," the site of most undergraduate studios.

Part of the meaning of community includes a relationship between faculty and students, which several design features frustrated. Systematic observation of the behavior of faculty in half-hour increments from 9:00 AM until 7:00 PM revealed that the faculty spent little time in buildings other than Building B, seldom lingering to speak with staff, students, or their colleagues on the perimeter path or in the courtyard. The semi-private nature of the mailbox area and adjacent restrooms, not accessible to everyone, further blocked possible spontaneous meetings between students and faculty out-side of office hours. The lack of a lobby area at the entry made it a poor place to foster student–faculty interaction. The overall congestion in the building limited privacy and therefore produced more closed doors, which confirms one of the recurring themes of human–environment relations, namely, that without privacy (individual control over interaction with others) commu-nity cannot flourish (Rapoport, 1975; Hayden, 1976). Students converted a classroom (A15 on the plan in Figure 9.1b.) into a lounge for City Planning grad students, and many other CED students used it. The creation of this lounge testified to the importance of semi-private space for students.

Faculty liked HFA insofar as it facilitated communication amongst faculty from different disciplines. Those in HFA reported more informal meetings and face-to-face contacts than those who were moved to different locations on campus and had to rely on e-mail and cell phones as their chief means of communication.

For staff, community was an elusive goal, and again design played its role, both positively and negatively. Most of the administrators responsible for the planning and operation of the complex seemed pleased with the amount of interaction among departmental staff, emphasizing its contrast to Wurster where the three departments were physically separated. This rosy image faded after talking with those in different roles. First, everyone noted a de-crease in privacy. Staff noted that staff–faculty and staff–student interaction had decreased. Observers noted that the relationships between staff mem-bers *within* each department were close-knit, while the relations *between* de-partments appeared distant. Even though the three departments shared one large office space, distinct boundary lines were drawn. Since the depart-ments were combined, observers expected to find a stronger sense of cama-raderie, exemplified perhaps by sharing office supplies and amenities, but each department had its own separate, locked supply cabinet and photo-copy machine. Even the shared stapler had a sign reading: "Property of . . ." Staff suggested that more staff interaction would have taken place if an in-door lounge with seating, a sink, and a link to an outdoor lounge had been planned. Instead, the conference room had a microwave oven to make up for having no kitchen.

The building did not have enough space to designate a private place for staff to counsel students, nor a reception area for waiting students and visi-tors. The lack of internal space to handle a crowd of students was particularly felt during the beginning and end of semesters or during registration when students needed counseling. Staff put up a Japanese-style folding screen be-tween their cubicle and areas of high traffic to create greater privacy. We

Fig. 9.2a. Courtyard in use, 2000. This was the main community space for the complex and was used for rest, socializing, and class work. (Photo by Galen Cranz.)

conclude that even in tight quarters, providing spaces for social differentiation and privacy is essential.

THE SUCCESSFUL COURTYARD

The courtyard (Figures 9.2a and b) served as one of the most successful features for community building. Two years after the opening of the HFA, the central courtyard gave students, staff, and faculty of the CED more than just a place to sit in or walk through, it gave them a flexible space, constantly adapted to the changing needs and uses of those who used it. Originally designed and installed as a simple, flat lawn with only three trees in front of the western facing windows of Building B, the courtyard became filled with sculptural installations, permanent furniture, and studio chairs pulled outside—all signs of continued use and alteration. The courtyard functioned as a kind of living room for the graduate students who usually spent 40 or more hours in the HFA complex per week.

Graduate students from all three departments used the area at many different hours of the day. While some only used the courtyard "when it's sunny," most passed through the space in between classes and most reported eating their lunch there. Over a third of the graduate students said they used the space in the evening or "late at night while working in studio." Most used the space for "taking breaks," "lounging," "mingling," "talking," and making cell phone calls; only one claimed not to use the courtyard for leisure purposes, but rather "just to walk by." Other activities included sunbathing, reading, smoking, meeting classmates, drawing, and taking photographs.

The courtyard contained some furniture (chairs, benches, and a platform). One person referred to chairs as, "good because you can rearrange them and bring out more if needed." This confirms one of the most important findings of Whyte's (1980) research on the social life of small urban spaces about the importance of moveable chairs.

Even though they liked the courtyard, many people had recommendations for improving it. Two-thirds of them mentioned the need for more seating, better furniture, movable chairs, and tables. Of the eight students who reported some dislikes about the courtyard, six complained about the lack of shade.

Yet, we should count the courtyard as a success. Many interviewees reported it as the main thing they would miss from HFA when they return to Wurster. Wurster has a courtyard, although it is less central to circulation. Instead, it has a first-floor internal lobby, the main thoroughfare, also used for informal reviews and exhibit space, where undergraduates can view graduate projects and vice versa, students can approach professors, and faculty can interact casually. This contrasts with the advantage of the outdoor location of the HFA courtyard at HFA, only steps away from the studios.

FINDING YOUR WAY AROUND

Wayfinding to the building had mixed success. Interviews with the general public confirmed that they perceived the buildings as convenient to the nearest public street, Bancroft Ave. However, first-time visitors had a difficult time finding the entry (Figure 9.3), because the complex is above eye level, which made the entrance difficult to predict from the street. Only a few outsiders knew that the "tin buildings by Hearst Gym" housed the CED, but many knew that they housed the PFA. The number of informal paper signs indicated a need for better signage. When asked to score the building as a representation of the Architecture Department, outsiders gave it a low score (1.9 out of 5). From the point of view of public perception and orientation, the building needed better use of signs and color.

Our researchers also observed problems with wayfinding and signage within the building. Having only one major entrance caused congestion and disorientation, especially for those who had business with one of the smaller two departments. Observers noticed that the one entrance to the three departments faced a reception-like desk, actually owned by the Architecture Department, that was misread as the information desk for the CED as a whole. Official signs hung from the ceiling in order to designate each department and assist in wayfinding, but they were too small, "barely visible." Sometimes unofficial signs were taped to the official ones, but both the official and the unofficial

Fig. 9.2b. (top) The courtyard has one of the ecological features of the complex. Trees planted in 1998 shade the west side of Building B as viewed from Building C today in 2005.

Fig. 9.3. (bottom) The sign for Building C is visible but the function of the building is not clear.

signs were inadequate to orient newcomers. Architectural form (in this case, entry-door reception desk) implicitly communicated more strongly than the explicit labels on signs. This misreading of the Architecture Department reception desk underscores the power of architectural configuration.

Many outsiders, including two-thirds of the undergraduates, did not understand the layout of rooms and had difficulty finding a specific room—rather surprising for such a small complex. The lettering system added to disorientation. The lettering system for the buildings did not correspond to the spatial hierarchy. (The most central building was labeled B instead of A). The signage for the buildings and rooms stood out only to those who repeatedly used the facility, or were accustomed to the layout. This problem applies to most cities in the United States (Muckenfuss, 1997).

Clearly, designers should give more attention to directional signage. Too often architects think of signage as a graphic design problem rather than an architectural one. Fraker had incorporated several urban design moves into the scheme, but was not as careful about signage. He aligned two of the buildings with the street and two with the grid of the campus to create a slightly skewed, asymmetrical plan, though users did not perceive this special layout. Instead, they complained about difficulties in wayfinding and lack of adequate signage.

SUSTAINABILITY

Dean Fraker's own professional expertise includes aspects of sustainability, so he had several aspirations for this building in this regard: prefabricated buildings that can be demounted (allowing the university in the far future, to dismantle, and transport the modular, pre-engineered structure to an off-campus storage facility), the efficiencies of sharing buildings and facilities, the use of fly ash, natural daylighting, operable windows, and natural ventilation. He referred to the building at the time as the greenest building in the state, saving a lot of money. He regretted the elimination of the more radical suggestion—a ventilation system relying only on ceiling fans—during construction, because it did not meet current codes.

Architecture Chair Cris Benton, himself an energy expert, expressed disappointment in the building as a missed opportunity. He explained that the buildings were *close* to being energy-efficient because they were thin in section, had high ceilings, were organized around a central courtyard, and had an adequate number of windows. But the building should have been "more porous" with bigger windows to allow more ventilation and should have had better shading. Instead of the vent and ceiling fan that Benton and Fraker

Fig. 9.4. This view is how most passersby from campus would experience HFA. Looking from Building B toward Building A, we see the relationship of the HFA to the PFA and the thwarted use of drought resistant potato vine for shading.

proposed to reduce heat in the summer, the university installed air conditioning, thereby creating cold drafts. Moreover, the use of drought resistant plants was an intentional shading strategy, and the trees on the west side do shade Building B in the afternoon, but the potato vines on the exterior trellises, which needed to grow profusely to function as shading devices, could not do so because the campus gardener kept them trimmed (Figure 9.4).

The present evaluation did not support the claims made for the building. The "observation" research team found that in the administration spaces (Building B) the arrangement of rooms did not allow efficient use of natural daylight and ventilation, even though many occupants were trying to save energy by turning down lights during daylight hours. The offices along the perimeter had windows on both their exterior and interior walls in order to light the larger interior space indirectly through the private offices. However, both these sets of windows had blinds to keep the light out, and, according to the observation team, even when the departmental heads were not in, the blinds were down, which kept the light out. In turn, this forced those in the central zone of cubicles to work with their desk lights on. This inefficient scenario could have been avoided if the professors' administrative offices had been located away from the windows toward the center, while the staff members, who spend most of their time at their desks, had been assigned to locations near windows. The status hierarchy implicit in traditional office design has caused similar problems in office planning throughout Europe and America (Duffy, 1997).

Ventilation suffered a similar problem: windows were not used for cross ventilation because most of the offices were empty with their windows and doors closed. As a result, many staff members used small fans on their desks.

The design of studio spaces used natural light directly, but overhead lights were on 24 hours, and occupants used desk lamps, giving the impression of ecologically uncaring behavior. The planning studio had a skylight, and so had a fewer number of desk lamps compared with other studios.

Regarding heat gain and ventilation problems, another research team noticed that some staff members used small heaters in the morning when Building B was very cold, and used fans in the afternoon when the place was overly warm. Temperature influenced the occupancy of studio rooms (Building D). On warm days, occupancy dropped to less than four people per studio around 2:00 PM and began to increase by around 6:00 PM.

Most students cared about Berkeley's "use of ecologically conscious building materials and techniques," but 30 out of 44 respondents could not agree that "HFA is a model for ecologically conscious building on campus." Thus, more than two-thirds of this sample did not feel that the building had fulfilled its goals as a host for environmental designers.

CONCLUSIONS

Faculty and students felt satisfied overall with HFA as a temporary facility. This building can work socially and physically for both instruction and administration and would be most suitable for smaller departments that do not have to divide their student body into groups. Those planning to use this building should take advantage of the courtyard and incorporate it into their organizational life. They might consider how to furnish it with seating, shading devices, and possibly more planting for greater enjoyment of informal use. Planners will also want to improve the buildings' dysfunctional ventilation system, increase storage, reduce noise, and increase privacy.

No matter who uses the space, it needs improved signage. Alterations should make the entire complex more legible by designing larger, more abundant, high contrast, color-coded signage and maps to orient visitors. They should add external signs in two key places for those passing by on the walk in front of Hearst Gym and for pedestrians and drivers on Bancroft Avenue. Improved signage will make the building complex more inviting to the public and more comfortable for visitors and the staff who receive them. The Pacific Film Archive remains in the complex and probably will stay there as other groups move in and out. Painting its façade might distinguish it.

Some lessons from the successes of HFA can transfer to Wurster Hall, the permanent home of the CED. The administration should seek to centralize some resources in order to get staff, faculty, and students to interact as an entire College. Given the effectiveness of the centralized courtyard, the seismic redesign of Wurster Hall probably should have lowered the height of the studio tower and filled in the fourth side of the current U-shape configuration in order to get a centralized courtyard and create continuous circulation through all the departments. The bright and warm atmosphere at HFA felt better than the notoriously cold mornings in the concrete Wurster Hall, but cool afternoons felt better than the notoriously hot metal buildings at HFA. Investigating the feasibility of fiber-optic sun scoops is one recommendation for exploring ways to bring warmth earlier and deeper into Wurster.

What lessons can we draw more generally for schools of architecture? First, try to keep undergraduate and graduate studios and classrooms in the same building. Second, in spite of reliance on computers, students still need space for models and large drawings. The tight quarters did not allow for storage, but students responded inventively by using the light fixtures or the trays that carry the electrical wiring as suspended shelving systems for models. Third, people valued the central place for gathering and informal interaction. Fourth, sacrificing privacy detracts from building a sense of community. Even in tight quarters, designs should provide spaces for privacy, territoriality, and personalization. Fifth, wayfinding adds to comfort for visitors and users. Architecture students and their visitors need clear wayfinding as much as any other group. Sixth, architecture buildings should demonstrate ecological building practices, but this may mean having to educate university administrators to change procurement practices and building codes.

LESSONS LEARNED

- Have a central gathering place, like the Berkeley courtyard, to help create a sense of community.
- Maintain adequate privacy, territoriality, or personalization to help strengthen a sense of community.
- Centralize administrative resources (rather than dispersing them) to foster greater communication among departments and faculties.
- Design for clear wayfinding as it yields greater user satisfaction with a place.
- Allow undergraduate students some exposure to graduate students to enhance peer education.
- Design for sustainability. Sustainable building and management practices require cooperation with administrators, suggesting that sustainability should be integrated into the architecture curricula, continuing education curricula, and management training.

Box 9.1

WOLFGANG F. E. PREISER

ARONOFF CENTER FOR DESIGN AND ART

THE UNIVERSITY OF CINCINNATI

SUMMARY

The College of Design, Architecture, Art, and Planning (DAAP) complex has had four phases of development, starting with the 1952 Alms Wing; the 1958 DAAP Wing; the 1976 Wilson Wing; and, the 1996 Aronoff Center for Design and Art. Previous evaluation studies were a POE carried out by a team of freshman students—the Aronoff Center POE Study Group (ACPSG) (1998)—followed by a "Vital Signs" project (Smith, et al., 1999). The post-occupancy evaluation reported here focuses on the latest development phase and design.

Although architect Peter Eisenman characterized his design in 1990 as "a rock concert in concrete," passersby gave the building low scores. As one critic, Adele Santos, said, "What astounds me is that a School of Architecture would pick an architect whose work is going to be so clearly defined at a point in time, knowing that would be the image of the school forever more. This is precisely one of the building types that require a certain kind of neutrality, flexibility, and future open-endedness" (1991).

On entry at Level 3000, one has difficulty getting one's bearings and knowing where to proceed, especially if there is no human being in sight to ask for directions. Wayfinding is circuitous and particularly difficult when changing levels, since first-time users cannot easily see the elevator and stairs.

Once in the building, users complained about the abysmal signage. Persons with disabilities face major problems getting around, since none of the three elevators connect the same stories, and one must travel long distances between them. Users also disliked the lack of natural light, sunlight, and views out, which make the interior feel like a dungeon for most of the year.

Users liked two spaces: the library and the atrium/food court. The latter succeeded in bringing the four schools of the college together in one cafeteria space. This large space, however, contributes to the overall low efficiency of only 50 percent net usable space in the building, and this comes at a relatively high building cost of more than $250 per square foot. The areas most disliked were the public areas/corridors and studios, exacerbated by poor wayfinding, lack of daylight, and harsh acoustics. Studios had problems with temperatures and poor ventilation.

The design has serious problems with waterproofing and leakage through the ceilings and walls, as well as maintenance, identified by other studies (Kristal, 2005). Regarding leakage, the design used an exterior insulation and finish system intended for light commercial construction, not for public buildings such as university facilities. The use of drywall, cheap carpeting, and omnipresent, inappropriately used caulking, has created a maintenance nightmare.

There are lighting and acoustic problems in the building, as documented by a "Vital Signs" study (Smith, et al., 1999). Since corridors and the stepped platforms of the concourse (which are not accessible to people with disabilities) are used for design critiques, student presenters complain about noise interference from people passing by. (See Figure 10.1.)

BACKGROUND

The Aronoff Center stands as an extreme expression of experimental architecture. The building's design tries to break radically with past traditions of order, hierarchy, symmetry, and the rules of aesthetic composition of facades, as well as the form and massing of the building elements. The designer, Peter Eisenman, attempted to accomplish these objectives through the realignment, twisting, and torqueing of the basic footprint of a chevron, which pre-existed in the adjacent, older buildings of the college complex, dating back to the '50s, '60s, and '70s. The design also has dizzying lines, shifted grids, and other disorienting features to achieve what Eisenman called "a geometry where the formal container is so fractured that the space is no longer contained by form."

Fig. 10.1.
Student
sign, "Quiet
Please!"
reveals
noise prob-
lems during
critiques in
the Aronoff
Center.

Eisenman achieved these visual/aesthetic effects primarily through surface manipulations of geometry, color, sculpted façade elements, fake windows, and tilted-looking east and west façades. These conceal the true and rather conventional structure of the building, which is not titled and has level floors to make it usable.

Eisenman stated that he does not care about the users of his buildings (DAAP, 1996), meaning he does not care about such fundamental concerns as function, human comfort, and ease of access. Echoing this, he claimed that obtaining user input through surveys and other means is a waste of time, implying that social science research and architectural programming is useless (DAAP, 1996). Perhaps a private client may want such a statement, but in a public building on a public campus, why try to create uncomfortable, destabilizing, dysfunctional, costly, and confusing architecture?

Why spend millions of taxpayers' dollars on it? In the case of the Aronoff Center, the cost per square foot in 1996 was about $250 per square foot, including fees and miscellaneous expenses. The project cost for new construction of 164,000 square feet was $31 million. An additional $3 million went to the renovation of the old buildings (i.e., about 140,000 square feet). At that time, typical costs of other new architecture buildings around the country were about $130 to $150 per square foot (Giovannini, 1996). Does "signature architecture" imply significantly increased construction cost when compared to regular architecture?

Several internationally known architects were approached for the project, but only Peter Eisenman was willing to develop a program for an independent Request for Proposal. That became the basis for an invited competition in which out-of-state architects would team up with local firms. Eisenman won in association with Lorenz & Williams of Dayton, Ohio. The architect selection for the building had little to do with the wishes of the faculty and students (Ward, 1995), but grew from the close affinity and collaboration of a triumvirate: then Dean Jay Chatterjee, whose vision was to have signature architects do most major building projects at UC; former Ohio State Senate President Stanley Aronoff, who got the dollars to make it possible; and, architect Peter Eisenman, who designed the building.

Groundbreaking took place in October of 1993, and the building was completed and occupied in June 1996. The renovations were finished in December 1996. The project won design awards along with praise in the architectural press. Five years prior to completion, the building won the 1991 Progressive Architecture Design Award, and it also represented the U.S. at the prestigious Venice Biennale that year. In 1996, it was selected from projects around the world for the 19th International Congress of the Union of Architects in Barcelona.

Now that the dust has settled, the time has come to take a more than cursory look at this building.

RESULTS

Results were grouped into two categories: building exterior, and overall building evaluation of the various spaces and building features. Beyond that, select findings from a similar, but earlier POE, which was carried out one year after the building was put into use, are presented.

BUILDING EXTERIOR

Eisenman claimed to base the design on a chevron shape, but such a shape occurs only once in the footprint of the older building; and following manipulation and fragmentation, the description of the design says that the chevron shape finally becomes so fuzzy that it takes on the undulating quality of the site. However, the site had the shape of a large knoll, until the landscape architect introduced the undulations, reminiscent of ancestral burial grounds of Ohio's Native American tribes. In the context of the Progressive Architecture design awards jury commentary (Dixon, 1991), Ralph Johnson remarked:

Fig. 10.2.
(right) East
"signature"
façade,
Aronoff
Center.

Fig. 10.3.
(below)
Passersby
had nega-
tive evalua-
tions of the
Aronoff Cen-
ter exterior
(mean 3.0).

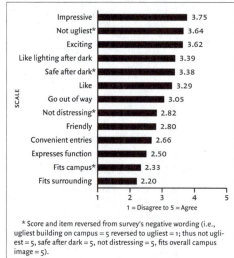

SCALE		
Impressive		3.75
Not ugliest*		3.64
Exciting		3.62
Like lighting after dark		3.39
Safe after dark*		3.38
Like		3.29
Go out of way		3.05
Not distressing*		2.82
Friendly		2.80
Convenient entries		2.66
Expresses function		2.50
Fits campus*		2.33
Fits surrounding		2.20

1   2   3   4   5
1 = Disagree to 5 = Agree

* Score and item reversed from survey's negative wording (i.e., ugliest building on campus = 5 reversed to ugliest = 1; thus not ugliest = 5, safe after dark = 5, not distressing = 5, fits overall campus image = 5).

"All of the manipulation occurs in the public space. Another quality I like about it is that it is an abstract concept and also very site specific. It makes sense with the existing buildings and with the site contours. It is not just an abstract imposition."

In fact, the POE shows that the building fails to relate to its site, context, and adjacent structures. It does not fit through its positioning, massing, and pastel colors (pink, light blue, and light green), which starkly contrast with the brick-and-concrete architecture of the University of Cincinnati (Figure 10.2).

Figure 10.3 highlights responses from a total of 45 respondents to the exterior survey. Passersby gave the exterior appearance neutral to negative evaluations.

They rated it as a bad fit with the campus, a bad fit with the surrounding buildings, dysfunctional, inconvenient, and unfriendly. They gave it neutral ratings for: walk out of the way to see it, like it, looks safe after dark, like the lighting after dark, exciting, not the ugliest building on campus, and impressive. Forty-five passersby who did not necessarily have any business in

Fig. 10.4. (left) North elevation of Aronoff Center in hillside.

Fig. 10.5. (below) The 3000 Level entrance area, Aronoff Center.

the building, disliked its appearance. While they may have seen it as mostly impressive and exciting, it left them with an overall negative impression. They responded that the building lacks convenient entrances and exits, the exterior does not indicate the interior functions, it does not fit the overall campus image, nor does its appearance fit in well with the surrounding buildings.

Some survey respondents liked the building. A fifth year English student characterized the building exterior this way: "It's an interesting concept to have a building with no right angles" (see Figure 10.4). But others did not. For example, a fourth year communications student said, "The colors are ugly, it (the building) doesn't fit in with the campus."

The negative evaluation may reflect in part the drive-up entrance experience. Visitors in cars must pass the loading dock and dumpsters before reaching the main entry (Level 3000) drop-off area. The 3000 level entrance area (Figure 10.5) has poorly executed, exposed concrete, and presents an obstacle course of handrails required by the Americans with Disabilities Act (ADA) for sloping traffic areas.

The monumental stair leading from the adjacent Crosley Tower to the 4000 level east entrance of the building forms the roof of the porte co-chere/drive up area. It is rarely used. The stairs are rarely used, and its ugly exterior wall treatment does not relate to the building at all, except for the color scheme.

Fig. 10.6. (top) Satis-faction with building features, Aronoff Center.

Fig. 10.7. (bottom) Satisfaction with Aronoff Center spaces.

OVERALL BUILDING EVALUATION

Figure 10.6 shows 216 survey respondents' overall satisfaction ratings for the quality of building features, ranging from exterior, interior, space, way-finding and overall environmental quality to ratings of jury areas, circula-tion, restrooms, and storage. Arranged in descending order, it shows that users gave fairly favorable scores to the interior aesthetics, adequacy of space and ceilings; and furniture. They gave unfavorable scores to security, maintenance, material quality, way-finding and accessibility. As one stu-dent noted: "I was on crutches, and life here sucked!"

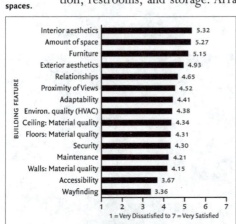

Figure 10.7 shows the rated satis-faction with each of the major space categories in the building. Users gave high scores to the library; small lec-ture spaces (30+ students); exhibition galleries; administrative offices; large lecture spaces (100+ students); pub-lic spaces (which refers to the atri-um/food court); and administration. Medium sized lecture spaces (21 to 40 students) and studios received neu-tral ratings (near the median for all spaces). Relatively low ratings went to the seminar rooms, probably due to their awkward shapes and thermal performance; jury spaces with poor acoustics; and computer labs which were woefully inadequate in size. Low-

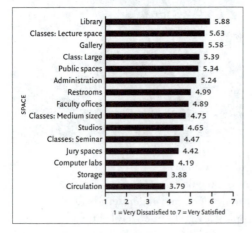

Fig. 10.8. Users judged the Atrium as one of the better spaces in the Aronoff Center.

est ratings were given to storage and circulation, agreeing with the low scores for wayfinding and accessibility.

Respondents gave the most favorable scores to the library and atrium / food court, 41.2 percent of the respondents agreed that the library was most successful, and 40.3 percent thought that the atrium / food court was quite successful. Regarding the library, its reading area under the sky-lights represents one of the few areas that receives actual daylight. Regret-tably, the sunlight harms the books. Architecture and interior design students described the library as, "High quality space, because of appropriate care, use of technology, and aesthetics. Very comfortable setup;" "Very well lit, no echoing sounds;" "Fairly easy to find things, nice spacing like the stacks."

As for the Atrium (Figure 10.8), users described it as, "Pretty good, very nice to hang out in and have crits;" "The atrium / food court—good open space accommodates many functions;" "The atrium with the tables and other seating areas—it serves as a nice meeting place, as well as a comfortable place to work during breaks;" "Exhibition spaces—good spaces to display; accessible."

Just 39.4 percent of respondents gave the most unfavorable scores to cir-culation / public areas, such as entranceways, hallways and connecting areas. Studios received an even worse rating with 35.5 percent of respondents. Here are some comments: "Although I like the grand stair, I find it inaccessi-ble and hard for disabled people to maneuver on." "Crit areas—bad lighting, walls to pin up on are not perpendicular to floor (the architect had designed crooked walls on purpose, in order to disorient and confuse building users, according to his own stated objectives), too loud."

While the large lecture hall ranked third among well-liked spaces, it has fake windows on the north side. (Figures 10.9 and 10.10) When the space does not need blackout for projection, real windows could have admitted daylight and a pleasant view of Burnet Woods. Instead, they represent a lost opportunity.

In response to the question about how much time was spent in an average week in each above-referenced space category, people reported the studio as used most often (about 18 hours per week). Next came the computer lab, library, and medium-sized classrooms (21–40 students), with approximately 7 hours each.

Fig. 10.9. Interior view of fake windows on north elevation of the Aronoff Center.

Fig. 10.10. Exterior view of fake windows on north elevation of the Aronoff Center.

PREVIOUS EVALUATION STUDIES: SELECT FINDINGS

The data and POE presented above extended a previous POE study (ACPSG 1998), but did not have the survey of the building exterior by passersby, and it used a 5-point instead of 4-point rating scale (Note in the Chapter 6 comparisons, we adjusted the 5-point ratings to 7-point scales to fit the other schools). That study had 364 respondents, consisting of faculty, staff, and students who were regular users of the Aronoff Center. Correspondence with the findings of the present POE is very strong. The most liked attributes/spaces included the amount of public space; the overall quality of the atrium (rated 35 percent excellent, plus 50 percent good); and, topping all other spaces, the overall quality and lighting of the library (43 percent excellent and 45 percent good). On the negative side, findings included poor wayfinding and signage; almost no views to the outside; and poor quality of surface materials for walls and floors. Short-, medium-, and long-term recommendations were made to solve identified problems.

At the time the POE was conducted, a "Vital Signs" project (Smith, et al., 1999) focused on physical measurements of the quality of lighting, acoustics, and temperature, mostly in the public areas of the DAAP complex, including the atrium/food court. Some of the key findings corroborated the findings from the two POE surveys. For example, although the atrium/food court is liked by most in terms of its aesthetic/experiential quality and its success as a social magnet, its lighting is marginal at best: the café area has 28 foot candles (fc) at night time; 45 fc with overcast illumination, 49 fc on a sunny morning; 45 fc midday on a sunny day; and, only 40 fc on a sunny afternoon. The skylights are partially blocked by the grid of permanently lit fluorescent lights, which are extremely expensive due to wasted energy and the annual re-lamping ritual with hydraulic cherrypickers. This low performance is caused by an eighth floor on the south side of the Atrium, which effectively blocks sunlight from entering through the skylight, except on summer solstice day.

METHODS

Post-Occupancy Evaluation (Preiser, Rabinowitz, and White, 1988) has evolved into building performance evaluation through the conceptualization of an integrative framework (Federal Facilities Council, 2001; Preiser and Vischer, 2005), which considers performance evaluation from the perspectives of the building delivery and life cycle processes. This field has now matured to the point where every architect can learn about and be tested on the topic of assessing and improving

LESSONS LEARNED

- Make designs more accessible and legible, with connected vertical circulation, and elevators located in a visible location. Cincinnati's monumental outdoor stair (linked to the chemistry building) goes unused and blocks access for wheelchair users. Elevators are hidden and fail to connect levels.
- Avoid innovative forms and materials that sacrifice basic protection from the elements, causing leaks, and requiring extensive annual repairs.
- The building should offer views to the outside and natural light, especially in the social hub or heart of the building. Although Cincinnati's concourse gets heavy use, better views and more natural light would have made it a more attractive space.
- For crit spaces, privacy and acoustic control should take priority, and such space should have adequate tacking areas. Cincinnati's crit spaces in corridors, while public, suffer from noise distraction and inadequate tack space.
- Avoid cheap materials and out-of-reach light fixtures, which create unnecessary operating and maintenance costs.

Box 10.1

the performance of buildings (NCARB 2003). The methodology used in the case study reported in this chapter followed the overall POE methodology for most case study chapters in this book (see Chapter 5). Two hundred sixteen respondents from the college completed the POE survey of building occupants. That sample included 15 percent from the School of Design, 34.7 percent from the School of Art, 13 percent from the School of Architecture and Interior Design; 32.9 percent from the School of Planning, and 4.2 percent library staff. Among 181 people reporting their gender, the sample had roughly half male (50.3 percent) and half female (49.7 percent). Ages of respondents ranged from 18 to 70 years old, with a median age of 23. Positions ranged from beginning freshmen to full-time faculty members.

There were 45 passersby (70.5 percent male, 29.5 percent female) who completed the survey about the building exterior. The sample included a diversity of people. Averaging 26 years old (ranging from 20 to 67 years old), and 3.09 years on campus (ranging from less than a year to ten years), the sample had undergraduates from every year (79.6 percent), graduate students (15.9 percent), faculty (2.3 percent) and staff (2.3 percent).

CONCLUSIONS AND RECOMMENDATIONS

The positive and negative findings reveal a partially successful design, with some serious flaws, including cost. One feature stands out as a notable success: the atrium/food court space. It brings students, faculty, and staff from all four schools together in one space, which serves social purposes, serves as a space for group discussions or individual work, in addition to serving as a cafeteria. It works because most traffic routes converge in the atrium, which has open architecture and visual connections with surrounding spaces, such as the concourse, the computer lab, the gallery / exhibit space, and others.

Yet the atrium has a flaw: It is an acoustically harsh environment with lots of reverberation, which is something difficult to fix. Furthermore, it has limited day lighting because, as already noted, an eighth floor blocks sunlight from the atrium skylight. The design also presents major problems for users in finding entrances, and wayfinding in the building. Finding elevators and staircases stand out as major issues, including a lack of building directories and poor signage.

Successful designs would do well to include a gathering space and magnet (such as a cafeteria) where routes converge. However, they should pay closer attention to circulation, wayfinding, and acoustics.

11

KATHRYN H. ANTHONY
AND MARINA PANOS

TEMPLE BUELL HALL

THE UNIVERSITY OF ILLINOIS
AT URBANA-CHAMPAIGN

SUMMARY

Long after they graduate, alumni re-member the buildings where they first studied architecture. Temple Buell Hall, a 1995 addition to the University of Illinois at Urbana-Champaign, is no exception.

Our post-occupancy evaluation of Temple Buell Hall included an analysis of archives about the building, physical traces, behavioral observations, and surveys of 424 students, faculty, and staff.

Results show students, faculty, and staff as highly satisfied with the build-ing. The exterior survey, completed by 141 individuals, revealed that re-spondents rated overall appearance of the exterior favorably, and also liked its impressive looks, excitement, and lighting features after dark. In particu-lar they liked the west glass wall, the use of glass, and the curve. They dis-liked the west entrance and the north façade.

The interior survey, completed by 283 occupants, yielded favorable but more mixed results. Respondents gave the most favorable rating to the aes-thetic quality of the exterior, maintenance, security, proximity of views, quality of building materials, aesthetic quality of interior, and ability to find

Box 11.1

ANATOMY OF A SUCCESS

- The university had many avenues of oversight.
    - It exerted a fair amount of control over size, form, and materials of buildings on campus.
    - It had strict design restrictions; the red brick exterior ties in with surrounding buildings in terms of massing, roof lines, and more. This may explain why respondents judged it as compatible.
    - The school administration played a significant role in overseeing the design of the building, monitoring just about every aspect of the design.
    - The university design review committee also oversaw the project.
- The architect—Ralph Johnson from Perkins and Will—designed a building that works for the users. He did not give making a statement a higher priority over fitting in with existing campus architecture.
- Good materials. Brick dominates the building inside and out, giving a solid, stable appearance.
- The Atrium is a star space; and perched atop it, the Eagle's Nest studio stands out as a visually impressive landmark.
- Wayfinding is one of the building's greatest strengths. Because the atrium is such a large, central, open space which can be seen from almost every spot in the building's interior, it is almost impossible to get lost. Circulation and wayfinding work well because most circulation areas are open to the atrium. The design has hardly any enclosed corridors.
- The studios and jury/crit spaces have huge windows, some studios feature two-story spaces with large expanses of glass, and most review rooms have glass doors that can be shut for privacy.
- The design successfully put one roof over the three academic units, Architecture, Landscape Architecture, and Urban and Regional Planning, which had formerly been split across the campus (although architecture still has a significant footprint in other buildings).

your way. They were least satisfied with its environmental quality. Responses to open-ended questions captured some complaints. Although occupants praised the building's visual quality, they criticized deficiencies in spatial programming; inconvenient functional provisions; a loud heating, ventilating, and air conditioning system; and a poor landscape design.

Three changes can improve the building: 1) Activate the atrium space with more exhibitions, ongoing events, and regular food service; 2) Activate the plaza with a greater variety of outdoor seating arrangements in sun and shade; and 3) Lower counters in administrative offices to make them more welcoming to persons with physical disabilities.

A BRIEF HISTORY

The project began in 1988 with a gift of $1 million from the Temple Hoyne Buell Foundation, followed in 1989 by a second gift of $5 million. The State of Illinois contributed an additional $6 million to complete site improvements and building construction. In 1991, a $1 million gift from alumnus Lawrence J. Plym resulted in the design and construction of the Plym Auditorium with seating for 200.

Temple Hoyne Buell was a 1916 graduate of the University of Illinois School of Architecture and a 1917 graduate of Columbia University, where he received his master's degree. He began his architectural career in Chicago working for the firm that built landmark hotels such as the Drake and the Blackstone. After a diagnosis of terminal tuberculosis in 1921, his doctors recommended the clean mountain air of Colorado. Buell moved to Denver where he launched T. H. Buell and Company in 1923. By 1940, with a staff of 150, it became the largest architectural firm in the Rocky Mountain States, achieving a national reputation for "the Western Style." Buell designed movie palaces; elementary, high school, and college buildings; private residences; an array of commercial buildings; and shopping centers. In 1948 after creating the Buell Development Corporation and transforming a 55-acre Denver dumpsite into the Cherry Creek Shopping Center, he earned the nickname, "the father of the shopping center" (University of Illinois Foundation, 1991). A philanthropist to public and private institutions across the country, his 1974 gift to the School of Architecture resulted in the Temple Buell Gallery in the Architecture Building, a presentation and exhibition space. At the same time, he made major donations to Columbia University and to several universities in Colorado.

The School of Architecture, the Office for Project Planning and Facility Management, and the Office of Capital Programs all participated in the selection of the architect for Temple Buell Hall. The commission was awarded to the Chicago firm of Perkins and Will, led by Ralph Johnson (Principal-in-Charge of Design), a 1971 University of Illinois architecture alumnus. The building committee visited five architecture schools in order to identify key issues to be addressed in Temple Buell Hall, and to incorporate them into the program statement.

When it opened, Temple Buell Hall was the first academic building in the Midwest to combine study and research in architecture, landscape architecture, and urban and regional planning. Its goal was to alleviate the physical fragmentation of these three disciplines, which had been housed in nine structures about a mile apart (University of Illinois Foundation, 1991). The School of Architecture was located in three buildings: the Georgian Revival style Architecture Building (1926), as well as two converted dormitories, Flagg Hall and Noble Hall (1954), on the west side of campus. The Department of Landscape Architecture was located in portions of another Georgian Revival classic, Mumford Hall (1924), as well as in two converted houses: 1203 West Nevada, an English Domestic style (1914), once the residence of the University President; and, the Neo-Classical house at 1205 West Nevada (1926). The Department

Fig. 11.1. An aerial view of the south quad at the University of Illinois at Urbana-Champaign campus. Temple Buell Hall, in the foreground, sits diagonally across the street from the Architecture Building. (Credit: Larry Kanfer Photography Ltd.,www. kanfer.com.)

of Urban and Regional Planning was located at the east edge of campus in three converted houses: 909 West Nevada Street (a 1929 American Foursquare), 1001 West Nevada Street (a 1918 Craftsman/Bungalow style), and 9071/2 West Nevada Street (1989). While the School of Architecture continues to use additional facilities for studio, classroom, and office space, the other two units moved almost entirely into Temple Buell Hall (Figure 11.1).

The building opened in August 1995 with ribbon-cutting ceremonies on October 13, 1995. *Chicago Tribune* architecture critic Blair Kamin (1995) gave it a rave review, contrasting Temple Buell Hall with Yale University's Art and Architecture Building, which students set afire in 1969. "No one seems likely to take a match to Ralph Johnson's new Temple Hoyne Buell Hall . . . Instead, top university officials are scheduling dinners in its light-washed atrium. Students are turning the atrium into a lively indoor courtyard, complete with coffee bar. And as often happens in Johnson's buildings, people are inquiring if they can use the place for weddings." (The coffee bar has since been removed.) Edward Keegan's (1996) description of the building in *Architecture* was almost equally glowing.

How did faculty, students, and staff evaluate Temple Hoyne Buell Hall? Overall they liked it, but open-ended questions revealed some problems.

TEMPLE BUELL HALL EXTERIOR

Results from the exterior building survey show that people liked its overall appearance (Figure 11.2). They also rated it favorably for these attributes: looks impressive, looks exciting, and lighting after dark. Students and faculty in Temple Buell Hall tended to have more favorable scores than others.

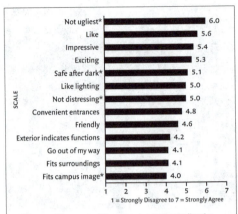

* Score and item reversed from survey's negative wording (i.e., ugliest building on campus = 7 reversed to ugliest = 1; thus not ugliest = 7, safe after dark = 7, not distressing = 7, fits overall campus image = 7).

Fig. 11.2. (top) Results from the exterior building survey.

Fig. 11.3. (bottom) The glass curtain wall along the west façade was one of the features respondents liked best about the exterior of Temple Buell Hall. (Credit: Larry Kanfer Photography Ltd., www.kanfer.com.)

When asked for exterior features they liked best, respondents most often cited the west glass curtain wall, the use of glass, and the curve of the building (Figure 11.3). When asked for the features they liked least, respondents most often cited the understated west entrance, the north façade, and the sterile, uninviting landscape design.

During special events, the courtyard works well. Yet even in excellent weather, the sunken outdoor courtyard and all outdoor spaces adjacent to the building are rarely used. The courtyard has linear concrete benches with no seat backs, not conducive to conversation or to long-term sitting, exactly the type of seating that Whyte's (1980) research on plazas found flawed. Other researchers who have conducted extensive studies of campus outdoor spaces have confirmed Whyte's findings (Cooper, Marcus, and Francis, 1990). Whyte's research also revealed the importance of visual connection to the street and pedestrians. Regrettably, the plaza offers nothing much to look at and no shade for protection. The grassy area, intended for seating, is rarely used. Had Whyte's widely known findings been incorporated into the design of Temple Buell Hall, its outdoor spaces could have been lively campus showpieces—a missed opportunity indeed.

TEMPLE BUELL HALL INTERIOR

Of the faculty, staff, and students who used the building regularly, a total of 283 people completed the interior survey. Results reveal high satisfaction with the interior. All but two features received ratings of 5.1 or above. Figure 11.4 shows that respondents reported highest satisfaction with the aesthetic quality of the exterior, maintenance, security, proximity of views, quality of building materials, aesthetic quality of interior, and ability to find your way. Environmental quality received the lowest rating. Spaces that respondents reported as ones they felt *most* satisfied with included public areas, along with computer lab and large lecture spaces. Those who cited the public areas (43% of those answering this question) praised adequacy of space (6.4), lighting (6.4), aesthetic appeal (6.4), and flexibility of use (6.3).

Yet many good public spaces have acoustic and temperature problems. Criticisms of environmental quality concerned both temperature and humidity, along with sounds from the heating, ventilating, and air conditioning system. Multiple hard surfaces—brick interior walls, concrete floors, exposed metal decking beneath the floors, metal handrails and guardrails, and large glass surfaces—exacerbate acoustical problems (Figure 11.5). In design studios, noise problems led to the removal of variable air volume system fans. Eagle's Nest, the building's premiere studio critique space overlooking the atrium, is especially noisy. While visually impressive, its walls do not meet the ceiling, so sounds from walkways and the atrium reverberate into the space, causing major distractions and exacerbating pressure for students in already stressful design reviews (Anthony, 1991).

Similarly, while the atrium works well for visual displays, any event that requires people to hear a speaker must have a microphone. Masters' thesis design reviews held here have had special problems, forcing them to relocate elsewhere. On occasion, a reviewer sitting less than 5 feet in front of student presenters could not even hear them. In retrospect, while the building is visually stunning, in other aspects of sensory design it falls somewhat short (Malnar and Vodvarka, 2004).

As for temperature control, faculty offices along the west glass wall often either heat up excessively or are over-air-conditioned during the summer and can be too cold during the winter. In addition, almost all year round, the Plym Auditorium feels too cold.

Fig. 11.4. (top) Results from the interior building survey.

Fig. 11.5. (bottom) Hard surfaces throughout the building exacerbate acoustical problems in the atrium. (Credit: Larry Kanfer Photography Ltd., www.kanfer.com.)

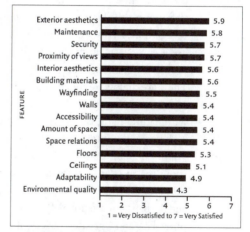

FEATURE

Feature	Rating
Exterior aesthetics	5.9
Maintenance	5.8
Security	5.7
Proximity of views	5.7
Interior aesthetics	5.6
Building materials	5.6
Wayfinding	5.5
Walls	5.4
Accessibility	5.4
Amount of space	5.4
Space relations	5.4
Floors	5.3
Ceilings	5.1
Adaptability	4.9
Environmental quality	4.3

1 = Very Dissatisfied to 7 = Very Satisfied

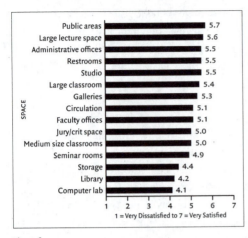

Fig. 11.6.
Satisfaction
with quality
of spaces.

Respondents also gave positive scores to most spaces in the building. As shown in Figure 11.6, all but four spaces had scores of 5.0 (fairly satisfied) or above. Spaces receiving highest scores included public areas, large lecture space, studios, restrooms, and administrative office area, large classrooms, and exhibition/gallery space. Lower scores (4.1 to 4.4) went to computer labs, storage, and seminar rooms. Even though restrooms received favorable ratings, some open-ended comments revealed two serious problems. Because restrooms are located at the north end of the building, many students, faculty, and staff must walk over a city block to reach them. The first floor has no restrooms, inconveniencing visitors and support staff—most of them females—who work in the building 40 hours a week.

Computer labs were rated least favorably, as architecture students must use a computer lab in the Architecture Building across the street. Seminar rooms were among the spaces with which respondents were least satisfied. They are below grade and windowless. Consequently, the only seminar room remaining in the Architecture Building across the street, a room filled with natural light, is usually booked to capacity.

In sum, the interior building design reflects a value system whereby the grand public areas and the spacious studios reign supreme and other classroom spaces—at least for the School of Architecture—are given somewhat short shrift. This is less true for the Departments of Landscape Architecture and Urban and Regional Planning, which have conveniently located computer labs and a greater variety of classroom spaces.

Some responses differed at a statistically significant level across groups. For example, urban planners and architects rated the aesthetic quality of the exterior and the aesthetic quality of the interior higher (by 0.8) than did the landscape architects. Architects also rated the amount of space more favorably than did the landscape architects (by 0.9), and they rated environmental quality more favorably than did the urban planners and landscape architects. Men rated environmental quality significantly better than did women. Students tended to report more favorable ratings than did faculty and staff, giving higher scores for the amount of space (by 1.5 points), environmental quality (by 0.8 points), and quality of floors, and quality of walls (each by 0.6 points).

Administrative offices in the old Architecture Building had superior natural lighting to that in the new building. Most support staff previously had south-facing offices with large multi-paned windows, whereas in Temple Buell Hall some now look out of narrow slits of glass. Even the Director's office in the new building has three windows measuring only 5 feet high by 1.5 feet wide. While most studio spaces are flooded in natural daylight, some staff offices require artificial lighting all day long.

When asked to select up to two spaces with which they felt least satisfied, most respondents cited public areas, medium-size classrooms, seminar rooms, and the large lecture space. Those who cited public areas (21 percent of those answering the question) were most critical of temperature (a mean of 3.1 on a 7-point scale) and acoustics (3.3). Ironically, these results reveal that public areas—most notably the atrium—were both the least satisfying and most satisfying spaces. (Figures 11.7 and 11.8). The atrium, the building's most prominent design element, elicits a strong reaction one way or the other.

Among the facilities currently lacking in Temple Buell Hall, respondents cited food service, computer labs for architecture students, a library, a faculty lounge, and better outdoor seating. During the first year of operation, the building had a food service kiosk offering only snacks, and it was closed during lunch hours, the peak usage times; it soon closed altogether. Student organizations occasionally sell pizza in the atrium. Adding permanent food service could enliven the atrium, which sits empty most of the time.

Fig. 11.7. (left) The Atrium elicited strong positive and negative responses, and it was the favorite building feature of many respondents.

Fig. 11.8. (right) Respondents were most and least satisfied with the design of public areas in the building. Shown here is the interior walkway and bridge system.

Although the survey did not pinpoint accessibility as a problem, the reception areas in the administrative offices need to be redesigned to accommodate visitors with physical disabilities. High counters in all three offices present any visitor in a wheelchair with a blank wall. Offices should send a more welcoming signal to all users, and a message to students about the importance of universal design.

METHOD

This post-occupancy evaluation was conducted during fall 1999. Methods included an analysis of archives about the building; physical traces; behavioral observations; and surveys of 424 students, faculty, and staff. We obtained 141 responses to the exterior building survey, and 283 responses to the interior building survey.

The first author of this chapter, Kathryn Anthony, oversaw the study. All 23 students in her seminar on "social and behavioral factors in design" participated in gathering the data. Students included both graduates and undergraduates with majors in architecture, industrial design, landscape architecture, and psychology. One student team distributed the exterior building survey at the north, west, and south entrances during mornings, afternoons, and early evenings. Another team distributed the interior building survey and asked instructors in all three academic units to administer the survey during class time. Another team contacted faculty and staff and distributed the surveys in their mail boxes.

CONCLUSIONS

Overall results reveal a relatively successful solution. On most items, respondents rated the building favorably, and open-ended comments tended to be positive. As one faculty member stated, "Recognize the building for the fine work of true architecture it is— poetry in light and space." And that it is. The natural light that floods the public areas of the building is perhaps its greatest quality, one that inspires and uplifts its occupants even on the darkest days. Without a doubt, the building offers something unique to the campus, and its atrium space is one of the most impressive of all the university buildings. Even the side stairwells— spaces often overlooked—are bathed in light. As architectural design critics have noted, the building is routinely in demand for official university functions; and for receptions, exhibits, and special events, it provides a stunning setting. It has become a showpiece.

As university administrators and architects had intended, Temple Buell

Hall has indeed served as a valuable teaching tool. Projects assigned in studio addressing Temple Buell Hall include acoustical installations in the atrium, gallery, and entry space; and expansions incorporating new programmatic uses. Students in seminar courses and studios routinely evaluate the outdoor plaza according to Whyte's (1980) principles.

What lessons can be learned from Temple Buell Hall? While placing such a strong emphasis on the grandeur of public spaces like the atrium paid off, some lesser spaces, such as faculty and staff offices, medium sized classrooms, and seminar spaces were shortchanged. Public spaces need to be designed with a greater level of activity in mind, so they do not sit empty much of the time.

Our recommendations for improving the building include activating the atrium space with more exhibitions, events, and regular food service. With the addition of a café offering lunchtime fare, the building has potential to become as lively as Berkeley's Wurster Hall or Harvard's Gund Hall, and a much greater draw for faculty, students, and staff from across campus. This would help achieve the benefactors' goals of linking the three disciplines. Communication occurs best when people are sitting, eating, and drinking together, not just when they pass each other on the bridges or dash down the walkways late for class.

LESSONS LEARNED

- Use campus design guidelines and design review to keep the building materials, proportions, scale, etc., compatible with the rest of campus and its neighborhood. The building can be unconventional inside while tying in with its contents.

- Provide livable outdoor public spaces, with seating, trees, water, and other features to enliven the area and attract outdoor use. (The outdoor screen and outdoor theater at Illinois did not work).

- Provide natural light throughout the facility (atrium, studios, classrooms, stairwells, and offices).

- Make sure that large atrium spaces have adequate acoustic controls and soft human features. These large spaces work exceptionally well (with a microphone) for special events (graduations, awards, ceremonies, exhibits) but they need better acoustics for more frequent uses as crit spaces. Designs should also soften and humanize these spaces in scale and materials.

- Crit spaces need acoustical privacy. The crit spaces with glass doors work better than those without.

- Include a café or eatery (preferably linked to the atrium or special event area) to enliven the building.

- Offices for architecture faculty with professional libraries must provide adequate space and shelf space.

- Make faculty mailrooms attractive, well-lit hubs, linked to Atrium spaces and outdoor pick-up. Avoid windowless faculty mailrooms, such as the ones at Illinois—hidden, claustrophobic, and lacking adequate storage and closet space.

Box 11.2

Ironically, when the building was still in the planning stages, a handful of faculty members stressed the need for a dining facility in the original design program. But it is still not too late. As Whyte (1980) demonstrated, public spaces where food is available are those that are most highly used. More seating in the atrium would also help in this regard. Ideally, new food-related activities along with both indoor and outdoor seating could spill over from the below-grade atrium up toward the west entrance of the building at grade level to attract more passersby.

Providing a greater variety of outdoor seating arrangements with opportunities for both sun and shade would help remedy problems with the adjacent outdoor space. Incorporating into the courtyard a landscape design that has more greenery and sitting space would help make it a more user-friendly place as well.

Many initial difficulties with the building's mechanical systems have already been addressed, although not fully resolved. The experience with Temple Buell Hall points out the need to incorporate mechanical engineers earlier on in the design process. Rather than attempting to fix costly problems repeated on a colossal scale, engineers can help architects prevent such problems. The building could have benefited at the outset from some softer surfaces, thus preventing acoustical problems and also allowing more flexible exhibit space throughout the corridors. Red brick wall surfaces along circulation ways remain empty most of the time; a notable exception was during a 2003 architecture accreditation visit when student work was posted all along the walkways with special fixtures to prevent damage to the brickwork. Rotating displays like this would no doubt enliven the entire building.

Is the University of Illinois at Urbana-Champaign a better place because of Temple Buell Hall? The answer is a resounding yes. That architecture, landscape architecture, and planning are now housed under the same roof is a major improvement. No longer are these units spread across campus with little or no contact with each other. Instead, students, faculty, and staff of all three disciplines see each other and products of their labor every day. And no doubt Temple Buell Hall will continue to inspire a new generation of designers.

KATHLEEN A. HARDER, JOHN CARMODY,
VIRAJITA SINGH, AND THOMAS FISHER

RAPSON HALL,
COLLEGE OF DESIGN

UNIVERSITY OF MINNESOTA

SUMMARY

The College of Design's new Rapson Hall at the University of Minnesota represents two styles of architecture from two different eras. The original Architecture Building, constructed in 1960, reflects the modern design approach of that time. The addition, designed by Steven Holl and completed in 2001, both complements and contrasts with the older building.

Despite the addition and remodeled older building, Rapson Hall still lacks adequate space to accommodate increased enrollment. To assess where to invest in future improvements, a post-occupancy evaluation (POE) was conducted. The POE primarily addressed the functional aspects of each type of space (e.g., library, classrooms, computer lab, offices/workspaces, studios) within Rapson Hall. The POE had two main tasks. We conducted (1) extensive surveys of faculty, staff, and students, and (2) focus groups with faculty, staff, and maintenance workers. In addition, detailed lighting measurements were obtained in several spaces. This chapter presents a representative sample of findings from the surveys and focus groups, as well as conclusions from the POE's broader set of data.

Results of the POE indicate that the building's users appreciate many of the spaces, but noted some problems with glare, acoustics, thermal comfort, and ventilation. Many of these problems can be traced to budget shortfall and decisions to place a higher priority on other design features. Attempts are underway to address these problems.

HISTORY

The addition to and renovation of the building began in the late 1980s, with the awarding of planning funds by the Minnesota legislature. The State Designer's Selection Board chose Ellerbe Becket as the architects of record, with Steven Holl as the design architect. That team designed a circular, 100,000-square-foot addition, with an arc-shaped library, auditorium, and offices and studios, punctuated by "light" towers containing review spaces and workrooms that terminated important axes on campus. The tall, doughnut-shaped addition, which was completed in 1960, extended over and to the north of the existing square courtyard building. Although that design won a Progressive Architecture Award (P/A) in 1990, for many years it never made it high enough on the University's priority list to receive construction funding.

In 1997, a new University president, Mark Yudof, proposed five interdisciplinary initiatives for funding by the legislature, including a design initiative that called for building the addition. The legislature, flush with money at the time, supported these initiatives, although their appropriation for the College addition matched that requested 10 years earlier. Even with substantial private funding, the College ended up having only enough money to build a 50,000-square-foot addition, half of what it had hoped to build the previous decade. The funding also called for the renovation of the existing building.

With the construction money awarded, the previous design team reconstituted itself, with Steven Holl now the lead architect, Vincent James Associates and Rozeboom Miller Architects as associate architects, and Ellerbe Becket providing engineering and landscape architecture services. While Steven Holl looked at the possibility of shrinking the original circular design, it quickly became clear that the design team needed to start over.

Instead of two inward-facing structures—the original square building around its enclosed court and the circular addition around its open court—the design evolved into a dialogue between the introverted original building and an extroverted addition (Figure 12.1). In contrast to the 1960s building's rational plan of squares within squares, wrapped in brick walls, with repetitive vertical windows, the new addition became an irregular cruciform whose arms extend out to the very edge of the site, wrapped in hori-

zontally seamed copper, with deep-
set, square windows and end-walls
of vertical, translucent channel glass.
Meanwhile, the design team, with Vincent James in the lead, returned the
existing building back to its original
1960s state, albeit with new mechanical and electrical systems, and new interior walls.

Holl thought of the cruciform addition as symbolic of the interaction
of architecture and landscape architecture disciplines in the College. He
designed the addition with four wings
of the building interleaved with four
gardens, providing large areas of glass
at the center of the cruciform so that

Fig. 12.1.
Exterior
photo of
Rapson Hall,
University of
Minnesota.

you can always see out into the landscape from inside the building, and see
through the center of the building from the gardens. The idea of interlocking
forms also informed the footprint and details of the building as expressed in
its overlapping L-shaped roofs; the section of the building with two-story,
interlocking L-shaped spaces stepping up through the center of the addition;
and even the L-shaped stairs, doors, and handles.

Holl also wanted the building to serve as an educational tool for the College's architecture program. He developed, in conjunction with the engi-
neer Guy Nordenson, a structural system of exposed concrete planks tied
into concrete bents, providing an exposed structure for the students to
study that also proved difficult to build. The lack of shear walls to maximize
flexibility in the moving of partitions in the future demanded that the con-
crete-plank floor system provide most of the shear resistance in the building.
This meant that the contractors had to support the planks up in the air and
then pour the concrete columns and beams up to them. Then they added a
topping slab over them so that the floor system worked as a single structural unit.

To reduce costs and keep the structure exposed, the engineers and
architects also decided to eliminate hung ceilings and most horizontal
mechanical-duct runs. Instead, they ran the mechanical ducts vertically
through two-foot-thick exterior walls, supplying rooms with air from wall-
and sill-mounted registers. Like a heavy winter coat wrapping the building,
these deep walls also provide, within their thickness, space for custom-
designed wood benches where students can sit and study. On the lowest

level, the ducts run along ceilings and along some walls on their way to the large mechanical room located below the auditorium.

The design team responded to environmental concerns in several ways. In addition to the thick, heavily insulated walls, large operable pivot windows provide cross ventilation in the narrow wings of the building. The large clear glass walls in the center of the cruciform plan, and the translucent walls of channel glass at the end of each wing and along the top studio floor also flood the interior with daylight, omitting the need for artificial lighting during the day. However, in some places they require shading devices to handle the glare.

The addition's exterior changed during the review and approval process. The original design called for a cladding of large interlocking slabs, which the Regents of the University rejected, asking the architects to restudy the exterior, at which point they proposed the current copper skin. While more expensive as a material, the lightness of the copper allowed the design team to reduce the size of the structural system and save $200,000 in overall costs. The copper also had the advantage of having the same color and hue of the surrounding brick buildings. It will blend into the trees and foliage over time as the copper develops its green patina.

Other aspects of the building's exterior recall aspects of the original 1980s scheme. The end walls of vertical channel glass, for example, recall the towers of light in the original design, glowing at night like lanterns, terminating views within the campus. Also, the detailing of the exterior wall with its tapered concrete slabs that allow for a thin edge at corners between the copper and glass, echoes the knife-thin detailing of the first design. Finally, the curved end of the addition's corner, facing a major intersection, brings to mind the tall, curving form of the 1980s addition, providing a commanding presence at a key entrance to the campus.

Although two outside estimators said that the building would come within budget, the bids came in at least 20% over budget because of the timing of the project during a building boom in the Twin Cities. The higher cost led to deletion of the furnishings and landscape. The delay in completing these aspects of the projects has allowed the College to go in new directions. The furniture now being installed uses recycled and low-energy materials. Meanwhile, the landscape, designed by landscape architect Rebecca Krinke and public artist John Roloff, demonstrates a more sustainable way of treating open space on campus and using public art in a functional role—in this case, large slabs of granite provide a terrace for people to sit or gather.

Overall, the renovation and addition have provided the College with more ample and functional, as well as more inspiring and challenging space than it ever had before. The College now has a building with a quality and presence that some people like more than others. Whatever the responses of different people to the building, the College felt an obligation to support the creation of a strong work of architecture, and with its winning of a New York AIA design award, the facility has lived up to that goal.

RESULTS

We conducted a POE to discover what the faculty, staff, and students think about Rapson Hall. Although the POE obtained ratings of spaces and features, it used a different questionnaire than the one used in most of the other case studies reported in this book. It also supplemented the questionnaire with focus groups to obtain more detailed information than was possible through the questionnaire by itself. The following section describes some key findings from the surveys and focus groups about the building, spaces, and attributes.

BUILDING OVERALL

The evaluation of the building used both focus groups and surveys. First consider the results from the focus groups.

Focus Groups

Focus groups were held to elicit more detailed information than can be obtained with surveys. A sample of the findings is presented here. Some participants said they felt a greater sense of pride when they enter the new building than they felt when they entered the old building before restoration. Some stated that it is gratifying to have a large lecture room in the building, because it is no longer necessary to walk one or two blocks to a large lecture room. Participants also reported that it is nice to have plenty of room for exhibits. Unfortunately, however, because the exhibit space is not secure, this limits the kinds of exhibits that might be held in the building.

The focus groups also revealed positive reactions to the library (Figure 12.2) and courtyard. The library is perceived by some to be well designed and attractive. Windows are plentiful and the space is functional. The interior courtyard is regarded as a really good social space, though the acoustics are a problem during reviews.

While the focus group participants highlighted a variety of positive building attributes, they also identified various kinds of problems with ventilation, thermal comfort, air quality, acoustics, lighting, and maintenance. The participants described the ventilation as uneven from room to room and from floor to floor. Some participants complained that cigarette smoke

**Fig. 12.2.
Respondents
liked the
Rapson Hall
Library.**

permeates parts of the building. Vents that return fresh air are located toward the ceiling so that some staff, with work stations near the vents, have a
continuous stream of air blowing on them. Unless the situation is corrected
with space heaters, they feel cold all the time. Some participants complained
about feeling too cold at various times during the day, particularly after 5:00
PM when the temperature is programmed to drop.

Faculty and staff in the old and new additions complained about acoustical problems. Some staff and faculty also complained about problems with
privacy and confidentiality in their workspace. And faculty reported that
during thesis reviews it is difficult to hear what the students are saying. Staff
working in the Visual Resource Center also complained that there is too
much daylight for their work with color. Moreover, other participants complained about significant glare problems near channel glass in offices and studios in the new addition.

Finally, maintenance employees reported that the new design makes it
difficult to clean properly. Faculty and staff have the perception that the
maintenance people are trying hard, but that their job is difficult.

Survey Results

Now consider the survey results. Figure 12.3 shows faculty, staff, and student responses to questions regarding overall impressions of the building.
For each question, the figure shows mean and standard deviation (SD) for
each group (faculty, staff, or students).

Figure 12.3 reveals some discrepancies between the response groups. Students, for example, rated the design of the building overall as unsatisfactory. Faculty and staff gave the building higher ratings, though both of these response groups do not rate the building higher than mid-point on the 7-point scale.

Figure 12.3 also reveals that faculty and staff had fairly similar assessments of how well the facilities meet their personal work needs. They rate the facilities as meeting their personal work needs moderately well. For space use in the building, neither the staff nor faculty judged it as effective, with staff giving it lower ratings than faculty.

Though the building did not receive high ratings for the overall design, users did like certain spaces and qualities of the design. As you can see in Figure 12.3, the building received more favorable scores for how effectively it serves as a recruiting tool for students. Of the three groups, faculty thinks the building functions effectively as a recruiting tool, while students and staff think the building functions somewhat effectively and moderately effectively, respectively, as a recruiting tool.

Figure 12.4 shows the ratings of spaces. The workshop received the most favorable ratings, followed by the library, classrooms, and computer lab. Regarding the computer lab, some members of the focus groups complained about insufficient airflow. The studios and workspaces received lower scores. In each case, with the exception of the studios, the faculty gave more favorable ratings than the students.

The workshop received fairly high ratings for how well it functions. Users rated the library as functioning somewhat well as a reading/research

Fig. 12.3. (top) Mean results for overall impressions of the building.

Fig. 12.4. (bottom) Mean ratings of different functions of the building.

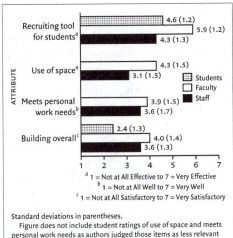

^{a} 1 = Not at All Effective to 7 = Very Effective
^{b} 1 = Not at All Well to 7 = Very Well
^{c} 1 = Not at All Satisfactory to 7 = Very Satisfactory

Standard deviations in parentheses.
Figure does not include student ratings of use of space and meets personal work needs as authors judged those items as less relevant to students.

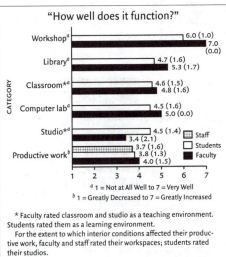

"How well does it function?"

^{a} 1 = Not at All Well to 7 = Very Well
^{b} 1 = Greatly Decreased to 7 = Greatly Increased

* Faculty rated classroom and studio as a teaching environment. Students rated them as a learning environment.
For the extent to which interior conditions affected their productive work, faculty and staff rated their workspaces; students rated their studios.
Figure shows staff responses for productive work only, as authors judged the other items as less relevant to staff.

environment. In the focus groups, some users described the library as well designed and attractive. They liked the plentiful windows and functional space. Because judgments of teaching and learning in a space may not mirror each other, faculty responded to a survey question about classrooms as teaching environments, while students responded to a question about classrooms as learning environments. The two groups were in agreement, rating the classrooms as functioning somewhat well as teaching or learning environments. The computer lab also received somewhat favorable ratings for how well it functions.

Individual Workspaces. The faculty mean response across six respondents indicates that respondents think the interior environmental conditions have no effect on their productive work. However, in this case the average does not tell the story because there is a split in the raw data among respondents: some thought the interior environmental conditions have increased their productive work, while others thought the conditions decreased it. The same bi-modal split is seen with the 27 staff responses, though more staff members judged the interior environmental conditions as decreasing rather than increasing their productive work.

Though students do not have designated offices in the building, they carry out much of their work in studios. When asked about their perceived productive work in the studios, the majority of respondents, unlike faculty and staff, thought the interior environmental conditions had no effect on their productive work.

Fig. 12.5. Mean satisfaction with various features of the studio.

Studio Space. Figure 12.5 shows student and faculty responses to a variety of questions about the studio space. The survey asked similar questions about each space, but we chose to showcase the studio findings because this space is where the greatest number of the building's users (students) spend most of their time. On average, faculty respondents rated the studio environment in which they teach as not functioning particularly well, though they had considerable variability in their responses. In contrast, students, on average, rated this learning environment as functioning somewhat well. Figure 12.5 shows the ratings for the following:

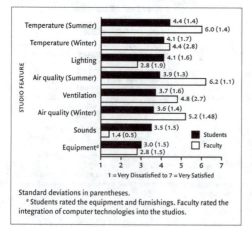

Standard deviations in parentheses.
a Students rated the equipment and furnishings. Faculty rated the integration of computer technologies into the studios.

- studio temperature during the cooling season (summer months)
- studio temperature during the heating season (winter months)
- amount of lighting
- air quality during the cooling season
- ventilation system
- air quality during the heating season
- sounds
- equipment and furnishings (students only); integration of computer technology (faculty)
- integration of computer technology

As you can see in Figure 12.5, faculty respondents were somewhat dissatisfied with the integration of computer technologies and the amount of lighting in the studio, very dissatisfied with the quality of the sound environment, but more satisfied with the temperature and air quality during the heating and cooling seasons. Students gave neutral responses, indicating neither satisfaction nor dissatisfaction with any of the various studio aspects investigated by the survey. However, they did express dissatisfaction with the equipment and furnishings.

METHOD

Faculty, staff, and students were surveyed regarding their perceptions of the functionality of various spaces in the building. Though each group (faculty, staff, and students) completed a survey designed for their particular response group, some of the questions were shared across the three surveys—findings from a sampling of the questions are presented in the "Results" section above. Following the analysis of the survey data, focus groups were held with each of the three survey response groups. Another focus group consisted of custodians responsible for cleaning the building. The intent of the focus groups was to elicit information at a greater level of detail than could be provided by the surveys. An unstructured interview technique was used. Each focus group lasted between 60 to 90 minutes and had four to seven participants. Two facilitators conducted each focus group. One-on-one interviews were also conducted with key design and facilities people who were involved in the development and construction of the building.

Respondent information about each of the three survey groups is presented below.

Seven regular faculty members responded to the survey. Four reported they are between 31–50 years old and three reported they are from 51–65 years old. Three of the respondents were female and four were male. Of the seven respondents, five were from the Architecture Department and two were from the Landscape Architecture Department. Respondents said they spend an average of 5.1 days (SD: 1.2) in the building during a normal work week.

Box 12.1

LESSONS LEARNED

This post-occupancy evaluation revealed that in some cases the building design does not meet user needs. Designers need to give careful consideration to the needs of the various users. Only by considering their needs can one produce a building that will function well for most users. For this reason a pre-occupancy evaluation should be conducted to discover user needs for incorporation into the building design process at the same time as the aesthetics of the design.

Building design should consider the following guidelines:

- Use a systems approach (as opposed to a piecemeal approach) to designing spaces. For example, in workspaces one should consider the placement of lighting fixtures, computers, desks, bookshelves, etc. before finalizing the layout. A piecemeal approach can produce problems. In Rapson Hall faculty offices, the positioning of the wall-mounted light fixtures makes it difficult for the occupants to place book-shelves in their offices. In the workshop, the low location of lighting and ventilation equipment has resulted in damaged light fixtures when users move materials and equipment.
- Where feasible, allow occupants to control the mechanical systems. Occupants prefer to control their own environment. In addition, mechanical systems often do not operate effectively. For example, the POE found that users perceived ventilation as a problem throughout the building—some participants report headaches in their offices. Allowing building occupants to open and close windows would likely help to mediate the ventilation issues.
- Carefully weigh the use of materials for aesthetic reasons against their effect on indoor environmental quality. The building has significant glare problems near the channel glass in studios and offices in the new addition. Shading devices are being added. Balance major expanses of glazing for aesthetic reasons against the impact on interior conditions.
- Carefully consider acoustics. Many areas in both the old and new building have acoustical problems. This stems from the hard surfaces on ceilings, walls, and floors. Acoustic baffles, floor coverings, and textiles, judiciously used, could alleviate the problem.
- Ease of maintenance should influence design decisions. For example, maintenance workers have difficulty keeping the black carpeting clean. In the winter they must vacuum it each evening. Maintenance issues should be considered when selecting floor coverings.

Twenty-two staff members responded to the survey. Four reported they were 30 or under, 13 reported they were between 31–50 years old, four were from 51–65 years old, and one did not give his/her age or gender. Eleven of the respondents were female and ten were male. Of the 22 respondents, two were from the Architecture Department, two were from the Landscape Architecture Department, and 18 were from the College. Respondents said they spend an average of 4.9 days (SD: 0.4) in the building during a normal work week.

One hundred fifty-four students responded to the survey. Twelve were between 17–19 years, 115 were from 20–25 years, 15 were from 26–30 years, and 10 were from 31–50 years. Two respondents did not indicate an age. There were 61 female respondents and 91 male respondents. Two respondents did not indicate their gender. Of the 154 respondents, 117 were undergraduate students in the Architecture Department, seven were undergraduate students in the Landscape Architecture Department, two were undergraduate students from areas other than the Architecture Department or the Landscape Architecture Department, 24 were graduate students in the Architecture Department, two were graduate students in the Landscape Architecture Department, and, two did not indicate their program. Respondents reported they spend an average of 5.0 days (SD: 1.5) in the building during a normal week.

CONCLUSIONS

The post-occupancy evaluation, which included an extensive survey and a number of focus groups, yielded a rich body of knowledge about users' perceptions of Rapson Hall. A modular approach was taken in which respondents were asked to evaluate each individual space in the building. Not surprisingly, the building's users like some spaces more and other spaces less. For example, users liked the library and the courtyard. The courtyard was a well-received center of activity. However, they disliked studio spaces. Functional issues such as acoustics, lighting, and comfortable furnishings were sacrificed for the sake of other design and budget priorities. The detailed information gained from this POE should be used to direct future efforts to improve the functionality of Rapson Hall.

JAMES POTTER

COLLEGE OF ARCHITECTURE

UNIVERSITY OF NEBRASKA–LINCOLN

SUMMARY

The College of Architecture at the
University of Nebraska—Lincoln has three Buildings: Architecture Hall
East, Architecture Hall West, and the Link, with the design of each having
taken place at different times. Participants in the study had favorable responses to the designs, especially about the aesthetic appeal of the exterior
and the Link. They rated the exterior of Architecture Hall East as more appealing than the exterior of Architecture Hall West. The Link had many
functions, and participants had few negative comments about it. The interior
of Architecture Hall provoked the most controversy. Participants loved
some spaces in it, such as the library, and detested others, such as the computer lab. Thus, the POE points to many good aspects of the design and exterior and some mixed evaluations of the interior spaces in Architecture
Hall.

BACKGROUND

Designed by Mendelssohn, Fisher, &
Lawrte, Architecture Hall East is the oldest building, completed in 1892

(Figure 13.1). It is the only university building to receive historic designation and was added to the National Register of Historic Places in 1975. The design of the building is sympathetic to the Richardsonian Romanesque style defined by its broad, low arches, octagonal shapes, high hip roofs, projecting dormer windows, and towers. It is a three and a half story, red brick structure with 95,800 square feet of space. Its T-shaped plan is symmetrical about the north-south axis. It is constructed with bearing walls, heavy timber columns and beams, and solid wood plank flooring. The rich wood detailing was magnificently preserved during renovation.

Designed by Lincoln architects Berlinghof & Davis and completed in 1912, Architecture Hall West (formerly the Law College, Figure 13.2) has a simple three-story plus basement rectangular plan with a long north-south axis. It has a brown brick exterior, built with steel beams and columns, and concrete slab. In the early 1960s, the Law College added a new building to the north for use as book storage (the stacks). Classrooms and offices occupied the first and second floors, and the law library occupied the third. The College of Law remained until the early 1980s, when it moved elsewhere, and the College of Architecture acquired the building (Logan-Peters, 1999).

In 1977, the University held a design competition for the connection and renovation of the two buildings. A local firm, Bahr, Vermeer, & Haecker (BVH), won the competition. The project remained unfunded until 1983, after which production began in earnest the following year (Spiry,

> **ANATOMY OF A SUCCESS**
>
> - The faculty in the College actively participated in the programming of the facility.
> - The university's facilities management department oversaw the renovation of the buildings.
> - A local firm did the design based on a competition.
> - The success has partly to do with having good buildings to begin with. The Architecture Hall East building is the oldest building on campus and is on the list of historical buildings. The new building is a well built, brick building that is a nice complement to the older building.
> - The renovation melded two buildings together with a Link that is not only a place of transition but also a social gathering place.

Box 13.1

Fig. 13.1.
Architecture Hall East.

Fig. 13.2.
Architecture
Hall West.

1999). Budget restrictions required a scaled-down version of the BVH winning design. The design had a contemporary, multi-level link with a glass atrium. The Link, completed in 1986, made circulation between Architecture Hall East and West more convenient (Figure 13.3). Renovations to the existing buildings included knocking out false ceilings and walls while leaving architectural features such as ductwork and the elevator shaft exposed. Alterations to make the renovation affordable were essential to the design. For example, using the former library stacks as studio space and excavating the space in the basement for a wood shop and computer lab were additions to the original plan. The exposed ductwork and other contemporary touches respected the original architecture of the buildings and served to integrate the old with the new. Renovations were completed in 1987 (Austin, 1988).

RESULTS

Overall, participants responded to the College of Architecture building in a very positive manner. They gave high ratings to both the exterior and interior appearance. The library and public spaces were considered very positive assets of the building. The areas least liked by the users were the slow elevator and the computer lab.

EXTERIOR OF ARCHITECTURE HALL

Participants liked the exterior features of the building (Figure 13.4). They gave it high ratings, and in response to the open-ended questions, they reported more likes than dislikes. This reinforced the responses to questions asking for their level of agreement with various statements about the building.

The participants were most in agreement with the following items: "I like its overall appearance," "It looks impressive," and "It looks exciting." On the other hand they tended to disagree with the following statements: "It looks distressing," "It feels unsafe after dark," and "It is one of the ugliest buildings on campus." One question had mixed responses, "Its appearance fits in well with surrounding buildings." Architecture Hall looks different. Some people like the contrast, others do not.

Twenty-nine participants offered responses to the open-ended question about what they liked best about the exterior. Responses fall into three categories: physical appearance, historical reference, and specific aspects of the structure. Physical appearance responses referred to the color of the bricks, texture, angles, and ornamental details. Participants liked the color of the building, the uniqueness of the building, and the details such as the turret, the owls, the clock, and the gables. One participant responded, "It is not just a square building. I like its curves, its jagged edges as well." Participants liked the "woodwork around the doors," the "carved stone archways" and the overall appearance. One participant noted that the building was a "nice variety from the rest of the buildings around. It is quite unique." Historical responses referred to comments about the integration of the old with the new as well as surrounding buildings. A common historical reference comment was that participants liked "how the old style and the new style were brought together in the middle." The specific aspects of the structure to which comments were directed included the arches, the doors, the towers, and the way the two buildings unite.

When asked what they disliked most about the exterior of Architecture Hall, many people had no comment. Only 20 percent of the 30 respondents reported dislikes. Their

Fig. 13.3. (top) The Link exterior.

Fig. 13.4. (bottom) Responses to exterior.

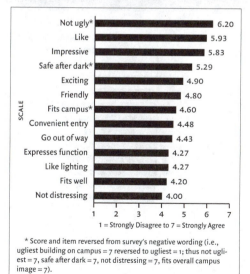

SCALE	
Not ugly*	6.20
Like	5.93
Impressive	5.83
Safe after dark*	5.29
Exciting	4.90
Friendly	4.80
Fits campus*	4.60
Convenient entry	4.48
Go out of way	4.43
Expresses function	4.27
Like lighting	4.27
Fits well	4.20
Not distressing	4.00

1 = Strongly Disagree to 7 = Strongly Agree

* Score and item reversed from survey's negative wording (i.e., ugliest building on campus = 7 reversed to ugliest = 1; thus not ugliest = 7, safe after dark = 7, not distressing = 7, fits overall campus image = 7).

dislikes included, "the clock doesn't work," "long rows of windows on the sides," and "no awnings." Five participants said they did not like the west building, calling it "bland" in comparison to the east building.

Fig. 13.5.
(top) The
Link interior.

INTERIOR OF LINK

Fig. 13.6.
(bottom)
Responses
to the Link.

Results for the interior of the Link space (Figure 13.5) revealed that overall participants were satisfied with the space (Figure 13.6). In particular, they gave the most satisfactory scores to, "I like its overall appearance," "It looks impressive," and "Its appearance fits in well with the surrounding buildings." (The last statement refers to the buildings that flank the Link, i.e., Architecture Hall East and West.) Likewise, they tended to disagree with the statements, "It is unsafe after dark," "It looks distressed," and "It is one of the ugliest buildings on campus."

In response to open-ended questions, respondents stressed the openness and large windows in the Link. Close to 60 percent of the respondents described the space as a good place to eat and socialize. They agreed that the appearance of the Link fits well with the buildings it connects. The responses to the Link survey paralleled the favorable responses to the exterior. Responses to the open-ended question about likes fit into two categories: structural and aesthetic. With regard to structure, users liked the staggered levels, the atrium space, the windows, and the lighting. With regard to the aesthetic character, they liked the openness of the space, the use of various materials and textures, and the use of both light and dark colors.

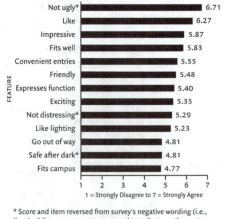

FEATURE	Score
Not ugly*	6.71
Like	6.27
Impressive	5.87
Fits well	5.83
Convenient entries	5.55
Friendly	5.48
Expresses function	5.40
Exciting	5.35
Not distressing*	5.29
Like lighting	5.23
Go out of way	4.81
Safe after dark*	4.81
Fits campus	4.77

1 = Strongly Disagree to 7 = Strongly Agree

* Score and item reversed from survey's negative wording (i.e., ugliest building on campus = 7 reversed to ugliest = 1; thus not ugliest = 7, safe after dark = 7, not distressing = 7, fits campus image = 7).

Most users (85 percent) described the Link as a place for social interaction, including eating, attending receptions, meeting friends, relaxing, and playing basketball. They also described the levels as great places to hang out, sit, and meet people. They liked being able to talk to friends on different levels, and they described the visual access to all the stairs and levels as pleasing. The communal space may well foster a sense of community, which the users value. Less than half of the respondents (43 percent) to the open-ended question wrote negative comments about the Link. They tended to complain about the slow elevators and the lack of maintenance of student work on display. Others commented on "feelings" about the Link, such as a general dislike for its eclectic nature.

INTERIOR OF ARCHITECTURE HALLS EAST AND WEST

Respondents gave relatively positive ratings to the interior of Architecture Halls East and West (Figure 13.7). The

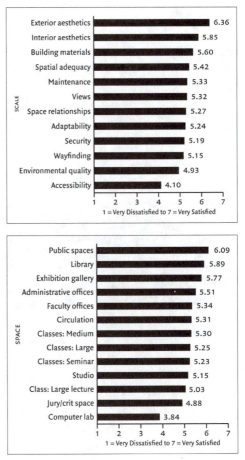

Fig. 13.7. (top) Overall satisfaction with Architecture Hall.

Fig. 13.8. (bottom) Most satisfying spaces.

aesthetic quality of the exterior and interior of Architecture Hall is the quality with which the participants were most satisfied. They were also moderately satisfied with building materials, spatial adjacency (distances among spaces), maintenance, views, space relationships (interconnectedness of spaces), adaptability, security, and wayfinding. On the other end of the continuum, the quality they were least satisfied with is accessibility for persons with disabilities.

If we consider which spaces the participants were most satisfied with, we see from Figure 13.8 that the public spaces, the library, and the exhibition galleries were the most satisfying. Reinforcing the quantitative assessments on the open-ended questions, 27 percent of participants listed the library as one of their most satisfying spaces, and 26 percent included the public spaces of Architecture Hall.

What made the library successful? Most users liked its aesthetic quality

Fig. 13.9.
Occupants loved the library for its aesthetic quality, lighting, acoustics, temperature, and security.

(Figure 13.9), lighting, acoustics, temperature, and security. The public spaces also received high marks for the individual qualities. Respondents gave the public spaces high scores to their aesthetic quality, acoustics, temperature, odor, security, and flexibility. Respondents gave lower ratings to accessibility.

As is obvious from Figure 13.10, the computer lab is the least satisfying space overall. In the open-ended questions, when asked which spaces they disliked most, respondents most often cited the computer lab (21 percent), studio rooms (16 percent) and circulation (10 percent). The computer lab is used for classroom, working, and presentation space. Ratings on it and the question about dislikes revealed that people disliked it due to problems with HVAC systems, aesthetics, odor, ventilation and temperature, adequacy of space, and security problems. Written comments showed an overemphasis on security measures, making the room inaccessible. Participants described the room as inconvenient because of the lock on the door and its being closed during term breaks.

METHOD

Three research teams concentrated on four study areas. One team surveyed people about Architecture Hall East, another team surveyed people about Architecture Hall West, and the third team surveyed people about the exterior of the building and the interior Link.

METHODS FOR ARCHITECTURE HALL EAST AND WEST

This study was done during fall semester 1999. In Architecture Halls East and West, interviewers gave the survey to faculty, staff, and students in the various disciplines of Architecture, Interior Design, and Community & Regional Planning. Every faculty and staff member received a survey and written description of this project in their mailboxes. The survey was distributed

:o students in each major based on 1999–2000 enrollment proportions. Students received the survey in their classrooms with a verbal description. We excluded people under 19 years old, thus excluding the need for paren-al consent, as well as excluding freshman students who lack familiarity with :he building. The West research team collected 65 completed surveys, and ιo partially completed surveys. The East research team collected 105 com-pleted surveys. More than 80 percent of the participants in these two sur-veys were students and the rest were faculty, staff, or other.

The Architecture Hall West research team encountered two problems. First, by mistake, two scales, which should have differed, had the same re-sponse scales (satisfied/dissatisfied twice instead of number of hours spent in each space). We corrected this expeditiously by attaching an addendum to :hose surveys not yet distributed, and in faculty mailboxes. Second, some confusion arose due to the two surveys (East and West) circulating. The re-search teams sometimes surveyed the same people.

METHODS FOR THE EXTERIOR AND THE LINK

The third research team examined user and non-user responses to two :hings: 1) the exterior of the buildings, and 2) the Link. The surveys were administered to a nonprobability sample, where interviewers stopped pass-ersby. For the Link, they stopped students, staff, faculty, and visitors who were in the Link. The teams did both surveys at various times of day, on

Fig. 13.10. The computer lab was disliked due to problems with HVAC, aesthetics, and security.

different days of the week, and at different locations within and outside of the building. Thirty-one people completed the Link survey, and 30 people completed the exterior survey. More than 70 percent of the participants in these two surveys were students. The rest were faculty, staff, or other. The sample had more males (55 percent) than females.

CONCLUSIONS AND RECOMMENDATIONS

The exterior of Architecture Hall works well. People see it as a positive contribution to the overall campus image, even though it differs from other buildings. Unlike the campus, which has primarily Collegiate Georgian buildings, Architecture Hall East looks Richardsonian. It has more complexity than the typical Georgian building on campus. The favorable responses to it suggest that people may like and find interesting a moderate level of novelty or atypicality (Berlyne, 1971 Gifford, 1997; Purcell, 1986). Architecture Hall has broad appeal, because many people find it "legible."

The adaptive reuse and the linking of Architecture Halls East and West is generally appreciated. The users find many aspects of the building quite pleasant and workable. Nevertheless, three key issues are paramount: the solitary slow elevator, the poor maintenance of the Link, and accessibility for persons with disabilities. In addition, the computer lab is an area that both faculty and students feel is a problem.

Clearly, the problems of the computer lab are multiple and may require special assistance. Consultants with the necessary expertise to deal with HVAC systems, aesthetics, odors, ventilation, temperature, functional adequacy, and security problems in the computer lab need to and have been engaged. Also there needs to be a balancing of the security needs with the need for accessibility. The security and HVAC problems have been tackled. A new HVAC system has been installed that has rectified the temperature, ventilation, and odor issues. Also, a new security system with a card sensor makes the computer lab much more user friendly for students and faculty. However, the aesthetics of the space have not been upgraded nor is it open during term breaks. The aesthetic issues have not gained enough support to bring about change, but the issue of the inadequacy of the computer lab to deal with the number of users has. Therefore, a new Media Center and a new GIS lab have been added to the College since the evaluation was done. These two additional facilities have taken some of the pressure off the computer lab. The operation of facilities over term breaks is a problem for most universities. Frequently the staff is not available to allow facilities to remain open and liability issues make this an added reason for not allowing access. Clearly, some problems are architectural in nature and others have to do with staffing, maintenance, or rules. Nonetheless, many of the problems of the computer lab could have been avoided with more careful pre-design analysis.

Given the participants' relatively low assessment of Architecture Hall with regard to accessibility for persons with disabilities, future designs might consider a couple of strategies for resolving such problems in the pre-design phase of the project. One strategy would be to do a more thorough analysis of user needs, e.g., modeling patterns of behavior. The other would be an adjacency analysis, which would clearly map the movement of people from one area of the building to another (tracking movement patterns and frequencies). These two strategies might help to alleviate many of the accessibility concerns of building users.

Messiness in the Link was an issue mentioned by some. The buildings may need more or better maintenance staff. The reality is that there have been some changes in the maintenance staff since the evaluation was done and the building looks much better. The staff members seem much more conscientious. Also, the faculty and students, with the prodding of the administration, have taken greater responsibility for cleaning up after themselves, which has made the tasks of the maintenance staff easier. This may not be an issue that is readily fixed through design. It has more to do with the efficient use of human resources and communication.

Clearly, the single slow elevator is a problem that requires a cost-benefit analysis. One elevator for a multi-story building is never a desirable solution. It will inevitably leave someone waiting and force them to take the stairs. The most obvious solution would have been to design the building with two elevators. (Given the

Box 13.2

LESSONS LEARNED

- Program comprehensively and with involvement of all users. Retrofitting spaces to rectify problems overlooked during the programming and design process can take time and money and still not achieve optimal results.

- Program for the adaptable and changing needs of teaching and learning over time. This suggests a loosely fitting building rather than one too tightly programmed and designed to begin with.

- Provide a building heart where all kinds of users flow through and linger to enliven the building. Places like the Atrium space can serve that purpose. Make sure it links parts together, is located at crossing points to encourage chance encounters, and has programmed activities, all of which can enhance informal interactions and sense of community.

- Give the design studios acoustic privacy between one another and other spaces. Otherwise, overlapping agendas can significantly interfere with teaching and learning.

- For spaces with specialized needs, such as computer labs, use consultants with special expertise to ensure that the program and design meet users' needs.

possibility of power outages and the concern for disabled users, emergency power should be provided, and if possible, a safe place within a fire proof area). While so-called safe havens with automatic steel fire doors can be found in the concrete cores of high rise buildings, they may not be realistic in this case, since the cost may have been prohibitive to implement any of these options. A less expensive solution to the elevator problem might be a long-term behavioral change of educating and convincing people that taking the stairs is good for them; it will benefit their health. But it would be helpful to have the cost-benefit analysis of adding another elevator during the pre-design phase of the project, so an informed decision could be made.

In conclusion, it makes sense to continue to re-evaluate the building, as functions may change over time. It is also clear that in schools of architecture with multiple functions and students, faculty, and staff moving throughout them, programming needs to place more attention on getting the accessibility requirements right. Finally, as suggested by a POE of the San Francisco Library, time spent in a space relates directly to the quality of materials used and the ambience, lighting, and other environmental influences of a space (San Francisco Public Library Commission, 2000). This might be worth future investigation in relation to spaces in design schools.

NANCY KWALLEK

14

GOLDSMITH HALL RENOVATION

THE UNIVERSITY OF TEXAS, AUSTIN

THE STORY BEHIND
THE BUILDING

In 1933, the architecture building, Goldsmith Hall, on The University of Texas at Austin campus was designed by famed architect, Paul Cret (1876–1945). Battle Hall and Sutton Hall are two additional architecture buildings that flank Goldsmith Hall designed by Cret's predecessor, Cass Gilbert (1859–1934). Composed of limestone, terra cotta, and red tile, together these buildings form an intimate complex (Figure 14.1) on The University of Texas at Austin campus that reflects a Spanish Mediterranean style.

Cret's vision in his master plan was to create a compact area within the campus. However, the feeling of intimacy began to be lost in the 1960s and 1970s with major university expansion and more monolithic campus buildings being added. Also, enrollment was reaching more than 600 students in the School of Architecture, and the administration realized a need for more studio space and classrooms, as well as offices for faculty and staff. Wanting to remain in these distinguished buildings designed by distinguished architects, they did not want to move from their premier site by creating a new architecture complex off campus. This decision led to plans of first renovating Sutton Hall, which primarily houses the architecture library and faculty

Box 14.1

ORIGINAL BUILDING SYNOPSIS

Designer: French-born and educated consulting architect Paul Cret.

Architects: Greene, LaRoche, and Dahl.

Supervising Architect: Robert Leon White.

Dates: 1933

Cost: $300,000

Construction: 51,800 square feet

RENAMED BUILDING AND RENOVATION SYNOPSIS

The Architecture Building was renamed Goldsmith Hall in 1978 in recognition of Professor Goldwin "Goldy" C. Goldsmith (1871–1962), who was the chairman of the School of Architecture from 1928-1935, and Architecture professor from 1935–1955. Goldsmith was influential in the construction of the original building.

Project architects: Thomas & Booziotis Architects, Dallas, Texas; and Chartier Newton & Associates, Architects, Austin, Texas—Bill Booziotis (partner-in-charge); Chartier Newton (partner-in-association); Donald W. Roberts (project architect); Lexa M. Acker (project manager for the University of Texas); Richard Dodge (associate dean, School of Architecture)

Renovation Dates: 1986–1988

Cost: $11 million

Construction: An additional 32,450 square feet were added to the original 51,800 square feet creating a total of 84,250 square feet of limestone, terra cotta, and red tile.

Occupants in 2005: 710 students in architecture, landscape architecture, and interior design; 26 faculty members, lecturers, and visitors; and 18 staff and administration members. Additional faculty and staff are in Battle Hall and Sutton Hall.

offices. When Sutton Hall was completed in 1982, a recession in the mid 1980s delayed the start of renovating Goldsmith Hall until 1986.

The plan for the renovation focused on a four-story wing on the south side, facing Sutton Hall and separated from the original building by a 12 foot-wide corridor. Faculty offices were located on the top and bottom floors, and studios were placed in between (Figure 14.2).

The new wing measures 38 feet wide by 182 feet long, and blends with Cret's original building. It preserved the massing and complexity of the original façade while adding a contemporary scale. The original building's Texas limestone was matched and the original cornice line was maintained. Sloping sills, simple medallions, and a black slate band were added to demarcate new from old. A loggia was added on the top floor to avoid

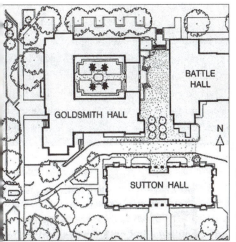

Fig. 14.1. (left) Plan layout of Architecture Complex with Goldsmith Hall, Sutton Hall, and Battle Hall.

Fig. 14.2. (below) South wing of Goldsmith Hall (photograph by Nancy Kwallek).

overwhelming the adjacent Sutton Hall. The original patio, with a simple
fountain than the original ornate one, was kept. It provides natural light to
the design and drawing rooms on two sides of the patio (Figure 14.3).

A unique interior feature is the ceiling of the north lobby. Major donor
are inscribed on the beams inside the south entrance; fresco caricatures of
professors are inscribed on the beams near the north entrance. The floor
are attractively covered with black and forest green slate. A dark green and
black granite stripe detail also delineates and adorns the new areas. The
color is carried to the upper hall areas.

EVALUATION OF THE
BUILDING EXTERIOR

Today, Goldsmith Hall houses the main
office for the school and serves as the school's headquarters. The University
of Texas at Austin restored an attractive architectural island in the middle of
a sprawling campus and achieved an improved and enlarged facility. Did the
school make the best renovation choices in an environment for students and
faculty?

The evaluations of the exterior were generally positive. The Exterior
POE revealed that the building fits very well with the surrounding buildings.
This is not surprising as the building is one of the 14 original buildings de
signed and created in 1933 by Paul Cret for the campus master plan.

Fig. 14.3.
Interior
Patio of
Goldsmith
Hall looking
west.

In general, respondents liked the overall appearance of Goldsmith Hall (Figure 14.4). They also rated it as having a good fit with surrounding buildings, looking friendly and impressive, and one of the best looking buildings on campus. They gave it neutral to low scores for excitement and feeling safe after dark, perhaps because the building abuts Guadalupe Street, the busy main drag, with a block of commercial shops and restaurants on the other side of the street. People of all backgrounds, including the homeless, often walk by or into the surrounding area and even wander into the building. At times, building occupants have found homeless individuals sleeping in some of the upper studios of the building.

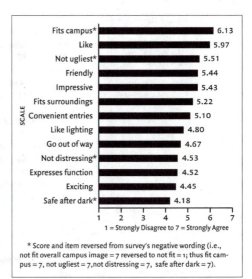

* Score and item reversed from survey's negative wording (i.e., not fit overall campus image = 7 reversed to not fit = 1; thus fit campus = 7, not ugliest = 7, not distressing = 7, safe after dark = 7).

Fig. 14.4. The exterior of Goldsmith Hall received consistently positive to average scores from the survey respondents (overall mean = 5.07).

Respondents also gave the exterior neutral to negative scores for how well it expresses the interior's function. The renovation focused chiefly on changes in the interior as a reaction to overcrowding. It improved the facilities to better reflect the demand of new technologies while retaining the style of the exterior to preserve the historical aspects of the building.

EVALUATION OF THE BUILDING INTERIOR

The interior received even more favorable evaluations (Figure 14.5). Occupants gave exterior aesthetics the highest satisfaction rating, but they also liked the overall appearance of the building. Other interior features receiving high satisfaction scores included interior aesthetics, the ease of finding one's way around, the amount of space in the halls, wall and floor quality, proximity to views, and spatial relationships.

Respondents gave the lowest ratings (though representing neutral evaluations) to security and the accessibility for persons with disabilities in the building. The lower security ratings might relate to the building location, as previously mentioned. The accessibility problems probably stem from limits in the original design, even though the remodeling process made substantial improvements, including the addition of an elevator.

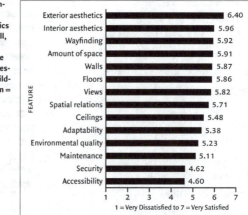

Fig. 14.5. Respondents liked the exterior aesthetics in Goldsmith Hall, but were less satisfied with the security and accessibility in the building (overall mean = 5.56).

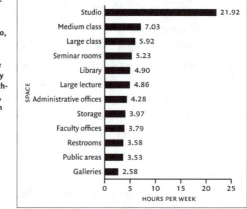

Fig. 14.6. Respondents spent the most hours per week in the studio, moderate hours per week in classes, and little time in the gallery (overall mean without studio = 4.52, overall mean with studio = 5.97).

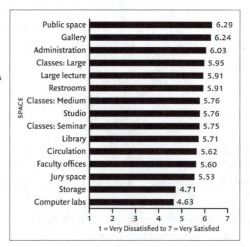

Fig. 14.7. Respondents liked the public space, gallery, and administrative offices, but were less satisfied with storage rooms and computer labs (overall mean = 5.69).

INTERIOR SPACES

In terms of space inside the building, respondents were most satisfied with the public areas, which included the entrances, atrium, and connecting areas. Other spaces with high ratings of overall satisfaction included the gallery and the administrative office area. Ironically, these public areas and the gallery were the two places where respondents spent the least amount of time (Figure 14.6). However, these areas are the most aesthetically pleasing compared to the usual messy condition of studio spaces. Nonetheless, respondents still rated their most used spaces positively, including studio, large- and medium-sized classrooms, and seminar rooms (Figure 14.7). Circulation, faculty offices, jury space, storage, and the computer laboratory received satisfaction scores below average. The lower scores for the latter make sense because of its location in the basement of the building, its poor lighting, and its makeshift arrangement.

The Least and Most Satisfying Spaces

Of all respondents, only a small percentage reported a space as among the least satisfying ones. Only 8 people (12 percent) indicated that the gallery area was the least satisfying space in the building (Figure 14.8), followed by 7 people (10 percent) for the computer laboratory, 7 people (10 percent) for seminar rooms, and 6 people (9 percent) for public areas. Among these

Fig. 14.8. The gallery received mixed evaluations.

respondents, they rated temperature, aesthetic appeal, and odor as the most unfavorable features in these spaces.

In contrast, more of the respondents reported spaces they judged as most satisfying. Nineteen people (28 percent) reported that they liked the public areas the most (Figure 14.9), followed by 13 people (19 percent) for the computer laboratory, 8 people (12 percent) for the gallery, and 5 people (7 percent) for the large lecture space. Among these respondents, the features they liked the most were the lighting, aesthetic appeal, adequate space, and acoustics.

Three spaces—the gallery, the public areas, and the computer laboratory (Figure 14.10)—received some ratings as the most and the least satisfying space. A look at the features

Fig. 14.9. (above) The public areas including this south entrance is a most liked space.

Fig. 14.10. (right) The least liked area is the computer laboratory.

associated with the respondents' experience showed that occupants often cited the quality of lighting and aesthetic appeal as features relating to their satisfaction with spaces. For the most satisfying spaces, respondents reported that they liked the lighting and aesthetic appeal. For the least satisfying spaces, they disliked the quality of the lighting and aesthetics. Overall, respondents of both kinds of spaces reported acoustics as a more favorable feature, and odor as a less favorable feature.

ANATOMY OF A SUCCESS

- The university had a solid program and budget.
- The College had a sensitive Dean, who kept an eye on construction to make sure the design met cost and user needs.
- The Goldsmith Hall renovation mixed modern and traditional elements to fit with neighboring historic buildings—Battle and Sutton Hall.
- The structure is built with high-quality materials.
- It has a great location on campus, near the desirable coffee shops, restaurants, and shopping.

Box 14.2

METHOD

The survey on the exterior of Goldsmith Hall was completed by 73 people. Most respondents were male (54.8 percent) and undergraduate students (56.2 percent). The sample also had 28.8 percent graduate students, 12.3 percent faculty members, and 12.3 percent staff members. The respondents ranged from 25 to 81 years old (mean = 34.9 years), and they reported spending from less than one year to more than 56 years on campus (mean = 6.0 years).

Sixty-seven people (41.89 percent males, 49.25 percent females, and 8.96 percent not reporting their gender) completed the survey on the interior of Goldsmith Hall. The sample included a variety of people (44.76 percent undergraduate students, 31.34 percent graduate students, 10.45 percent faculty members, 7.47 percent staff members, and 5.9 percent not reporting their position). Their reported ages ranged from 24 to 77 years old (mean = 34.03 years); and their reported time on campus ranged from less than a year to more than 25 years (mean = 4.03 years).

CONCLUSIONS

Passersby and occupants were very positive about Goldsmith Hall. Passersby judged this historic building as appealing and an appropriate environmental setting within the campus as a whole and its adjacency to surrounding buildings. These favorable assessments of the exterior carried into the interior. Occupants liked the interior;

LESSONS LEARNED

- It is particularly challenging for a building that will be scrutinized by an architecturally sophisticated population to achieve a highly positive evaluation.
- Occupants appreciate the character of a landmark restored building if it works and is well done.
- The juxtaposition and selection of appropriate materials is critical to providing a building that is well received and comfortable.
- Most occupants enjoy the gallery and design of the wings that wrap around an interior patio.
- People respond well when access to nature is provided through windows, gardens, and courtyards.

Box 14.3

---

they found it an attractive environment, not only aesthetically, but also for its functionality, such as the amount of space, the relationship between spaces, and the ease of finding their way around and moving through the interior. They were particularly positive about the public areas. The few areas that some occupants disliked could be improved with changes in the basic amenities and ambient design characteristics such as lighting, overall appearance, temperature, and odor. Otherwise, with its consistently favorable ratings, Goldsmith Hall at The University of Texas at Austin stands as an example of the design features that make for a successful School of Architecture building. Individuals planning to build or renovate a design building should visit and examine this building's plans and site.

STUDENTS' ASSESSMENT OF ARCHITECTURE SCHOOLS

SUMMARY

The study of architectural building types, which embody functional and formal properties, can be used as an analytical tool to develop a fund of shared knowledge. As an analytical tool, the historical and cultural context provides a framework for understanding societal conventions. Objects such as buildings have not only a "use" value but also a "message" value. A connection, therefore, exists between the concepts of type and meaning. The meaning, however, must be shared and understood by the makers and the users of an object if it is to serve the intended purpose. Meanings are constructed in accordance with context-dependent conventions and change over time. This investigation is an analysis of architecture schools as a building type. Beginning with a historical perspective through an assessment of several recent buildings (chapter 3), it will be shown that building types change slowly, but they do evolve over time.

A post-occupancy evaluation was developed to compare notable architecture buildings from the users' perspectives. A comparative assessment of six architecture buildings was conducted, using a walkthrough evaluation rating scale. The buildings selected were at Florida A&M University, University of North Carolina–Charlotte, University of Wisconsin–Milwaukee,

University of Cincinnati, North Carolina State University, and Roger Wil
liams University. This approach sought direct responses from architecture
students according to six elements: *context, massing, interface, wayfinding, socio
spatial environment,* and *comfort.* By using a series of checklist questions and
numeric ratings from satisfactory to unsatisfactory, scores were assigned to
each element being appraised. Individual scores were graphed to establish a
building profile, and profiles were compared. The results demonstrate that
wayfinding and *comfort* were consistently identified as the least satisfactory
building element for all buildings in the study. In a similar vein, buildings
touted by architectural critics received mixed responses from students.

RESEARCH PROBLEM

Buildings designed specifically for ar
chitectural studies in a university setting are a recent phenomenon. The past
several decades has witnessed more than 20 new and renovated university
architecture buildings in America alone, many of which have been documented in the architecture press. In very few instances have there been any
systematic attempts at gauging responses to the new facility by the building's
occupants. There have, however, been anecdotal reactions from critics, students, and faculty. For example, the Yale School of Architecture is housed
in the 1963 Art and Architecture Building by Paul Rudolph, which was
purportedly set afire by students in 1969. The building was in bad shape,
butchered by renovations, dirty, leaky, bombed daily by pigeons that roost in
its towers, cold in winter, hot in summer, and unbelievably cramped for
space (Crosbie, 1988a). Too little daylight reaches the internal areas of the
workspace since remodeling divided two story spaces into separate single
stories. The original concept was for the drafting rooms to be multi-level affairs, so you couldn't help but see and be quite aware of what other people
were doing. (Crosbie, 1988a). According to Rudolph, the division of major
spaces and resulting change in light levels was most damaging to the original
design intent. The library is overstuffed and there is too little classroom and
administration space (Crosbie, 1988a). The building was designed to grow
to the north, yet it was not large enough for its intended purpose on the day
it opened. An addition is underway.

In a similar vein, the College of Environmental Design at Berkeley was
established in 1959 under the guidance of William Wurster, for whom
Wurster Hall is named. Designed by a collaborative group including Joseph
Esherick, Vernon DeMars, Donald Hardison, and Donald Olsen, the building was intended to look like a ruin (as noted in chapter 3). Built out of

rough concrete with the internal workings all exposed, the building presents a rough and aggressive appearance.

At Philadelphia, expansion in the late 1950s meant a new building for the University of Pennsylvania School of Architecture. The building was not well received by many of the students and instructors. For all the building's shortcomings, Penn's experience was not unique . . . protest also occurred at Yale, Harvard, and Berkeley, each of which built new buildings for the design schools, and each of which found these buildings attacked by their users (Strong and Thomas, 1990).

A building for the teaching of architecture should engage not distract the inhabitants of such a building. However, the lack of any systematic documentation of user responses to architecture school buildings clearly leads to a repeat of previous malfunctions and unnecessary dissatisfaction. A universal solution is not the purpose of acquiring such a knowledge base, but rather the knowledge should allow designers to predict consequences that may result from their design decisions. Therefore, this study represents an initial attempt at seeking responses from a sample of architecture building users—the students.

METHOD

There are many feasible approaches to assessing building performance. Post-occupancy evaluation (POE) is the process of evaluating buildings in a systematic manner after they have been built and occupied. POE is said to derive its name from the occupancy permit that is issued when a building is completed, inspected, and deemed safe according to building codes and regulations. A building's performance can consist of a variety of technical, functional, and behavioral elements (Preiser, Rabinowitz, and White, 1988). Elements such as health, safety, and security, as well as the psychological and social aspects of user satisfaction, can comprise a POE. Markus (1994) described the distinct elements of our experience of buildings to be form, or what things look like; what people do in the building; and how we sense where we are, in relation to other spaces inside and outside the building.

The POEs in this chapter used a different approach from that used in most of the other chapters. The present approach, which relied on an understanding of the built environment, used a self-guided tour with a checklist. Unlike other assessment strategies that rely upon conventional social science techniques for describing and judging the environment, the checklist offers individuals a procedure for taking a structured walk through a building. The results of such a walkthrough encourage responses to the views, walkways, barriers, daylight, orientation, wayfinding, and appearance. For building oc-cupants, the walkthrough represents a rediscovery of a building's features and characteristics that may have influenced the users' accommodation or adaptation. This analysis allows observers to appraise building quality in terms of six key elements (Bishop, 1977; Sanoff, 1990). The element catego-ries were identified through an extensive literature review of building de-scriptions by numerous authors. They are as follows:

- CONTEXT—the building's setting.
- MASSING—the organization of building parts into a form. Massing of the parts gives both form and meaning as well as variety to the building.
- INTERFACE—the meeting place where the inside of the building con-nects with the outside.
- WAYFINDING—the ability for people to discern routes, traffic patterns, or passageways in and around the building.
- SOCIO-SPATIAL ELEMENTS—the ability of the building to accommodate diverse human needs.
- COMFORT—the environmental conditions affecting human comfort.

By using a series of checklist questions and numeric ratings, scores from 1 (very unsatisfactory) to 7 (very satisfactory) were assigned to the element being appraised. The process used notes and photographs to supplement the elements described in the checklist. Numeric scores were assigned to each question in the checklist. Individual scores were then averaged and an over-all building score was assigned. An appraisal report considered:

1. A description of the building appraised with supportive photographs.
2. Appraisal of the building according to the six elements using the check-list, with responses and numeric scores for each question provided.
3. A paragraph describing the success or lack of success with which each el-ement is achieved or satisfied.
4. A descriptive profile of the ratings by computing average scores for each element of the appraisal and the overall building score.

Samples of six recently constructed architecture schools were selected for this study. Individual faculty members from each school were contacted and requested to use 20 students as a sample population for this study. In ad-dition to survey responses, secondary data sources, such as articles about each building in the survey as reported in the architectural press supple-mented the discussion.

FLORIDA A&M

The Florida A&M University (FAMU) School of Architecture, designed by Clements/Rumpel Associates, sought to push the limits of definitions of architecture. The FAMU School of Architecture was perceived as a continuing experiment and teaching tool. It was intended for students to learn by studying how the building was designed and constructed and by observing what works and wears well over time and what does not. Both the successes and shortcomings of the facility are teaching tools, and the entire building becomes a valuable resource in the educational program. Several of the experimental aspects of the facility involved the passive heating and cooling system. Other features of the school included the use of small individual studios, the reduced size of faculty offices in favor of shared meeting space, and the open circulation system to facilitate human interaction (Sanoff, 1994). The design competition for the new School of Architecture stressed a structure that emphasized economical construction, programmatic flexibility, community accessibility, and energy conservation (Fisher, 1985).

The building is located on a sloping site along a major campus road. The library, computer lab, and lecture hall are contained within a front and central block, partially buried to relate in scale and material to the houses nearby. Perpendicular to the front block are four wings containing offices, labs, and studios. The wings are constructed with low-cost steel framing and corrugated steel and fiberglass cladding.

One of the objectives for the new architecture building was to avoid the large, barn-like rooms in favor of smaller, separate studios, which hold only one class of 16 students each. The intention was to create an atelier atmosphere in the design classes, a sense of ownership of the space, where students have their own workstation and are encouraged to move in. A major program goal was to demonstrate state-of-the art techniques in passive heating, cooling, ventilation, and lighting systems. Other related goals were to utilize advantages in the area's climate, and to present an image of leading edge quality of school. This was the basis for selection of the design from the competition. In addition, promoting social interaction among students and faculty and effective workspaces were equally valued goals. Using the concept of community as an organizing element, it was hoped that a new building would support a sense of social community among the students: a place where people would want to go, where they would want to spend time. Comfort was also seen as important: Environmental factors have a significant impact on the teaching and learning processes.

From the profile of student responses (Figure 15.1), it can be observed that their consistency in responses signifies that the building achieves a general level of satisfaction or fittingness with the building's primary purpose. The highest level of agreement is with *comfort*, which is the least satisfactory

Table 15.1
ELEMENT DESCRIPTION (FLORIDA A&M)

CONTEXT	MASSING	INTERFACE	WAYFINDING	SOCIO-SPATIAL	COMFORT
• building respects vernacular context • building fits the scale of the campus	• functions are identified by different masses • difficult to identify functions from exterior • variety of materials and connecting structures blur the massing • reception area unclear	• no visual access to outside from studios • no distinction between public and private spaces • interior does not relate to exterior • entrances are not clearly marked • assigned assembly spaces and atrium underutilized	• open circulation facilitates visual connections • difficult for visitors to locate entrance • signage confusing • ground level is underutilized • wheelchair accessibility problems	• separation of studio spaces from faculty offices • studio spaces not well maintained • no provisions for eating • poor interaction between students due to individual studio spaces	• poor climate control • numerous technological breakdowns

Fig. 15.1. Six-element profile (Florida A&M).

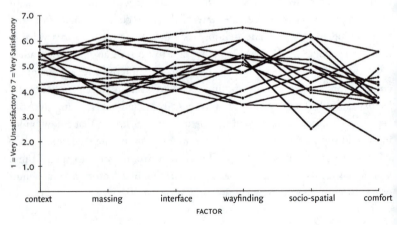

1 = Very Unsatisfactory to 7 = Very Satisfactory

7.0 — 6.0 — 5.0 — 4.0 — 3.0 — 2.0 — 1.0

context   massing   interface   wayfinding   socio-spatial   comfort

FACTOR

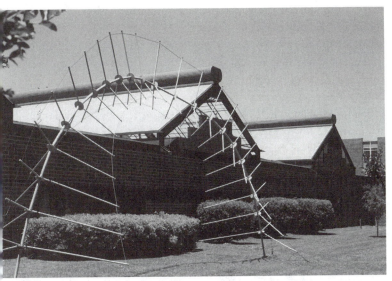

Fig. 15.2.
Exterior view
(Florida
A&M).

element, though is still considered to be satisfactory as reported by the element scores. *Comfort* problems are associated with breakdowns of the HVAC system and the inability to adequately control the temperature in the building. Students commented about their separation from faculty offices as well as their isolation from other students due to individual studio spaces. *Wayfinding*, too, appeared to be a problem for visitors since entrances are not clearly marked (Table 15.1). The most successful element, with the highest level of agreement, is the *context*. Here, it was agreed that the building respects the vernacular context and responds to the scale of the campus (Figure 15.2).

UNIVERSITY OF NORTH CAROLINA AT CHARLOTTE

The University of North Carolina at Charlotte's College of Architecture, designed by Charles Gwathmey, separates studio spaces from offices with a long, two-story exhibition salon, with narrow corridors providing second-floor access while overlooking the salon. Although the salon was not part of the original program, Gwathmey argued that it was needed to serve as the college's "living room"—a place for everything from crits and impromptu discussions to art exhibitions and formal receptions (Pearson, 1991). A library with an exhibition gallery and a lecture hall anchor the ends of the salon hallway. In line with the building's main entry is a cylindrical stair elevator, intended to orient visitors to the main interior axis. Faculty offices look onto the long space from both the first and second floors and are accessed by corridors on either side of the salon.

The building's design studios—with their 14-foot ceilings on the lower level, north-facing skylights on the upper level, and outdoor work space on both floors—underscore the importance of studio experience in the school's curriculum. In the studios, columns (18 feet on-center) form a grid within which low partitions separate the various teaching sections without closing off the space. Located on the site of a former parking lot, the 86,000-square-foot building intends to define an open space, linking the architecture school to the rest of the campus.

Table 15.2
ELEMENT DESCRIPTIONS (UNIVERSITY OF NORTH CAROLINA)

CONTEXT	MASSING	INTERFACE	WAYFINDING	SOCIO-SPATIAL	COMFORT
• massive entrance • studio elevation not too large for human scale • unclear entrance • poor face to campus	• does not reflect functions • ground floor circulation clear • building defined into zones • window arrangement unclear	• clear location • lobby often dark • entry lobby opens to a blank wall	• lack of clear entrances • bathroom locations unclear • recognizability from street is poor • confusing for first time visitors • corridors define circulation	• large unoccupied areas • opportunities for personalization • nodes for casual contact not clear • faculty separated from students	• lack of light penetration into deep studio spaces • noise in studio space • crit rooms lack ventilation

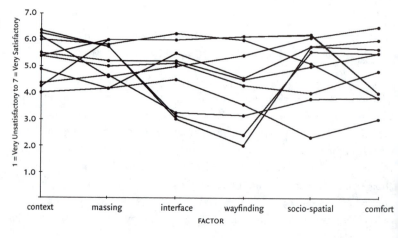

Fig. 15.3. Six-element profile (University of North Carolina, Charlotte).

Fig. 15.4.
Exterior view
(University
of North
Carolina,
Charlotte).

Strongest agreement among students is the *context* and *massing* which are both perceived to be positive (Figure 15.3). Student observations, if compared with the remaining elements, vary widely for *wayfinding* and *socio-spatial element*. Student responses to the open ended part of the survey suggest a lack of clear entrances and a poor face to the campus (Table 15.2). Figure 15.4 shows a view of the entrance locations. Once inside the building, however, circulation is somewhat clear, though it may confuse first time visitors. Students noted that faculty offices separated from studio spaces did not allow for casual contacts, and there were large unoccupied areas, namely Gwathmey's salon. Poor lighting and noise in the studio spaces were also cited as inadequate *comfort* features.

UNIVERSITY OF WISCONSIN
AT MILWAUKEE

The University of Wisconsin–Milwaukee School of Architecture, is housed in Englemann Hall, an undistinguished 1930s high school, barely large enough for its 750 students (Stubbs, 1988). The basement houses a lounge/pin-up room, but many of the classrooms are awkwardly proportioned for studios and crits (Stubbs, 1988). An addition completed in 1993 by Holabird & Root of Chicago, with Eppstein Uhen Architects of Milwaukee, provided an additional 142,000 square feet of interior space.

The L-shaped building frames an interior courtyard with 4-story window walls set within a concrete structural grid. The new building's exposed structure and utilities are intended to work hand in hand with the educational philosophy of the school. "We stress construction. We stress realism and materiality," asserts the then and current Dean, Robert Greenstreet (Litt, 1996). Design is made public since student drawings can be tacked to walls anywhere in the building, and jury spaces are located in large hallway

Table 15.3
ELEMENT DESCRIPTIONS (UNIVERSITY OF WISCONSIN, MILWAUKEE)

CONTEXT	MASSING	INTERFACE	WAYFINDING	SOCIO-SPATIAL	COMFORT
• entrance difficult to locate • conforms to context • lack of ornamentation • corridor noise in classrooms • building turns its back on public area	• massing divided into circulation and non-circulation • monotonous building, except for west façade • no variety in size, form, or material • too many hard surfaces	• mundane main entrance • no protective covering over entrances • court not utilized • no sheltered setting in court • wasted space due to locked doors	• stairways inconvenient • circulation paths cross activity nodes • bathrooms inconveniently located • sameness of size, color, and texture • orientation is difficult for visitors	• stairs are primary location for interaction • pockets of social spaces work well • no sufficient informal meeting areas • transparent interior facilitates visual contact • lack of individual control by users	• difficult to control temperature in studios • lighting fixtures generated noise, and illumination was ineffective • high ambient noise level in building

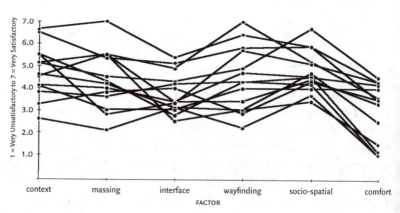

Fig. 15.5. Six-element profile (University of Wisconsin, Milwaukee).

Fig. 15.6. Exterior view (University of Wisconsin, Milwaukee).

alcoves. Although Greenstreet observed that the main façade of the building facing the campus is a little harsh, the experience of entering a light-filled interior comes as a pleasant surprise.

Student responses to the survey concur with many of Greenstreet's observations. They feel that the main entrance is mundane, a sameness of size and color, in contrast to Greenstreet's description of the dramatically stripped-down interior (Table 15.3). While the building's exposed structure and utilities are an expression of realism, students gave *comfort,* including lighting, ambient noise level, and temperature control, their lowest ratings (Figure 15.5). Litt (1996) explains that the layout of offices and classrooms is aimed at guaranteeing that students and faculty bump into one another continuously. He further observes that the principal area for socializing is the two-story main space. Student perceptions are that the pockets of social spaces work well; that the stairs are the primary location for interaction; and that the transparent interior facilitates visual contact. Generally, students gave the *socio-spatial* element the highest rating. Figure 15.6 shows an exterior view.

THE UNIVERSITY OF CINCINNATI

The University of Cincinnati's Aronoff Center for Design and Art, designed by Eisenman Architects, is a building that houses studios for different disciplines interspersed among each other and 40 offices. The 146,000-square-foot addition combined old and new in a public space containing a bookstore, cafeteria, library, gallery, and corridors used for reviews that are open to passersby. The program of the addition called for turning a central atrium into a main street for 2,000 students and 130 faculty members. The purpose of the addition was to consolidate under one roof a college with departments dispersed around the campus. In a *New York Times* article, Wilson (1996) claimed that the building "resembles a stack of pastel blocks appearing as if they are about to fall." In a critique of the building, Giovannini (1996) suggested that "Its unexpected

Table 15.4
ELEMENT DESCRIPTIONS (UNIVERSITY OF CINCINNATI)

CONTEXT	MASSSING	INTERFACE	WAYFINDING	SOCIO-SPATIAL	COMFORT
• building fits landscape and topography • color and materials not suited to context • not visible to students on campus • building is unique in its context	• clear and interesting subdivision of building parts • parts unidentifiable as to their function • massing integrates old and new parts • interior spaces are differentiated	• visitors are disoriented • welcoming entrance • exits difficult to locate • building contains a central core • interesting interior spaces	• interior and vertical circulation confusing • no signage • poor connection in between old and new part • interior routes interesting	• atrium cafeteria is a social focal point • building materials constrain pin-up • no opportunity for personalization • few opportunities for student/faculty socialization	• acoustic problems in studios • poor illumination in studios

Fig. 15.7. Six-element profile (University of Cincinnati).

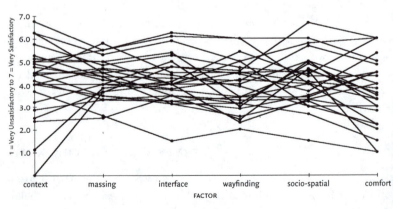

Fig. 15.8.
Exterior
view (Uni-
versity of
Cincinnati).

success is its ability to act as a social condenser—Eisenman feeds all floors and parts of the combined building into a stepped promenade that centers on an atrium lined with activities." He further acknowledged "disappoint-ments," such as too few windows that look directly out, and a perimeter that turns its façade and public face away from the campus. An observation made by one student was that "Eisenman's building (not our building) does not fare very well based on these six categories. If he were asked for six catego-ries on which to judge his building, I feel certain there would be little over-lap." From the profile, it can be observed that this is a controversial building. (See also chapter 10.) Students had strong reactions to each of the elements. They lamented the lack of opportunity to personalize their environment, since the building materials constrain pin-up. They noted problems of noise and poor illumination in the studios. While they felt that the interior spaces were interesting, they also commented that they were disorienting. *Massing,* the most positive element (Table 15.4), was described as a clear and inter-esting subdivision of building parts. Interior spaces were differentiated, though many did not have a clear and obvious function. Interior routes were reported to be interesting though confusing. *Context,* the most controversial element (Figure 15.7) was responded to from different viewpoints. While some students felt strongly that the colors and materials were not suited to the context, others believed that their distinctiveness was a virtue and made the building unique in its context (Figure 15.8).

NORTH CAROLINA STATE UNIVERSITY

Wolf Associates designed the 37,000-square-foot addition to the College of Design in Raleigh. The building was intended to reflect not only the functional needs of the client—the studios, offices, lecture rooms, and other spaces required for a design school—but a reflection of architectural principles that the faculty wanted to impart to the students. By exposing the pre-cast concrete structure and the mechanical systems, the design reflects an educational concept that students can and should learn from about how architecture functions (Wood, 1978). The architects designed the building so that studio spaces would vary in size, shape, and volume while the interior walls are painted white and floors are carpeted. Certain floor levels have operable windows while others have fixed glass. The studios generally face east with a few openings on the west side. The architects have reflected the building's relationship to adjoining sections of the campus and established traffic patterns (a street used to run where a courtyard is now) by including pedestrian colonnades on the ground floor that anyone, not just those in the College of Design, may use. The site's former occupant, the old university YMCA, also had a colonnade;

Table 15.5
ELEMENT DESCRIPTIONS (NORTH CAROLINA STATE UNIVERSITY)

CONTEXT	MASSING	INTERFACE	WAYFINDING	SOCIO-SPATIAL	COMFORT
• fits well with surrounding buildings	• no visual cues to functions	• entrances difficult to locate	• no visual cues to circulation	• no opportunity for casual contact with faculty	• uneven thermal comfort
• lack of detail clashes with adjacent buildings	• massing oversized for human scale	• no sense of entry	• no signage	• difficult to personalize	• not effective in responding to illumination or comfort needs
• poor connection with the outside	• difficult to identify ground floor from others	• good visual connection between interior and exterior	• people continually getting lost	• lack of privacy	
	• no distinction between floor levels	• no front façade	• auditorium difficult to locate	• all studio spaces public and noisy	
				• social needs of students and visitors not met	
				• studio spaces show student activity	

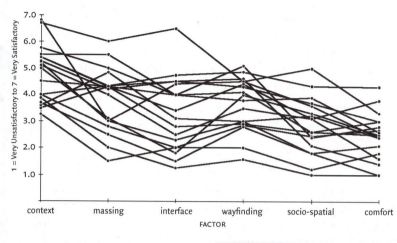

Fig. 15.9. (left) Six-element profile (North Carolina State University).

Fig. 15.10. (below) Exterior view (North Carolina State University).

and the new colonnade and fenestration reflect those of the adjoining neo-classical, main building of the school.

Wood (1978) reported that as the building opened for classes, both the client and architect were pleased with the way the process of designing it had worked out. "It was a very special kind of linkage that developed between the architect and client," recalled Claude E. McKinney, the dean of the college at that time. Descriptions of this award-winning building included statements like *multiplicity* and *variety* and Charles Gwathmey, a juror for the South Atlantic Regional AIA competition, called the addition "terrific." Students indicated that the building scale, massing, and use of materials fit well with surrounding buildings, with the exception of the building's lack of detail. They also felt that the massing lacked human scale (Table 15.5). The building's direct connection with the outside was seen as less successful, though the visual connection was good. From the profile (Figure 15.9) it is evident that *wayfinding, socio-spatial* (the element which accommodates a diversity of human needs) and *comfort* have the largest number of negative responses. People are continually getting lost because entrances are difficult to locate (Figure 15.10). From a more personal point of view, the studio spaces are regarded as too public and too noisy; illumination is poor and thermal conditions are uneven. The author infers that the noticeable positive responses in the profile came primarily from international graduate students who experienced substantially inferior working conditions in their native countries.

ROGER WILLIAMS UNIVERSITY

The architecture building at Roger Williams University in Bristol, Rhode Island, is the product of a national design competition won by Kite Palmer Architects. Kite's winning entry seemed to the jury to embody the program's call for "an outstanding design, compatible with existing campus buildings, consideration for cost effectiveness and energy conservation" (Crosbie, 1988b). The building program called for accommodation of 280 undergraduate students, faculty, and administration offices, flexible studio space, jury rooms, computer labs, a library, and social spaces.

The design is a two-story, day-lighted spine, anchored at one end by the library and at the other by a lounge. The building steps along in one large studio that relies on setbacks and movable partitions to define studio groups. A mezzanine level overlooking the studio is used for review spaces and a computer lab. Student responses were generally favorable in all categories (Table 15.6). They noted that the architecture building was a significant contribution to the visual character of the campus, although it was poorly located. While the building is well organized with a clear separation between studio and office spaces, the large studio space was reported to have some

Fig. 15.11. Six-element profile (Roger Williams University).

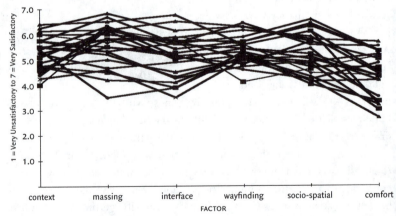

Table 15.6
ELEMENT DESCRIPTIONS (ROGER WILLIAMS UNIVERSITY)

CONTEXT	MASSING	INTERFACE	WAYFINDING	SOCIO-SPATIAL	COMFORT
• building enhances surroundings • scale and materials related to context • poorly located on campus	• massing reflects different uses • clear separation between studio and office space • clear axial organization • main entry not clearly marked	• exterior circulation is clear • lack of entry/exit definition • orientation creates heat and glare problems • clear separation of public and private areas	• meeting area created in front of building • studio circulation confusing • 2nd floor layout confusing • visitors often wander	• lounge is remote and unused • no privacy in studio • no gathering spaces in studio • good teaching tool to observe good and bad features • need for more social spaces • not enough review spaces	• excessive heat gain • lack of HVAC control • harsh lighting

disadvantages (Figure 15.11). The lack of privacy, social spaces, and confused circulation were noted as problems with the large studio space. The large amount of overhead glass and building orientation were also noted as a source of excessive heat gain and glare problems (Figure 15.12).

CONCLUSIONS

This pilot study, with responses from approximately 20 students from each school, had a relatively small sample, but their similarity of responses have interesting implications. From the combined element scores (Figure 15.13), using the median value from each school, students rated Roger Williams highest on all scales except *comfort*. UNC Charlotte's school of architecture scored highest on *comfort*, while its *socio-spatial* quality received the lowest rating for all schools. The Aronoff Center in Cincinnati scored lowest on *massing* and *context*. NCSU scored lowest on *interface* and *comfort*.

Fig. 15.12. Exterior view (Roger Williams University).

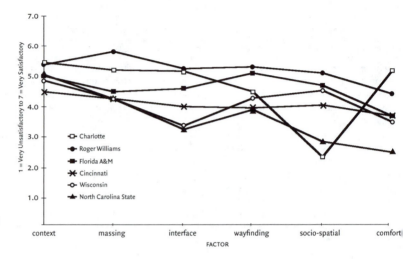

Fig. 15.13.
Combined
element
profiles.

Almost all scores reflect a positive response to each element in spite of a number of problems noted by the respondents. Clearly, the median values are used here for comparative purposes. When examining element scores for individual buildings, it can be observed that the variation between positive and negative responses was substantial in all cases except for Florida A&M and Roger Williams, which reported the highest level of agreement (lowest standard deviation from the mean). Comparing element profiles for *all buildings,* it appeared that the least successful ones were *wayfinding* and *comfort.* For *wayfinding,* it was consistent from responses to each of the buildings that visitors would find entrances and circulation confusing and that bathrooms and stairways were inconveniently located. In some cases circulation paths generated unwanted noise. Equally consistent was the reported dissatisfaction with the illumination and acoustics of studio spaces as noted in the *comfort* category.

The study results still leave some doubt whether current architecture buildings reflect the program and function. Each of the buildings' architects responded to a program established by the client, which in most cases consisted of a faculty committee. Programs vary with their explicitness, and consequently allow for a different interpretation of needs and equally reflect the ideologies, memories, and personalities of the architect. But, a program is incomplete if an assessment of its validity has not been conducted. Every programmatic assumption may have a consequence, or side effect, which building users may perceive as a positive or negative factor. While several schools opted for individual studio spaces, for example, this produced a side effect of lack of contact with other students. The assessment also revealed unresolved environmental problems. An exposed building structure that provides a teaching role also requires maintenance and may well suffer visible deterioration over time.

While the value of a program cannot be denied, it is equally important to anticipate the consequences of programmatic requirements. In some cases the building program may have lacked sufficient detail, or the building architect placed a low priority in solving the problems identified. Nonetheless, it is evident that a well detailed building program can help ameliorate many dissatisfactions students experience on a daily basis. Since a program cannot anticipate every potential problem, it should be assumed that building modifications might be necessary after initial occupancy.

Sampling only the student population represents a bias, since faculty and staff members are important users whose viewpoints also require consideration. The focus of this study, however, is the student population. This report represents the first step of an analysis of American and international schools of architecture constructed within the past 20 years with the aim of constructing a knowledge base about a building type.

LESSONS LEARNED

Shared strengths and weaknesses from student assessments of the six architecture buildings highlight six directions for improving future designs.

- Fit the appearance of the architecture building exterior to its context in scale, massing, and materials.

- Provide natural gathering places for informal interaction and socializing. A café serves this purpose, as do transparent stairways with wide landings.

- Provide a legible circulation system. This includes having clear entrances and exits, simple layouts, good signage, you-are-here maps, and points of differentiation (such as a landmark stair), all of which can reduce disorientation and make it easier for visitors to find their way around.

- Design studios should have well planned acoustics, temperature controls, and illumination. Most of the studios suffered from problems with illumination, glare, noise, and temperature.

- Give each studio and the students in them privacy.

- Faculty offices should allow for relatively easy student access, but afford faculty adequate privacy and control of access. Students preferred faculty offices close to studios for easy access, but research suggests that faculty members favor greater distance for privacy (and may flee offices lacking such privacy).

Box 15.1

EVALUATION
CASE STUDIES
(INTERNATIONAL)

PART IV

THE SCHOOL OF ARCHITECTURE

DOKUZ EYLUL UNIVERSITY, IZMIR, TURKEY

SUMMARY

The building for the Dokuz Eylul University School of Architecture (DEU-SA) opened in September 2004. The Architecture Department occupies one wing, and the City and Regional Planning Department occupies the other wing. In May 2005, 159 people (students, faculty, and staff members from two departments) participated in a post-occupancy survey to evaluate the interior and exterior of the facility.

Overall, the building received negative scores. Respondents rated the exterior unfavorably. They gave the least favorable ratings to the lighting after dark, their willingness to walk out of their way to see it, and its excitement. Occupants reported neither satisfaction nor dissatisfaction with the interior. They had the lowest satisfaction for accessibility for the disabled, environmental quality, security, and wayfinding. They had the highest satisfaction (roughly equal to neutral scores) for the quality of building materials— floor, wall, ceiling, and maintenance. Open-ended responses agreed with these findings. For the exterior, respondents criticized the building size and color, entrance and security, and poor landscape. The only favorable comments were on uniqueness and window details. While a few participants found the articulation on the façade unnecessary and overdone, more people liked it because it distinguishes the building from the campus architecture. For the interior, respondents criticized accessibility for persons with a disability, security, environmental quality concerning temperature, and acoustics.

Ratings of specific spaces revealed that most spaces did not score well. The cafeteria emerged as the least liked space. Occupants complained about its furniture and poor connection to the outdoors and the atrium. The medium classrooms emerged as the most liked spaces, receiving praise for their large, shaded windows. Occupants also liked the restrooms, praising their upkeep and newness.

On a campus, architecture buildings should draw students from other departments, but this architecture building does not. With small improvements such as landscaping the surrounding area, adding activity to the atrium and cafeteria, the building has the potential to draw people to socialize. Students and faculty members spend most of their time in studios; and they tend to find the design of the studios unsatisfactory. Softening the wall and floor surfaces (to reduce acoustical problems) and adding comfortable and movable seats can improve the studio spaces. While digital technologies have become more important, the building works against their use with its inefficiently used computer laboratories. Relocation (closer to entrance, darker room, fewer windows) and better equipment (e.g., cameras and digital key entrances) would allow the labs to stay open day and night. Up-to-date computers would also increase lab use by students.

BACKGROUND

Educational units at Dokuz Eylul University are located at different parts of Izmir. The old building for the School of Architecture, which housed Architecture, City and Regional Planning, Theater, and History, was close to the city center. The new building for the School of Architecture, which has two departments (Architecture, City and Regional Planning), is located at Dokuz Eylul Kaynaklar Campus at the north edge of the city, close to the intercity highway, and far from the city center.

While the faculty and the students would have preferred to stay in the old building for its location, it was in poor condition with humidity problems and damage from the 1974 earthquake. The project for a new School of Architecture (DEU-SA) building began in 1994 and was scheduled for completion in 1997. The Office of Facility Planning and Management estimated the project cost at about $5 million. After the bidding process, the winning contractor proposed to complete it for about $3.6 million. By May 2005, the

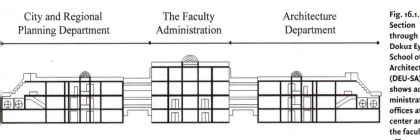

City and Regional Planning Department	The Faculty Administration	Architecture Department

Fig. 16.1. Section through Dokuz Eylul School of Architecture (DEU-SA) shows administration offices at center and the faculty offices, classes, and studios in the two wings.

.otal cost reached about $10 million. The building was opened in September 2004, but some parts were still incomplete by May 2005, such as the furnishings in the conference hall with seating for 500 and the lighting and the green areas surrounding the building.

The Office of Facility Planning and Management and the President of Dokuz Eylul University selected Prof. Dr. Mehmet N. Tureyen as the architect who produced about 50 university buildings and designed 5 university campuses in Turkey, including Dokuz Eylul Kaynaklar Campus (Tureyen, 2003).

Professor Tureyen designed the building for Architecture, City and Regional Planning, Industrial Design and Interior Design (Tureyen, 1999). As of summer 2005, the Architecture and City and Regional Planning Departments occupied the building. Industrial Design and Interior Design have yet to be established. The 245,616-square-foot building has a U-shaped composition surrounding a central court (Figure 16.1), with the faculty administration located in the center of the U, and the departments located in the two symmetrical wings (Tureyen, 2000). In the original design, Architecture was in one wing, and the other wing had City and Regional Planning, Industrial Design, and the Interior Design Departments. Until the other departments get launched, City and Regional Planning Department has the wing to itself. The central section has a cafeteria in the basement; a main entrance, an exhibition hall, and a conference hall on the first floor; and administration offices on the second and third floors. The department entrances and the stairs are at the center of each block. The faculty offices are on the first and second floors in the front. The studios and the classrooms are on the first and the second floors in the back. These two spaces are separated by a two-story-high atrium (Figure 16.2).

The Office of Facility Planning and the contractor changed Tureyen's original plan. The changes eliminated a circular stairway connecting the first and second floor studios in City and Regional Planning. In Architecture, some classrooms were divided with walls for use as faculty offices. The departments' administrative offices were replaced with faculty offices.

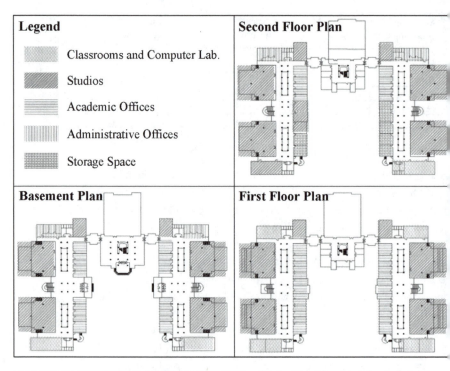

Legend

- Classrooms and Computer Lab.
- Studios
- Academic Offices
- Administrative Offices
- Storage Space

Second Floor Plan

Basement Plan

First Floor Plan

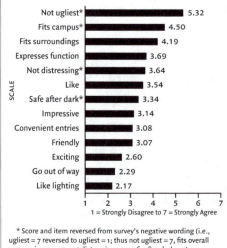

SCALE	
Not ugliest*	5.32
Fits campus*	4.50
Fits surroundings	4.19
Expresses function	3.69
Not distressing*	3.64
Like	3.54
Safe after dark*	3.34
Impressive	3.14
Convenient entries	3.08
Friendly	3.07
Exciting	2.60
Go out of way	2.29
Like lighting	2.17

1 = Strongly Disagree to 7 = Strongly Agree

* Score and item reversed from survey's negative wording (i.e., ugliest = 7 reversed to ugliest = 1; thus not ugliest = 7, fits overall campus image = 7, not distressing = 7, safe after dark = 7).

Fig. 16.2. (above) The original plans for the building show departments located symmetrically in three floors.

Fig. 16.3. (left) The DEU-SA exterior received unfavorable ratings (Grand mean = 3.43).

THE BUILDING EXTERIOR

Respondents rated the DEU-SA exterior unfavorably, agreeing with negatively worded items (such as it feels unsafe after dark) and disagreeing with positively worded items. Figure 16.3 shows the results from the exterior building survey. They gave the least favorable ratings to the lighting after dark (new lighting around the building has been added), their willingness to walk out of their way to see it, and its excitement (all below 3.00 somewhat disagree), to its friendly look, its convenient entrances and exits, and its impressive look (all below 3.15). Only one response on a positive item exceeded a neutral rating, it fits well

Table 16.1
OPEN-ENDED RESPONSES ABOUT THE BEST AND LEAST LIKED
FEATURES OF THE DEU-SA EXTERIOR

| | Percentage of respondents selecting features as | | |
Physical Features	Best Liked	Least Liked	Total Mentions
Building Form	15.4 percent	14.5 percent	29.9 percent
Building Color	8.5	14.5	23.1
Entrance and Security	0.0	6.8	6.8
Landscape	0.0	4.7	4.7
Building Size	0.0	2.1	2.1
Windows	10.3	6.4	16.7
Uniqueness	11.5	5.1	16.7
TOTAL	45.7	54.3	100.0

with the surrounding buildings (4.2), and one response on a negative item was below a neutral rating, it is one of the ugliest buildings on the campus (2.68).

When asked for features they liked best and features they liked least about the exterior, respondents reported more disliked features (54.3 percent) than liked ones (45.7 percent) (see Table 16.1). They disliked the building size (2.1 percent), entrance and security (6.8 percent) and landscape (4.7 percent). After the POE, new landscaping around the building was completed. While a few respondents liked the building color, more disliked it (liked = 8.5 percent, disliked = 14.5 percent). According to some respondents, the exterior color reminds them of an elementary school, rather than an architectural education building.

Respondents tended to like the uniqueness, windows, and form (liked = 11.5 percent for uniqueness, 10.3 percent for windows, 15.4 percent for form; disliked = 5.1 percent for uniqueness, 6.4 percent for windows, 14.5 percent for form). The photographs in Figure 16.4 show the building exterior from different perspectives. People commented on the articulation on the façade. While a few participants found the articulation on the façade unnecessary and too much, more liked it for giving information about the interior functions and distinguishing the building from the campus architecture. People also commented on the window details. They liked the windows for looking dark from the outside, providing privacy.

THE BUILDING INTERIOR

Figure 16.5 shows the results from the interior building survey, which reveal moderate dissatisfaction with the design (grand mean 3.73 out of 7). Respondents gave the lowest satisfaction scores to accessibility for the disabled, environmental quality, security,

Fig. 16.4. (right) People liked the exterior for its uniqueness, windows, and form, and disliked its color, size, entrances, and landscape.

Fig. 16.5. (below) Although respondents liked the building materials, they disliked the design's accessibility, environmental quality, security, and wayfinding, and the grand mean (3.73) shows an overall negative evaluation of the interior.

From South to North

From West to East

From Northwest to Southeast

Dokuz Eylul University School of Architecture

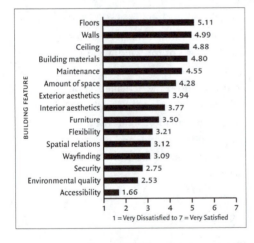

BUILDING FEATURE	
Floors	5.11
Walls	4.99
Ceiling	4.88
Building materials	4.80
Maintenance	4.55
Amount of space	4.28
Exterior aesthetics	3.94
Interior aesthetics	3.77
Furniture	3.50
Flexibility	3.21
Spatial relations	3.12
Wayfinding	3.09
Security	2.75
Environmental quality	2.53
Accessibility	1.66

1 = Very Dissatisfied to 7 = Very Satisfied

and wayfinding. They gave the highest scores to the quality of building materials—floor, wall, ceiling, and maintenance.

With regard to accessibility, DEU-SA has two exterior ramps between the entrance and the first floor. Otherwise, stairways connect all floors. Turkey lacks a building code that enforces accessibility for persons with a disability. Such accessability for persons with disability is a problem in most buildings in Turkey, and this building is no exception.

Criticisms of the environmental quality in the building concerned the temperature and acoustics. The large size of the atrium and design studios require specially designed temperature control systems. Some faculty offices et natural sunlight, and some do not. The offices have no cooling system. Faculty members in offices with natural sunlight complained that they get oo hot in summer. Others in offices without natural sunlight complained about the cold in winter, stating the need for personal heaters. The design studios have a major problem with noise, because of their size and hard surfaces. They are arranged in the form of two-story-high galleries (Figure 16.6). Consider that a circular stair should have connected the two floors for use by the same class of students. Without the stairs, different classes occupy each floor. As the classes meet at the same time, noise from each floor interrupts classes in the other. In some cases, the noise causes faculty to postpone classes. The two-story-high studios now have soundproof glass dividing them into two spaces.

The building has a 24-hour security office near the front door (Figure 16.7). Respondents still had security concerns, because the building has multiple entrances. Features such as the huge columns in the atrium space make users feel unsafe at night because they obstruct views, create possible hiding places, and block possible escape (cf. Nasar and Fisher, 1993).

Dokuz Eylul University
School of Architecture

Fig. 16.6.
Two-story
galleries in
the design
studios drew
complaints
about noise.

Users also note problems with wayfinding. The symmetrical form may account for some of the problem. In addition, respondents noted that stairs between the basement and first floor do not connect to the stairs between first and second floors.

Regarding the quality of spaces in the building, most did not score well (Figure 16.8). Respondents gave low satisfaction scores to the cafeteria, computer laboratory, and design studios. They gave more favorable scores to the restrooms, faculty offices, and administrative offices. Open-ended responses to most and least liked spaces agreed with this finding. While the cafeteria and design studios appeared on the top of the list of the least liked spaces, medium-sized classrooms, restrooms, faculty offices, and atrium appeared on the top of the list of most liked spaces (Table 16.2). Now consider the settings that people said they liked most, and those they said they liked the least.

People who liked the medium sized classrooms (19 percent of the respondents) praised lighting, odor, adequacy of spaces, temperature, and acoustics (higher than 5.0). In open-ended responses, participants pointed out the spacious rectangular shape and the wide, dark glass windows on one of the long sides of the building. They noted that the amount of natural light in medium sized classrooms is superior to the other classrooms, such as design studios with narrow windows.

Those who cited restrooms as liked (18 percent of the respondents) gave positive ratings to the restrooms' aesthetic appeal, furniture, and adequacy of space (higher than 5.0). In open-ended responses students said they liked the number, location, upkeep, and newness of the restrooms. (Figure 16.9) Students use the restrooms on the south end of the corridor and faculty use the ones on the north ends. This separated use was the only criticism about the restrooms.

Those who selected the faculty offices as liked (13 percent of the respondents) gave favorable ratings to the furniture, adequacy of spaces, odor lighting, aesthetic appeal, and acous-

Fig. 16.7. Respondents had security concerns due to the columns.

Dokuz Eylul University School of Architecture

cs (higher than 5.0). The old building had ruined wall and floor materials. Most faculty members shared small offices, with up to four people in an office. Some had class desks as an office desk. The new building gave most faculty members larger, private offices with new furniture. In the open-ended responses, participants praised the new furniture, large size, and nice view. (Figure 16.10) The criticism about the faculty offices referred to the location and temperature. Some faculty offices face north, have a view to a forest or city, and get natural sunlight. Others face courtyard and do not get much natural sunlight. Participants criticized this inequality.

Those who selected the atrium as liked (13 percent of the respondents) gave favorable ratings to the lighting, adequacy of space, and aesthetic appeal (higher than 5.0). In open-ended responses, participants pointed to the spaciousness and the lighting as liked

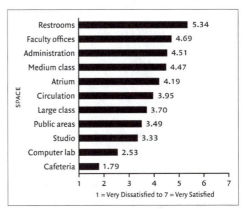

SPACE	Rating
Restrooms	5.34
Faculty offices	4.69
Administration	4.51
Medium class	4.47
Atrium	4.19
Circulation	3.95
Large class	3.70
Public areas	3.49
Studio	3.33
Computer lab	2.53
Cafeteria	1.79

1 = Very Dissatisfied to 7 = Very Satisfied

Dokuz Eylul University
School of Architecture

Fig. 16.8. (top) Respondents liked the restrooms, faculty offices, and administrative offices, and disliked the studio, computer lab, and cafeteria.

Fig. 16.9. (bottom) Respondents rated the restrooms as good for their location and upkeep.

Table 16.2

USERS PICKED THE MEDIUM SIZED CLASSROOMS AND RESTROOMS AS THE MOST LIKED SPACES, AND THEY PICKED THE CAFETERIA AND DESIGN STUDIOS AS LEAST LIKED SPACES

Space	Percentage of People Picking Space as	
	Most Liked	Least Liked
Medium Sized Classrooms	18.9 percent	1.2 percent
Restrooms	17.6	0.6
Faculty Offices	13.2	0.0
Atrium	12.6	1.9
Circulation	10.1	1.9
Administrative	7.5	0.0
Large Size Classrooms	3.1	2.5
Public Areas	1.9	3.1
Computer Laboratory	0.0	10.1
Design Studio	8.8	17.6
Cafeteria	2.5	60.4
No Response	3.8	0.6

features of the atrium. While they liked the student-project exhibitions in the atrium space, they complained about the frequency of change and short term of display of the exhibitions. They also mentioned the lack of plants and sittable spaces as disliked features of the atrium.

People who disliked the cafeteria (60 percent of the respondents) gave negative ratings to everything. They gave the lowest ratings to its odor, acoustics, lighting, and aesthetic appeal (below 2.0), and low scores to its accessibility, temperature, security, furniture, adequacy of space, and flexibility (below 3.5). In open-ended responses, they complained about its location. The cafeteria is placed in the center of U-shaped structure in the basement. The architect saw "no disadvantage originating from the obstruction of natural view for the cafeteria . . . on the level of basement because of the sloping site" (Tureyen, 1999). However, due to its small windows, this cafeteria space does not get much natural sunlight (Figure 16.11). These small windows also do not permit efficient ventilation and fresh air, and do not ease odor problems. The hard floor and wall materials make it noisy. While large, it has many columns that divide it into smaller spaces and decrease the perceived safety. Participants indicated that a cafeteria should be open to the exterior and have large windows. Without these features, fewer people use the cafeteria as a socializing space, despite the wide variety on the food menu.

Fig. 16.10. Participants liked the amount of space and the furniture in academic offices.

Dokuz Eylul University School of Architecture

Those who cited the design studios as the least liked space (18 percent of the respondents) gave low scores to their acoustics, accessibility for persons with a disability, temperature, and furniture (below 2.5), but the studios also received low scores for aesthetic appeal, odor, lighting, security, flexibility, and adequacy of space (below 4.0). In open-ended responses, participants criticized the form, columns, windows, and furniture. Most of the participants stated that having overlapping classes in two-story-high galleries causes acoustical interruptions. Their large size and hardscape material add to this noise problem. The columns dividing the large area into smaller spaces interrupt the interaction between the instructor and students. Despite its aesthetic appeal, the narrow windows in the slanting roof cause temperature control problems, and they are not functional. For the furniture, footstools with no seatback or no soft surface are not comfortable for long-term sitting and studying.

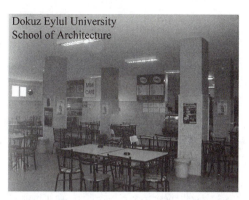

Dokuz Eylul University
School of Architecture

Fig. 16.11.
Respondents
disliked the
cafeteria for
its location
and narrow
windows.

Most respondents spent less than five hours per week in almost all spaces, except the design studios. Most respondents spent between 11 to 20 hours in design studios, and some individuals spent as much as 40 hours or more per week. Almost 20 percent of participants have never seen the computer laboratories. Each department has its own computer laboratory, located in the basement. This inaccessibility may help explain their underuse, but they are also often locked and of insufficient quality.

METHOD

In October 2004 (a month after moving into the building) 150 people participated in the study. In May 2005, 159 people (77 males, 82 females) participated in a follow-up study. Because the results of these two groups are similar, the results for the survey of May 2005 are reported here. Ninety-four participants were from the City and Regional Planning Department, 55 were from the Architecture Department, and 10 were administrative staff members working for both departments. Most participants were students (72 percent) and some were faculty members (21 percent). Their ages ranged from 19 to 62 years with a mean age of 26.

The interviews took place in various locations in the building such as the cafeteria, classrooms, and faculty offices. Each participant responded to the interior and exterior building survey.

CONCLUSIONS

Overall, DEU-SA building received negative scores for both its exterior and interior. Although people like the exterior for its windows and uniqueness, they disliked its size, color, and landscape. As for the interior, although occupants liked the materials on the walls, floors, and ceilings, plus some classrooms and faculty offices, they

LESSONS LEARNED

- Use warm and friendly materials for the exterior, and plan on a scale that fits surroundings.
- Enliven the space around the building with landscaping and a variety of comfortable seats.
- Provide lots of openness, natural lighting, and views to outside.
- Connect community gathering areas (such as a cafeteria) to the outdoor and indoor gathering space (atrium).
- Make the design easier for visitors to find their way around by simplifying the layout, connecting vertical circulation systems, having adequate differentiation at key decision points, and providing multiple entrances, visual connections, and well designed you-are-here maps at key decision points.
- Scrap open studio plans and give studios adequate acoustical protection. The acoustic problems of the open-plan, two-story-gallery shape of studios interfere with teaching and learning.

Box 16.1

expressed dissatisfaction with spatial relationships, wayfinding, HVAC, accessibility, security, the furniture, and the dysfunctionality of the cafeteria and studios (the most used space in the building).

The architecture building should draw students from other disciplines. For outdoor areas, the school of architecture achieved this through its distinguished form, landscaping, and comfortable seating which activate the space around the building. The vertical and horizontal movement on the front and sides and the step-like form of the studio windows distinguishes this building form from the campus architecture, while helping it to fit into its surroundings. However, it is out of scale and unfriendly. A sensitive landscape design with comfortable seating around the building would make the building friendlier.

For indoor areas, DEU-SA could become a social hub for the campus by having an active atrium and an attractive cafeteria. To improve the design of architecture buildings with atrium spaces, designers should include features that add activity and soften the spaces. This might include places for student presentations, plants, sittable spaces, movable seats, and visual access to pedestrian activity. A cafeteria needs a good connection to the outdoors and to the atrium space. With such improvements in and around the building, it may become a socialization area for the campus.

When different departments share a building, occupants may want to stay connected. As in this case, the wing form and the large size design may work against that purpose. The addition of common indoor and outdoor gathering spaces, in equal distance to departments, could help to increase interaction between the users.

Because students spend so much time in studios, the design of the studios should inspire creativity and productivity. Unfortunately, acoustical problems and inappropriate furnishings decrease student efficiency. The design can be improved via several modalities including shape, materials, and furniture. To protect studios from the noise of other studios, the two-story-high gallery shape of studios can be divided into two pieces, upper and lower, using sound-proof windows. Softening wall and floor surfaces would also help. Comfortable and movable seats could help to remedy the problem of interrupted interaction between the instructor and students by columns.

As digital technologies continue to affect architectural academia, a school of architecture should have a well designed and well equipped computer laboratory. In this building not many people report using the lab, and those who used it report dissatisfaction with it. The computer laboratory should be open day and night for frequent use, and safety should be achieved with cameras and digital key entrances. An easily accessed location in the building may also increase security. In addition, instructors often use overhead projectors in computer laboratories, and they need darker rooms. Large windows in such areas work against that purpose.

Although the architecture building at Dokuz Eylul University has its deficiencies and limitations, small changes could make it a better place. These improvements include landscaping the surrounding area, adding activity to the atrium, cafeteria, and computer laboratory, as well as overcoming the furniture and acoustical problems in studios.

TAKEMI SUGIYAMA, ROHAN LULHAM,
AND GARY T. MOORE

EVALUATION INFORMING CHANGE:
THE WILKINSON
ARCHITECTURE BUILDING

THE UNIVERSITY OF SYDNEY, AUSTRALIA

**FROM ONE OF THE TEN
UGLIEST TO A NEW LIFE**

Built in three stages beginning in
1984, the five-story Wilkinson Building at the University of Sydney is home
to the Faculty of Architecture, a 1500-student, multi-disciplinary faculty including architecture, urban and regional planning, urban design, design
computing, digital media, environment-behavior studies, facilities management, and six other environmental design disciplines. The University, the
oldest and best in Australia, has built an international reputation for its outstanding research and teaching excellence, including leading the nation for
many years in competitive funding from the Australian Research Council
(equivalent to the American National Science Foundation).

The university is in an urban location, on a hill 1.9 miles from and overlooking the Sydney central business district, in a tranquil setting of parks,
sporting ovals, and 150-year-old trees. The University includes the country's
best examples of Gothic Revival architecture combined with contemporary
buildings by some of Australia's leading architects. Australasia's first Professor and Dean of Architecture, Leslie Wilkinson, after whom the Wilkinson
Building is named, designed part of the Main Quadrangle and several other
buildings. The Main Quadrangle is an icon in Australia, used as a TV back-

drop for important national media stories. In contrast, the Wilkinson Building, seen in Figure 17.1, is brutalism at its best or worst (O'Brien, 2004) with exposed concrete now marred by concrete spalling visually dominating the exterior. Like many Brutalist designs, it has rough concrete exposed structure, and a blocky look. Perhaps, as a result, The Wilkinson Building was listed in one of Sydney's weekend tabloids in 2000 as one of the 10 ugliest buildings in Sydney —hardly befitting the country's finest architecture faculty in the premier national university.

Fig. 17.1. The Wilkinson Architecture Building at the University of Sydney, Australia. (Source: Ricardo Gutierrez © 2007 Faculty of Architecture, University of Sydney)

Not surprisingly, faculty, staff, students, and alumni unanimously felt that that the premier school of its type in Australia could not be housed in one of the city's 10 worst buildings. In addition, interior changes were needed to respond to a doubling of the number of students the building was originally planned for, changes in curriculum, a burgeoning research program, and new Occupational Health and Safety requirements. In 1999, early in his appointment as dean, Gary Moore accepted this considerable challenge of improving the aesthetic, amenity, and functional performance of the building.

Moore commissioned a five-stage master plan for the building's refurbishment. In addition to demands of locating funding and harnessing institutional support, the master plan needed to respond to the issues of the building users and stakeholders. A user-oriented post-occupancy evaluation (POE) was undertaken. The POE informed the master plan, highlighting environment–behavioral issues of particular importance for faculty, staff, and students. It also facilitated renovations consistent with institutions aims, involving faculty and Ph.D. research students while providing other students with a learning environment to help them develop into leading professionals in their fields. Serendipitously, soon after the commissioning process began, the opportunity arose to be involved in the present book's international project to evaluate architecture buildings worldwide.

Four of the five stages of renovation have been completed, with tremendous pedagogic, social, and visual effect. While the exterior façade has yet to change, we have revitalized both major entryways and created a social meeting place in the main entry forecourt. Inside, we have enlarged and renovated studio teaching spaces, expanded and revitalized research spaces, created additional Ph.D. offices and associated research spaces, and designed a series of gathering spots throughout the building—a hearth and café at the heart of the building à la Alexander, et al. (1979); a social urban forecourt à la Whyte (1980); and a number of social break spaces. Staff, students, alumni, and visitors now comment that the building is alive, with people getting together everywhere for casual conversation or debate, a true symbol of the *new* Faculty of Architecture, once again, considered the premier faculty in the nation.

SYNOPSIS OF THE RESULTS

The POE took place in 1999 at the start of the master planning and renovation process. It obtained responses from 350 students, faculty, administrative and technical staff, and passersby. The data were analyzed statistically and interpreted relative to other information about the building, its history, and public media concerns.

In response to the exterior survey, both passersby and occupants of the Wilkinson Building concurred with the tabloid, finding that its exterior was unfriendly and even "distressing."

Respondents had mixed reactions to the interior of the building. While occupants considered some spaces satisfactory, such as a new Boral Timber Gallery and existing Denis Winston Architecture Library, they considered other spaces quite unsatisfactory, including architecture, urban design and urban planning studios, computer labs, and washrooms. Similarly, they found some qualities of the building such as the floor material and *amount* of space satisfactory, but they found the aesthetic *quality* of spaces unsatisfactory.

Principal component analysis revealed four dimensions that characterized participants' responses to the interior spaces of the building: material aesthetics, functional requirements, layout, and security / care. Of these four, poor material aesthetics and poor response to functional requirements contributed the most to user dissatisfaction with the building interior.

This chapter examines these results, outlines the methods used, and concludes with recommendations and a discussion of the findings and their impacts on the recent program of renovations.

BUILDING EXTERIOR: SUPPORT FOR BEING ONE OF THE TEN UGLIEST IN SYDNEY

Most participants of the exterior survey saw the Wilkinson Building negatively. Figure 17.2 displays the mean scores of the passersby for responses to statements about the exterior qualities of the building (see also Appendix C Exterior Ratings). Participants did not express satisfaction with *any* of the building exterior items. Most were very dissatisfied with the aesthetic architectural qualities of the building. It was judged as "unexciting," "unimpressive," "unfriendly," and even "distressing." On items which compared the building with others in the university context, participants were again dissatisfied, though less so. Overall, there was little ambiguity in interpreting assessments offered by passersby of the exterior of the building—most were dissatisfied to very dissatisfied with just about every aspect of the building.

Occupants of the Wilkinson Building also assessed the building exterior on satisfaction / dissatisfaction. In accord with passersby, students and staff members were also generally dissatisfied with the exterior of the building (mean = 2.59 out of a possible 7).

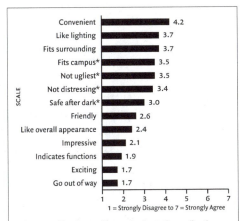

SCALE

Convenient	4.2
Like lighting	3.7
Fits surrounding	3.7
Fits campus*	3.5
Not ugliest*	3.5
Not distressing*	3.4
Safe after dark*	3.0
Friendly	2.6
Like overall appearance	2.4
Impressive	2.1
Indicates functions	1.9
Exciting	1.7
Go out of way	1.7

1 = Strongly Disagree to 7 = Strongly Agree

* Score and item reversed from survey's negative wording (i.e., does not fit campus = 7 reversed to not fit = 1; thus fits campus = 7, not distressing = 7, not ugliest building on campus = 7, safe after dark = 7).
See Appendix C Building Exterior Ratings for statistical comparisons.

Fig. 17.2. (top) Mean score of user responses to Wilkinson exterior qualities.

Fig. 17.3. (bottom) Exterior view of the brutalist tradition inspired Wilkinson Architecture Building, University of Sydney, Australia. (Source: © Faculty of Architecture, University of Sydney)

Many buildings at the University of Sydney were built 120 to 150 years ago of beautiful Sydney sandstone, and, in the Australian context, they stand as genuinely historic. Users and passersby of the Wilkinson Building, however, overwhelmingly agree that the exterior of the building was (dare we agree with the tabloids): "ugly." Some passersby mentioned the gloomy color of the exterior of the building, designed in the popular brutalism of the 1950s (Figure 17.3). In general, there was little appreciation among the majority of passersby and occupants for the exterior brutalist-modernist aesthetics of the building. In support of this assessment, and paralleling the sentiments in the tabloid article several years earlier, was a piece of amusing washroom graffiti discovered during the time of the POE that asked the rhetoric question: "What is the definition of irony?" The answer: "Architecture is in the ugliest building on campus."

Fig. 17.4.
(top) Mean
satisfaction
scores for
Wilkinson
interior
qualities.

Fig. 17.5.
(bottom)
Mean
satisfaction
scores for
Wilkinson
interior
spaces.

BUILDING INTERIOR: NEED FOR AESTHETIC, STUDIO, LAB, AND SOCIAL SPACE UPGRADING

The interior of the Wilkinson Building received some positive, some negative, but largely neutral responses from occupants of the building. Figure 17.4 shows mean satisfaction scores for various qualities within the building (for more details see Appendix C Interior Quality Ratings). Participants were especially dissatisfied with three items (interior aesthetics, wayfinding, and ceiling materials). On the other hand, they were satisfied with four items (floor materials, amount of space, security, maintenance, and, less so, accessibility). They were neutral to mildly favorable for all other qualities.

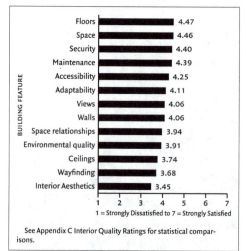

See Appendix C Interior Quality Ratings for statistical comparisons.

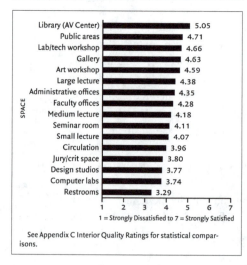

See Appendix C Interior Quality Ratings for statistical comparisons.

Figure 17.5 indicates respondents' mean satisfaction with various *spaces* in the building (for more details see Appendix C Interior Space Ratings). These rating were mixed, indicating that many interior spaces were appreciated while others had problems. While the participants rated some spaces favorably (e.g., the library, public areas, labs, and technical workshops) before the renovations, they rated other spaces unfavorably (especially the restrooms, but also computer labs, design studios, jury/crit spaces, and lecture theatres). The composite satisfaction score for the interior of the Wilkinson Building revealed an overall neutral evaluation for the spaces (for details see Appendix C Composite Space Rating).

When asked in an open-ended question what *features* they "least liked" about the interior, occupants most often cited aesthetics. More than a quarter of the participants mentioned the interior aesthetics as disliked. Sixteen percent of the respondents said they

Fig. 17.6.
The Boral
Timber Gal-
lery showing
extensive
use of native
Australian
timbers.

least liked the layout of the building. This agrees with the dissatisfaction with wayfinding (shown in Figure 17.4). Some respondents (11 percent) mentioned the concrete as a least liked feature. They may consider the extensive use of exposed concrete in the building to be drab, which may contribute to the overall low rating of the interior aesthetic quality of the building.

When asked about the features they *liked most* in the building, occupants most frequently cited the use of wood. A year before the POE, with a donation from Boral Timber Australia, the Faculty refurbished the entrance foyer of the building, which included a change of floor material from deteriorating red carpet to a variety of Australian native woods (Figure 17.6). This change may account for the appreciation of the wood. Note that in Figure 17.3, floor materials scored the highest satisfaction rating among various features. The respondents also mentioned the amount of space in the building as a most liked feature. This comes as a surprise, as the building was originally designed for about half the current student numbers.

Comparing the number of participants mentioning most liked features (6 to 8 percent) with number mentioning least liked features, reveals a much higher frequency of least liked features. Thus, the responses to both structured and open-ended questions suggest that the occupants of the Wilkinson Building judge the interior in the range of neutral to dissatisfied.

The survey had participants also pick two least liked and two most liked *spaces*. The disliked spaces included the restrooms, computer labs, and design studios (Figure 17.7). One third of the participants mentioned the restrooms as least liked. In a separate set of questions regarding the qualities of

Fig. 17.7.
A typical
architecture
design stu-
dio, BEFORE
Wilkinson
renovations.

the restrooms, they gave low ratings (below 2.0 out of 7) to aesthetics and odor. (See Appendix C Disliked Spaces for ratings of the qualities of the restrooms and other disliked spaces). Free description responses revealed dissatisfaction with both the quality of the restrooms and the inadequate number of them in the building. Except for the first and second floors, each floor has only one restroom for men or women, forcing students, faculty, and staff members to use the stairs to access a restroom.

More than a quarter of the participants mentioned the computer labs and design studios as least liked spaces. For the computer labs, they gave low ratings (below 3.0) to aesthetics, adequacy of space, and temperature. The architectural, urban design, and urban planning studios received low ratings (below 3.0) for aesthetics, security, adequacy of space, and lighting. Figure 17.7 shows one of the architectural design studios in the building, before renovation.

When asked what spaces they *most* liked, respondents often cited the Denis Winston Architecture Library, the public areas and exhibition galleries, and, ironically, some design studios (see Appendix C Liked Spaces for ratings of the qualities of these most liked spaces).

More than a quarter of the respondents cited the Library. They gave it high scores for the quality of lighting and acoustics. Located on the fourth floor, the Winston Library surrounds an atrium that provides considerable natural light. Like many libraries, it has good acoustics, attracting students, staff, and members of the professional communities to read or work quietly.

Although the respondents liked the library, they did not give it particularly high ratings for other environmental qualities. Perhaps they liked it more for its location and content (the largest architecture, urban planning, and related disciplines library in Australasia), along with its lighting and acoustics, than for other aspects of its design.

Some participants cited the public areas (24 percent) and exhibition galleries (18 percent) as most liked spaces. The public areas received high scores (means above 4.5) for lighting, aesthetics, and adequacy of space. The galleries received high ratings (means above 4.5) for aesthetics and lighting.

The design studios were the fourth in the list of most liked spaces, but they also were third in least-liked spaces. The Wilkinson Building has a number of different design studios, which vary in overall design quality, amount of natural light, vicinity to outside views and openness. Thus, the evaluation probably depended on the particular studio space a respondent had in mind when answering the POE questionnaire.

The interior POE questionnaire also asked respondents to name building features they thought most needed to be improved. Since the aesthetic quality was the least-liked feature of the building, it is not surprising that aesthetics was the most frequently mentioned item as requiring improvement. Interestingly, however, the second item was seating/furniture. Although the questionnaire did not include this feature in the qualities of the building, the open-ended question disclosed that the quality of seating/furniture was an important user concern. Some participants also felt that the signage in the building needed improvement—recall that respondents rated wayfinding in the building as very difficult (Figure 17.4).

The questionnaire also asked participants to list spaces that needed to be added or improved. Significantly, more than a quarter of participants spontaneously suggested the need for more and improved common/lounge/social areas, including suggestions for a canteen, café, cafeteria, bar and/or recreation spaces—most of which have since been added. This feature, suggested by participants, indicates the importance of providing opportunities for informal social interaction in and around the building.

In order to explore the perceptual dimensions of the interior qualities, a principal component analysis with varimax rotation was conducted. The analysis extracted four components or perceived dimensions of the building interior (for details see Appendix Table C.1): material aesthetics, functional requirements, layout of spaces, and security/care. The POE used regression analysis to understand the relative impact of each of the four dimensions on people's overall satisfaction with the building interior (for details see Appendix Table C.2). These four dimensions accounted for 31 percent of the variance in people's overall satisfaction. Functional requirements and material aesthetics each had twice the impact on satisfaction than did layout and security/care. This analysis suggests that improvements in the aesthetic qualities of the materials and functional aspects of interior spaces could significantly improve users' overall satisfaction.

METHOD

The POE took place in August 1999. An interviewer approached people passing by the Wilkinson Building and carried out the exterior POE survey. The interviewer asked questions orally and recorded the answers verbatim from respondents. A total of 34 people who walked past the Wilkinson Building (who were not Architecture students or staff members) participated in the exterior survey.

For the interior POE survey, the investigators collected data from undergraduate and graduate students, faculty, and administrative and technical staff members in the building. Students had the POE questionnaire distributed in several classes. The faculty and staff members received it with a letter of request in their mailboxes. These approaches yielded 316 valid interior POE responses (55 percent male, and a mean age of 28.0 years ranging from 18 to 69 years old).

Fig. 17.8. The new Faculty Hearth at the heart of the second floor.

Analyses included various descriptive and inferential statistical analyses, including Fisher's *t*-tests, principal component analyses, and regression analyses.

CONCLUSIONS

Based on the analysis of the data, we suggested the following recommendations to improve the quality of the building.

EXTERIOR AESTHETICS

The exterior of the building emerged as clearly the worst feature of the building. Although the renovation carried out in the Wilkinson Building had not yet included upgrading the exterior façade, modifications in this respect would likely affect the way users and passersby perceive the building and value what they expect to find inside.

MATERIAL AESTHETICS

The POE suggests that the material aesthetics of the building are important factors in occupants' positive regard for the building. As the wood-floored main entry foyer, renovated just before the POE, was successful, and the participants found exposed concrete unattractive, it seems clear that similar, more natural material changes would likely improve occupant satisfaction with the building.

Since the POE and master plan, the amount of usable interior space has been increased and improved in functional and aesthetic quality. The Boral Timber Gallery has been connected to a much larger hearth and café at the center of the building, all done in Australian native timbers and connected through floor-to-ceiling bi-fold doors to an exterior wooden deck court-yard, which brings natural light and visibility to all parts of the main floor of the building (Figure 17.8).

FUNCTIONAL REQUIREMENTS

The analysis found that wayfinding and access to outdoor views are relevant to the overall quality the building. Careful allocation of spaces would provide easy navigation and good exterior views. Better interior transparence, visibility, and signage may also enhance people's evaluations of the building.

The four stages of renovation completed to-date have visually opened up spaces, creating flexibility for today's and tomorrow's curricula and pedagogy (see Figure 17.9), creating visual connections (previews) between corridors and use spaces, bringing light across corridors into functional spaces, and creating more views through spaces to the outdoors.

RECTIFYING UNSATISFACTORY SPACES

The renovation has improved restroom space aesthetics, resolved the odor problem, and increased the number of restrooms, as indicated by the post-occupancy evaluation.

In addition, the computing labs were redesigned and expanded, and now comprise six new, well lit, contemporary designed, and spacious labs serving various critical teaching and learning purposes in a number of disciplines (Figure 17.10).

Fig. 17.9. (above) The new first-year architectural design studio, Wilkinson.

Fig. 17.10. (right) A new design computing lab on the second floor of Wilkinson.

Box 17.1

LESSONS LEARNED

- **The Architecture Should Facilitate Social Interaction.** The post-occupancy evaluation found the Wilkinson Architecture Building design to be outdated and oppressive, not providing amenity for the social interactions, informal dialogue, and debate yearned for in any learning and creative environment. Social interaction is an important part of how knowledge is tranferred, professional identity developed, and skill nurtured, and as such is an important component in the evaluation—and design—of any learning and creative organization.

- **Improve Wayfinding.** The Wilkinson Building had serious wayfinding problems, due to a complex interior based on three stages of expansion, each on a different structural grid. To make it easier for people to find their way around, provide a simple, legible plan with clear circulation and signage. Increased visibility and transparency provide a better environment for exhibiting and viewing student work.

- **Material Aesthetics: Wood over Concrete.** Material aesthetics have proven to be imporant factors in the overall evaluation of the Wilkinson Building, not only among architects and archtecture students, but also among passersby from non-architectural disciplines. Consistent with other findings from environment-behavior studies, most people see the exposed concrete as cold and unfriendly. They see natural woods as warm and inviting.

- **POEs and Strategic Master Planning.** Post-occpuancy evaluations can be about academic research; they can be about gaining user feedback from a variety of buildlings of a building type. They can also be—and in this case were—integral in a strategic view of master planning, uncovering user opinions at the formative stage of setting priorities and developing an overall *strategic* facility master plan and program or brief for new construction or significant upgrade and renovation.

- **Don't Downplay Functionality.** It's not sexy; it sometimes doesn't make the red carpet on awards night, but it's one of the main determinants of good architecture. In the case of the Wilkinson Building, functionality, and the provision of social spaces were deemed imporant to users, and ultimately, to the university administration and to alumni and Friends of the Faculty who supported and funded the master plan and renovation project.

While mixed opinions of the design studios reflected differences in the studios and suggests a need for the separate evaluation of each one, appropriate pressure from the teaching staff led to an upgrade of three clusters of studios—the undergraduate Architectural Design Studios, the Art Workshop Studios, and the graduate Urban Design and Urban and Regional Planning Studios. In addition, the new Design Computing Labs with audio-visual teaching facilities have resulted in these spaces developing a dynamic atmosphere more consistent with a design studio than an austere laboratory.

Substantial opportunities for further expansion of research and teaching facilities exist if or when the Denis Winston Architecture Library moves to a
planned new combined Sciences and Technology Library.

CREATING MORE COMMONS

Although occupants rated the public areas as satisfactory, many participants
indicated a desire for more and improved common lounge areas where they
could relax, have a cup of coffee, and chat with friends. In response to this
demand, we have improved the so-called "secondary" need for indoor and
outdoor social spaces, funding for which was the most difficult to obtain.
The renovated facility now has a newly improved social forecourt, a Faculty
Hearth and café in the heart of the building surrounded by display space, a
Graduate Student Common Room, two open-access Internet/social spaces,
and smaller breakout spaces with flexible furniture on each of the upper
floors of the building.

CARA D. ANDERSSON AND
NATHAN H. PERKINS

THE DEPARTMENT OF LANDSCAPE ARCHITECTURE (INSTITUTIONEN FÖR LANDSKAPSPLANERING)

SWEDISH UNIVERSITY OF AGRICULTURAL SCIENCES, UPPSALA, SWEDEN

SUMMARY

The POE of the Department of Landscape Architecture at the Swedish University of Agricultural Sciences (SLU) revealed a range of responses to the design, with notable differences between faculty members and students. The newer wing, constructed in 1992 and 1998, contained the most successful areas in the school, due to an abundance of natural light and spaciousness. Problems were identified with other areas of the building, such as poor ventilation and inadequate storage space, which may become worse with projected increases in student numbers. Faculty and students described the least successful spaces in the building as cramped, stuffy, or having conflicting uses. Due to the inadequate space, possible growing student enrollments, and demand for studios and larger classrooms, the department will likely need more space in the near future. Thus, the results of this POE may prove useful.

BACKGROUND

A relatively new university, SLU was formed in 1977 when the colleges of agriculture, forestry, and veterinary medicine were merged. The University, headed by the Ministry of Agriculture, has several campuses. SLU Ultuna, the location of this study, is 3.1 miles from Uppsala, and about 45 minutes by automobile north of Stockholm. SLU has approximately 2,000 students. In 2000 the Institution of Landscape Architecture (ILA) had 120 full-time students in the five-year M.Sc. program, 16 Ph.D. students and approximately 50 staff and faculty members.

In 1992, Dunge Arkitekont was selected to redesign the existing microbiology building into suitable quarters for the ILA. While the department and the technical division of SLU had some influence in the renovations of the 1959 structure, for the new addition it could only specify the number of studios and offices required. According to the Director of the Technical Bureau, the governmental agency that builds and leases all university buildings at SLU, more money per square foot was allotted to the project than was typical for other campus buildings. The rationale was that a building for a school where design took place should have better materials and attractive features. In 2000, the ILA building had a yearly lease rate 56 cents per square foot higher than the average for buildings on campus.

Built at a total cost of approximately $3 million USD, the renovations occurred in two phases. The first phase, completed in 1992, converted the existing microbiology labs into studio spaces, renovated the offices and restrooms, and created a library and computer lab. The second phase, completed in 1998, consisted of a 5,974-square-foot addition with red wood siding and ample windows that housed a new foyer, exhibition gallery, studio, kitchen, and student dining area. The second phase also included the exterior landscaping (Figure 18.1).

EXTERIOR

The exterior survey was conducted over a four-day period in November 2000. Thirty-one respondents completed the questionnaire at the same location (identified in Figure 18.1 by an asterisk) to keep the view of the school consistent. Some of the respondents felt uncomfortable with completing what they considered to be a design critique. Explained one subject: "I don't know beans about design." In order to encourage as much participation as possible, respondents had the option of answering the survey in either Swedish or English.

The analysis showed that 45 percent of the survey group liked the building's appearance to some degree, while 50 percent felt that the building was "not exciting." Of these respondents, some cited such things as the building's "overall boring impression—it looks like the 1970s," or that "the color and

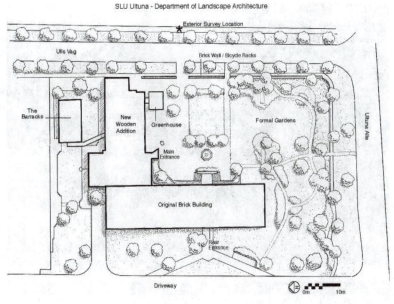

Fig. 18.1.
Site plan.
Asterisk
(top center)
shows
location of
question-
naire admin-
istration.

style remind me of grade school." Less than a third of the respondents felt that the building appearance was exciting to some degree. Areas that generated visual interest were such things as "the different additions" or "its irregularity." The areas of the building that generated the most interest are located where the old microbiology building and new wood addition meet.

While the building exterior did not rate high in terms of excitement, most people agreed that the building looked "friendly." Sixty percent felt that the facilities fit in well with the surrounding campus, because the building materials were consistent with the rest of the campus architecture. The red-stained wood siding of the addition is seen in many places on campus (and throughout Sweden, for that matter) and the red bricks in the main building were, according to one particular respondent, "very Ultuna."

Although the exterior of the school may be considered consistent with the discipline of landscape architecture—the building is fronted by formal gardens containing perennials, clipped hedges, sculpture, and a fountain— results of the survey found that the majority of respondents reported feeling neutral, or they disagreed with the statement that the exterior "clearly indicates" the interior functions. This lack of functional clarity may arise from the fact that, from the roadway, it is fairly difficult to see the unique features of the landscaping, due to a brick wall at the edge of the property that obscures much of the view (Figure 18.2).

Divisions arose among the open-ended responses as to the most-liked

Fig. 18.2. Exterior brick wall, which blocks the view, may explain the low score for "exterior clearly indicates interior functions."

Fig. 18.3. Respondents uniformly liked the garden.

and least-liked exterior features. Many of the same features that were most-liked by some also appeared to be least-liked by others. Five respondents (16 percent) felt that the greenhouse was the best physical feature, and another five respondents felt it was the worst. Five people cited the bricks as a favorite feature, while two disliked them stating they were "not so charming," and referring to the amount of brickwork as "colossal." In terms of the clay tile roof, two respondents liked it—one did not. One respondent liked the brick wall, while another questioned the need for it. Similar results were found for other elements such as the building proportions and stairs. The only element that all respondents reported to be positive was the formal garden (Figure 18.3).

INTERIOR

Students in each of the undergraduate years responded to the interior of the ILA, as did faculty and staff members at the institution during the fall semester of 2000. A total of 74 surveys were completed. Of the 52 student respondents, 84.6 percent were female, which was consistent with the female/male ratio in the department. Results were divided into faculty and student responses.

Light and spaciousness were the two physical characteristics most liked by the students. Light was cited by 58 percent of the respondents, with references such as "big windows that give much light," and, "the newly built section since there is light and air."

References to space accounted for 35 percent of student responses. Comments dealing with space often referred to specific locations. Of the 18 respondents citing positive feelings about space, 83.3 percent mentioned such specifics as "The Ateljé's big space" and "the foyer" (Figure 18.4). Most respondents considered the spaces in the new addition positively.

The lack of space in certain places of the school also emerged as a dissatisfying physical characteristic. Of the respondents citing dissatisfactions, 30

Fig. 18.4. Participants mentioned the foyer as a well-liked space.

percent complained about inadequate space saying, for example: "There is not enough room! It is cramped" and that "the building's spaces/rooms are bad," and "There are too many students."

The likes and dislikes of the faculty members were less clearly defined as those of the students. For both the best and least-liked characteristics, the highest percentage of the faculty (38 percent) mentioned specific places in the school. Space, as a general characteristic was rated as best-liked by 18 percent of the faculty, while 14 percent mentioned light as being a favored characteristic tied to aesthetic appeal. Space and light may have a higher significance among the faculty members than the figures indicate, since these may have been motivating factors for singling out specific areas of the building such as the Ateljé (which is associated with both space and light).

The data indicated a general level of satisfaction by both the faculty and students overall; however, students' satisfaction levels with the school exceeded those of the faculty for each of the variables. The students were particularly pleased with the flooring material in the building, with 80 percent of them reporting they were either "satisfied or very satisfied." Faculty satisfaction for the same variable was only 47 percent. This difference may be due to the fact that the most aesthetically pleasing flooring materials, such as the pine flooring in the Ateljé and the clay tile in the foyer, is in the part of the school where the students spend most of their time. The flooring in the faculty areas is predominantly linoleum and lacks the elegance of the other materials.

Responses to the question of space adequacy were also divided in terms of the respondent group. Sixty seven percent of students felt satisfied to some degree with the adequacy of space in the building, compared with 50 percent of the faculty members. A possible explanation for this may lie in the fact that faculty members are dispersed throughout the building. Offices are located on the second, third, and attic floors, and in a temporary annex called "the barracks." Because of this distribution, it is likely that faculty members have spatial experiences that differ from the student body.

In assessing satisfaction levels with various areas around the school, the faculty members generally reported a higher level of satisfaction with the teaching spaces (e.g., seminar rooms, classrooms, and the exhibition gallery) than did the students who are the primary users of these spaces. Evaluations of the computer lab were mixed in both respondent groups.

Students were most satisfied with the public areas, studio, and circulation. Not surprisingly, approximately 70 percent of the students rated the faculty offices and administrative offices as either "neutral" or "don't know." This was expected since the students spend very little time there. What is surprising, though, is the fact that almost 25 percent of the faculty members reported their satisfaction level with the faculty offices as "don't know." Ph.D. students in the attic, for example, reported feeling "isolated."

While 75 percent of the faculty members gave the Exhibition Gallery a positive rating, students gave the space a mixed evaluation. Thirty-three percent of the students expressed either slight or moderate dissatisfaction with the space and another 12 percent responded that they did not know how to rate the space.

LEAST-LIKED SPACES (TIGHT AND POORLY VENTILATED)

When asked about their least-liked spaces faculty members mentioned administrative office areas (26 percent) and the seminar room (17 percent). In comparison, the students identified the medium sized classroom (31 percent) and the computer room (21 percent).

If the areas selected for the least-liked spaces varied, the motivations for students and faculty picking these spaces were quite similar. The criticisms common to the least-liked spaces were that they were cramped and had bad ventilation. Approximately 46 percent of faculty members and students mentioned the lack of space as a reason for selecting their least-liked place. Almost a third of the respondents referred to poor ventilation as a motivating factor. Crowded conditions may engender psychological discomfort in addition to physical discomfort. In the computer lab, "people cannot sit anywhere without people who are walking by looking over one's shoulder." Another responded, "It [the computer lab] feels unsafe and one becomes interrupted in one's work. The air becomes depleted very quickly."

In an effort to make the most of the space, areas are sometimes used for more than one purpose, which can also prove to be a source of frustration. One student remarked, "There are insufficient places to get together, for example, for reading, conversing in groups, and sitting in cozy places. It is irritating to have to present work in the student café, when others are in the café or kitchen." Another respondent complained that "the double functioning student café is also a place for critiques. It often becomes conflicting or irritating."

Among staff and faculty members, administrative offices were mainly criticized for being cramped or stuffy. One faculty member cited her own room as being bad because "there is not enough space." She added, "We are five Ph.D. students in one room." Noise was also a factor in spaces being least liked, specifically, the attic and the barracks. Another person commented that, "Silence is lacking in the attic where I have my faculty place."

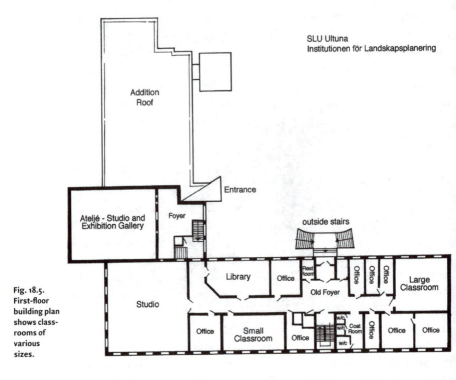

Fig. 18.5.
First-floor
building plan
shows class-
rooms of
various
sizes.

Office equipment is working almost constantly, and the noise is obvious. When it is turned off on occasion, one notices how satisfying the silence is."

In spite of their names, the two classrooms in the building with the small and large lecture rooms both fit into the medium size classroom range (the plan in Figure 18.5 shows the sizes of the two classrooms). One-third of the students chose these rooms as the space that was least-liked. Although adequacy of space received the lowest median score for this area (2.5), in the open-ended part of the questionnaire, students cited ventilation problems with these rooms twice as often as lack of space. One student recounted, there is "not enough ventilation until you open the windows—then it becomes cold instead."

BEST-LIKED SPACES (LIGHT AND SPACIOUS)

There seemed to be a clear agreement between the students and the faculty members in identifying the best-liked spaces in the school. In both cases, the public areas, including the atrium, café, kitchen, and the exhibition hall were the two highest ranked spaces in the school. While the amount of natural light and spaciousness seemed to be the most important factors among the students, the faculty members identified the aesthetic appeal of these areas. The best-liked spaces had many windows, high ceilings, and quality building materials.

The public spaces in the department of Landscape Architecture are concentrated in the new addition of the building. The area features windows that run along the length of the student eating area, clay tile flooring, and an elevated ceiling, particularly in the foyer area where the ceiling reaches to the third floor. The public areas were rated most liked by 37 percent of the faculty and 34 percent of the students.

While respondents were satisfied to some degree with all of the variables with an average median 6.0, the median scores for "Odor" ranked the lowest in both respondent groups (5.0 and 4.5 respectively). Temperature also received a comparatively low median score, which was substantiated by such comments referring to a "huge cold area from the windows in the cafeteria," or that the window frames in the café should be insulated as "it becomes cold there in spite of the triple glass windows."

Light and space are the two words that are most frequently associated with the Ateljé. Although the floor area is the same or slightly smaller than the other studios, the sloping ceiling is very high, making the room feel very spacious. This exhibition gallery also has windows in all four of the walls, and skylights in the ceiling that allow for maximum light penetration and reflection off the light pine floor. "Airy, light, beautiful, appealing with the light wood floor, much glass in the wall; good light penetration," said one respondent. The highest median scores were given for space, lighting and flexibility. As in the case of the public spaces, faculty rated the aesthetic appeal as 7.0—one point higher than did the students.

When asked what could be improved in the building, most respondents (70 percent) suggested new spaces and amenities, such as new classrooms (25 percent of the students), particularly those that can accommodate 40 or more people. Eighteen percent of the respondents cited smaller areas suitable for group activities or meetings.

Respondents had a sense of belonging to the school, viewing it as a "home away from home." This sense is present even though students do not personalize their spaces in the same way found at the University of Guelph (Woolham, 1999). For example, they reported valuing the building for its "family atmosphere," "feeling of home," a "sense of community," and comfort. Among the staff, requests for spaces for recreational or relaxation opportunities were of highest importance for the group (19 percent). Among the students, requests for "a small sleeping room" and the "possibility to relax with a shower and sauna" were indicative of this home-like sentiment. Such suggestions strengthen the argument that design schools are distinct from many other university faculties.

CONCLUSIONS

In many ways the building for landscape architecture at SLU functions well. People like the space and light of the new addition. They expressed general satisfaction with the building, but they also had problems with crowding and poor ventilation.

Areas that are not being actively used during certain times of the year could be temporarily reassigned. Finally, installing more coat hooks or bringing in lockers may provide a partial solution to the storage issue, especially for those students who lack a studio space of their own. Improved ventilation and lighting systems would be the next best thing to actually building new facilities, since they would likely increase the comfort levels of the occupants.

Of course, additional space could alleviate the bulk of the crowding problems. The school recognizes this and is, in fact, intending to build another addition in the near future. What becomes clear from this POE is that the most successful additions should incorporate elements identified in this study as important, including openness, light, and amenities such as comfortable areas for group work and increased storage. While such recommendations may be important in terms of the Institutionen för Landskapsplanering at SLU, they certainly apply to other design programs. What implications does this POE have for design schools in general? Design schools may differ from schools in other disciplines—a point supported in part by

Box 18.1

LESSONS LEARNED

- Have participation in the initial design and plan for ongoing monitoring and evaluation throughout the process. Changes occur in people, needs, programs, constraints, and the possibility of such changes should be built into the earliest design program. Ongoing monitoring and evaluation by users will insure that design flexibility respects the design integrity.
- Provide lots of natural light, especially in the far north (or south) latitudes.
- Use quality materials (such as the wood floors) for their perceived warmth.
- Design to give users lots of latitude to modify their work and learning spaces. Building occupants should have the means to alter their space. By anticipating, and even encouraging this behavior, designers can foster a richer and more diverse building community. Individual ownership, pride of place and a host of other benefits accrue when users (students, faculty or staff members) can claim space through personalization.
- Respect history and evolutionary change in defining the character of a facility. Just as a subdivision takes time to become a neighborhood, a design school takes time to acquire the quirks and character that come with use. The designer should learn to let go and see where it goes.

the occupants' desire for a "homelike" level of comfort by providing easy so-cialization opportunities. In addition, design students have a sensitivity and awareness of the spaces that they occupy. While a successful design should have high quality materials, lighting, and adequate quantities of space, that represents only part of the picture. Not only are design schools places that facilitate formal learning, they are also a complex network of social inter-actions, influenced by spatial relationships (Andersen, 1993; Huang, 1998; Woolham, 1999). Design schools should not only supply adequate space, lighting, and amenities, they should also create a building where the occu-pants are an essential component of the design itself— a building that lives.

A general finding that seems to arise from this POE study and is likely ap-plicable to most, if not all, design school facilities is that the basics matter. HVAC systems that function, quality lighting and building materials, stor-age, and adequate and flexible space seem so simple yet elusive. The authors, based at the University of Guelph, see the same issues in the School of Land-scape Architecture in Ontario. Our recommendations for the designers of design schools might therefore be best summed as, "More or less, do less, but do it better."

APPENDIX A
DATA GATHERING INSTRUMENTS

After the post-occupancy evaluation (POE) instruments were developed through email exchanges, and potential investigators received standardized instructions (below) for administering the POEs. Readers can use these instructions to create their own POEs.

GENERAL INSTRUCTIONS

The POE has five parts:

1. Gathering background information on the project
2. Evaluation of the exterior appearance of the building
3. The POE of the building and its spaces
4. Standard coding format
5. How to analyze the data

You can download them at: http://facweb.knowlton.ohio-state.edu/jnasar/archpoe/poeindex.htm. See Preiser and Vischer (2005) for additional tool kits for evaluation.

1. The next section lists the *background information* to try to get. For this, give a point of contact (dean, director, university architect) for potential follow-up information.
2. The survey of the *exterior appearance* of the architecture facilities should obtain responses from at least 30 passersby (preferably non users of the building, as we will already have similar information from them). The interviewers should take a position and select every *nth* passerby until they get the necessary interviews. If the building location does not have much pedestrian traffic, then photograph it and take the photograph to a public area on campus. Stop pedestrians in a similar fashion and have them complete the survey.
3. For the *POE of the building and its spaces,* we recommend a standardized procedure. Rather than leaving surveys in mailboxes or calling people, schedule times to meet in classes and studios. During that time, have all students and the faculty complete the survey. This should get a large response rate. (Students who already filled one out would not complete it again). For staff members, the interviewer could bring the survey to them directly. Posting the instrument on-line in sites such as Survey Monkey or Zoomerang works well, because these sites code the responses into excel files for you.

4. We have a standardized *coding format* for the surveys for transferability.
5. We suggest some simple *analyses* that you can use to make sense of your data.

BACKGROUND INFORMATION TO GET

Information to get from School Director/Dean/Administration or University Architect

- The designer(s) and other consultants
- Dates
  - Start of Construction
  - Completion of Construction
- Type of construction:
  - New
  - Addition
  - Renovation
- Total square footage of architecture facilities
- Net to gross square footage
- Net usable space lumped together for categories such as studios, all other classrooms, crit spaces, and library
- Degree of university oversight/control/design review from the program to final construction
- Total Project Cost
- Any information on operating costs, maintenance, heating, and cooling
- Typical cost per square foot of other campus buildings
- How the designer was selected
  - Open competition
  - Invited competition
  - Two-stage competition
  - Bidding
  - Interview process
  - Other
- Number of students enrolled by discipline
- Number of faculty members
- Number of staff members
- Photos of the building exterior
- Digital photos of selected spaces in the interior (entry, one studio, one small lecture room, one large lecture room, computer lab, gathering space). Particularly, include photos of the most liked and least liked places.

- Floor plans
- Local, national, or international reviews (what did the critics say and where). Designate a point of contact who can be reached for clarifications.

EXTERIOR SURVEY

This section presents the oral request for participation, followed by a sample building exterior POE survey form, which meets Human Subjects standards. If at a university, you should clear the survey with your university's Human Subjects review board.

Oral Introduction

Could you please help me out on a short survey about the appearance of a new building on campus? It should take less than two minutes to do. The questionnaire asks you to rate the building on some scales. Will you help me out?

(Name of School Building) Survey

I'm interested in your opinion of the exterior of the new building for the School of Architecture. The school houses programs in X, Y, and Z. Your answers will be kept confidential and anonymous. There are no right or wrong answers, so feel free to give your honest opinions. You can refuse to answer any question you do not wish to answer and you can refuse to participate or withdraw at any time without penalty or repercussion.

Please complete the form and return it to me.
It should take no longer than two minutes to complete!

Please rate how much you agree or disagree with each of the following statements about this exterior, where:

SD = Strongly Disagree   D = Disagree   FD = Fairly Disagree
N = Neither Disagree nor Agree   FA = Fairly Agree   A = Agree
SA = Strongly Agree   NA = not applicable

	SD	D	FD	N	FA	A	SA	NA
1) I very much like its overall appearance.	☐	☐	☐	☐	☐	☐	☐	☐
2) It looks exciting.	☐	☐	☐	☐	☐	☐	☐	☐
3) It looks distressing.	☐	☐	☐	☐	☐	☐	☐	☐
4) It looks friendly.	☐	☐	☐	☐	☐	☐	☐	☐

5) It looks impressive. ☐ ☐ ☐ ☐ ☐ ☐ ☐ ☐

6) It does NOT fit the overall
   campus image. ☐ ☐ ☐ ☐ ☐ ☐ ☐ ☐

7) It feels unsafe after dark. ☐ ☐ ☐ ☐ ☐ ☐ ☐ ☐

8) Its appearance fits in well with
   the surrounding buildings. ☐ ☐ ☐ ☐ ☐ ☐ ☐ ☐

9) I would go out of my way to
   experience it. ☐ ☐ ☐ ☐ ☐ ☐ ☐ ☐

10) I like the lighting after dark. ☐ ☐ ☐ ☐ ☐ ☐ ☐ ☐

11) The exterior clearly indicates
    the interior functions. ☐ ☐ ☐ ☐ ☐ ☐ ☐ ☐

12) It has convenient entrances
    and exits. ☐ ☐ ☐ ☐ ☐ ☐ ☐ ☐

13) It is one of the ugliest
    buildings on campus. ☐ ☐ ☐ ☐ ☐ ☐ ☐ ☐

14) In my opinion the physical features I like best about the exterior are:

_____

_____

15) In my opinion, the physical features, I dislike most about the exterior are:

_____

_____

16) Please tell us a little about yourself. What is your:

    a) Position:

        ☐ Faculty

        Dept: _____

        ☐ Staff

        Dept: _____

        ☐ Student

        Major _____

        Year: (Check the one that best applies)

            ☐ First year undergraduate

            ☐ Second year undergraduate

            ☐ Third year undergraduate

            ☐ Fourth year or higher undergraduate

            ☐ Master's student

            ☐ Ph.D. Student

            ☐ Other _____

    b) Your Year of Birth: 19____

    c) Your Gender: Male   Female

    d) Number of years on campus: _____

▌INTERIOR SURVEY

This section presents the oral request for participation, followed by a sample interior POE survey form, which meets Human Subjects standards. If at a university, you should clear the survey with your university's Human Subjects review board.

Oral Introduction

Could you please help me out on a survey about the performance of the new school of architecture building? It should take about fifteen minutes to complete. The questionnaire asks you to rate the building on various scales. Will you help me out?

Post-occupancy Evaluation

We wish to conduct a post-occupancy evaluation (POE) of your facilities. Our purpose is to assess how well the facilities perform for your health, safety, security, functionality, and psychological comfort. We hope the POE will identify areas for improvement, areas that work well, and will provide information to improve facility utilization, and the design of future buildings. Your answers will be kept confidential and anonymous. There are no right or wrong answers. So feel free to give your honest opinions.

Please complete and return your survey now.
It should take less than 15 minutes to complete!

1) What physical features do you like best about the new facility (addition)?

_____

_____

2) What physical features do you like least about the new facility (addition)?

_____

_____

3) On each item below, rate your satisfaction with the overall quality of the design of the facilities where:

VD = Very Dissatisfied   D = Dissatisfied   SD = Somewhat Dissatisfied
N = Neither Dissatisfied nor Satisfied   SS = Somewhat Satisfied
S = Satisfied   VS = Very Satisfied   NA = Not Applicable

	VD	D	SD	N	SS	S	VS	NA
a) Aesthetic quality of exterior	☐	☐	☐	☐	☐	☐	☐	☐
b) Aesthetic quality of interior	☐	☐	☐	☐	☐	☐	☐	☐
c) Amount of space	☐	☐	☐	☐	☐	☐	☐	☐

d) Ability to find your way ☐ ☐ ☐ ☐ ☐ ☐ ☐ ☐

e) Environmental quality
(lighting, acoustics,
temperature, etc.) ☐ ☐ ☐ ☐ ☐ ☐ ☐ ☐

f) Proximity of views ☐ ☐ ☐ ☐ ☐ ☐ ☐ ☐

g) Adaptability to changing
uses ☐ ☐ ☐ ☐ ☐ ☐ ☐ ☐

h) Accessibility for persons
with disabilities ☐ ☐ ☐ ☐ ☐ ☐ ☐ ☐

i) Security ☐ ☐ ☐ ☐ ☐ ☐ ☐ ☐

j) Maintenance ☐ ☐ ☐ ☐ ☐ ☐ ☐ ☐

k) Relationship of
spaces / layout ☐ ☐ ☐ ☐ ☐ ☐ ☐ ☐

l) Quality of building
materials:

a. Floors ☐ ☐ ☐ ☐ ☐ ☐ ☐ ☐

b. Walls ☐ ☐ ☐ ☐ ☐ ☐ ☐ ☐

c. Ceilings ☐ ☐ ☐ ☐ ☐ ☐ ☐ ☐

m) Other (specify) _____ ☐ ☐ ☐ ☐ ☐ ☐ ☐ ☐
_____ ☐ ☐ ☐ ☐ ☐ ☐ ☐ ☐

4) For each space listed below, please rate your overall satisfaction with its quality, where:

VD = Very Dissatisfied   D = Dissatisfied   SD = Somewhat Dissatisfied
N = Neither Dissatisfied nor Satisfied   SS = Somewhat Satisfied
S = Satisfied   VS = Very Satisfied   NA = Not Applicable

	VD	D	SD	N	SS	S	VS	NA
a) Public Areas (entrance, atrium, and connecting areas)	☐	☐	☐	☐	☐	☐	☐	☐
b) Seminar Rooms (5–20 students)	☐	☐	☐	☐	☐	☐	☐	☐
c) Medium Size Classroom (21–40 students)	☐	☐	☐	☐	☐	☐	☐	☐
d) Large Classroom (41–100 students)	☐	☐	☐	☐	☐	☐	☐	☐
e) Large Lecture Space (more than 100 students)	☐	☐	☐	☐	☐	☐	☐	☐
f) Computer Lab	☐	☐	☐	☐	☐	☐	☐	☐
g) Studio	☐	☐	☐	☐	☐	☐	☐	☐
h) Library	☐	☐	☐	☐	☐	☐	☐	☐

i) Administrative Office Area	☐	☐	☐	☐	☐	☐	☐	☐
j) Faculty Offices	☐	☐	☐	☐	☐	☐	☐	☐
k) Exhibition Galleries	☐	☐	☐	☐	☐	☐	☐	☐
l) Jury/Crit Space	☐	☐	☐	☐	☐	☐	☐	☐
m) Circulation (elevators, stairs, corridors)	☐	☐	☐	☐	☐	☐	☐	☐
n) Restrooms	☐	☐	☐	☐	☐	☐	☐	☐
o) Storage	☐	☐	☐	☐	☐	☐	☐	☐
p) Other (specify) _____	☐	☐	☐	☐	☐	☐	☐	☐
_____	☐	☐	☐	☐	☐	☐	☐	☐

5) For each space listed on the left, indicate how many hours you spend in it in a typical week.

				HOURS PER WEEK					
SPACE TYPE	0–5	6–10	11–15	16–20	21–25	26–30	31–35	36–50	40+
a) Public Areas (entrance, atrium, & connecting areas)	☐	☐	☐	☐	☐	☐	☐	☐	☐
b) Seminar Rooms (5–20 students)	☐	☐	☐	☐	☐	☐	☐	☐	☐
c) Medium Size Classroom (21–40 students)	☐	☐	☐	☐	☐	☐	☐	☐	☐
d) Large Classroom (41–100 students)	☐	☐	☐	☐	☐	☐	☐	☐	☐
e) Large Lecture Space (more than 100 students)	☐	☐	☐	☐	☐	☐	☐	☐	☐
f) Computer Labs	☐	☐	☐	☐	☐	☐	☐	☐	☐
g) Studio	☐	☐	☐	☐	☐	☐	☐	☐	☐
h) Library	☐	☐	☐	☐	☐	☐	☐	☐	☐
i) Administrative Office Area	☐	☐	☐	☐	☐	☐	☐	☐	☐
j) Faculty Offices	☐	☐	☐	☐	☐	☐	☐	☐	☐
k) Exhibition/Galleries	☐	☐	☐	☐	☐	☐	☐	☐	☐
l) Jury/Crit Space	☐	☐	☐	☐	☐	☐	☐	☐	☐
m) Circulation	☐	☐	☐	☐	☐	☐	☐	☐	☐
n) Restrooms	☐	☐	☐	☐	☐	☐	☐	☐	☐
o) Storage	☐	☐	☐	☐	☐	☐	☐	☐	☐
p) Other (specify) ____	☐	☐	☐	☐	☐	☐	☐	☐	☐
____	☐	☐	☐	☐	☐	☐	☐	☐	☐

6) From the previous list of spaces, pick up to two spaces that you feel Least Satisfied with, and for each, tell what physical features leads your dissatisfaction.

a) Space _____ _____

b) Space _____ _____

7) For your Least Satisfying space listed in question 6a, how would you rate each of the following?

VP = Very Poor   FP = Fairly Poor   P = Poor   N = Neither
FG = Fairly Good   G = Good   VG = Very Good   NA = Not Applicable

	VP	FP	P	N	FG	G	VG	NA
a) Adequacy of Space	☐	☐	☐	☐	☐	☐	☐	☐
b) Lighting	☐	☐	☐	☐	☐	☐	☐	☐
c) Acoustics	☐	☐	☐	☐	☐	☐	☐	☐
d) Temperature	☐	☐	☐	☐	☐	☐	☐	☐
e) Odor	☐	☐	☐	☐	☐	☐	☐	☐
f) Aesthetic Appeal	☐	☐	☐	☐	☐	☐	☐	☐
g) Security	☐	☐	☐	☐	☐	☐	☐	☐
h) Flexibility of Use	☐	☐	☐	☐	☐	☐	☐	☐
i) Accessibility for Persons with Disabilities	☐	☐	☐	☐	☐	☐	☐	☐
j) Other (Specify) _____	☐	☐	☐	☐	☐	☐	☐	☐
_____	☐	☐	☐	☐	☐	☐	☐	☐

8) For your least satisfying space listed in question 6b, how would you rate each of the following?

VP = Very Poor   FP = Fairly Poor   P = Poor   N = Neither
FG = Fairly Good   G = Good   VG = Very Good   NA = Not Applicable

	VP	FP	P	N	FG	G	VG	NA
a) Adequacy of Space	☐	☐	☐	☐	☐	☐	☐	☐
b) Lighting	☐	☐	☐	☐	☐	☐	☐	☐
c) Acoustics	☐	☐	☐	☐	☐	☐	☐	☐
d) Temperature	☐	☐	☐	☐	☐	☐	☐	☐
e) Odor	☐	☐	☐	☐	☐	☐	☐	☐
f) Aesthetic Appeal	☐	☐	☐	☐	☐	☐	☐	☐
g) Security	☐	☐	☐	☐	☐	☐	☐	☐
h) Flexibility of Use	☐	☐	☐	☐	☐	☐	☐	☐
i) Accessibility for Persons with Disabilities	☐	☐	☐	☐	☐	☐	☐	☐
j) Other (Specify) _____	☐	☐	☐	☐	☐	☐	☐	☐
_____	☐	☐	☐	☐	☐	☐	☐	☐

9) From the previous list of spaces, pick up to two spaces that you feel Most Satisfied with, and list physical features that lead your satisfaction.

a) Space _____   _____

b) Space _____   _____

10) For your Most Satisfying space listed in question 9a, how would you rate each of the following?

VP = Very Poor   FP = Fairly Poor   P = Poor   N = Neither

FG = Fairly Good   G = Good   VG = Very Good   NA = Not Applicable

	VP	FP	P	N	FG	G	VG	NA
a) Adequacy of Space	☐	☐	☐	☐	☐	☐	☐	☐
b) Lighting	☐	☐	☐	☐	☐	☐	☐	☐
c) Acoustics	☐	☐	☐	☐	☐	☐	☐	☐
d) Temperature	☐	☐	☐	☐	☐	☐	☐	☐
e) Odor	☐	☐	☐	☐	☐	☐	☐	☐
f) Aesthetic Appeal	☐	☐	☐	☐	☐	☐	☐	☐
g) Security	☐	☐	☐	☐	☐	☐	☐	☐
h) Flexibility of Use	☐	☐	☐	☐	☐	☐	☐	☐
i) Accessibility for Persons with Disabilities	☐	☐	☐	☐	☐	☐	☐	☐
j) Other (Specify) _____	☐	☐	☐	☐	☐	☐	☐	☐
_____	☐	☐	☐	☐	☐	☐	☐	☐

11) For your Most Satisfying space listed in question 9b, how would you rate each of the following?

VP = Very Poor   FP = Fairly Poor   P = Poor   N = Neither

FG = Fairly Good   G = Good   VG = Very Good   NA = Not Applicable

	VP	FP	P	N	FG	G	VG	NA
a) Adequacy of Space	☐	☐	☐	☐	☐	☐	☐	☐
b) Lighting	☐	☐	☐	☐	☐	☐	☐	☐
c) Acoustics	☐	☐	☐	☐	☐	☐	☐	☐
d) Temperature	☐	☐	☐	☐	☐	☐	☐	☐
e) Odor	☐	☐	☐	☐	☐	☐	☐	☐
f) Aesthetic Appeal	☐	☐	☐	☐	☐	☐	☐	☐
g) Security	☐	☐	☐	☐	☐	☐	☐	☐
h) Flexibility of Use	☐	☐	☐	☐	☐	☐	☐	☐
i) Accessibility for Persons with Disabilities	☐	☐	☐	☐	☐	☐	☐	☐
j) Other (Specify) _____	☐	☐	☐	☐	☐	☐	☐	☐
_____	☐	☐	☐	☐	☐	☐	☐	☐

1 2) Select and rank in order of importance the facilities that are currently lacking in your facility:

_____

_____

1 3) Please make any other suggestions for physical improvements in your facility:

_____

_____

1 4) Now we want to know a little about you. What is your:
   a) Room no. / Building area? _____
   b) Your Position? (Check the one that applies)
      ☐ Faculty
      Department of Organizational unit: _____
      ☐ Staff
      Department of Organizational Unit: _____
      ☐ Student
      Major _____
      Year: (check the one that best applies)
         ☐ First year undergraduate
         ☐ Second year undergraduate
         ☐ Third year undergraduate
         ☐ Fourth year or higher undergraduate
         ☐ Master's student
         ☐ Ph.D. student
         ☐ Other _____
   c) Your Year of Birth: 19_____
   d) Your Sex: Male   Female
   e) No. of years with the present school: _____

SAMPLING AND CODING

For exterior surveys, interview at least 30 people. For comparison, you might try to do a similar size sample at some other comparably aged buildings on your campus. For the interior surveys, try to get all of the staff (assuming they are a relatively small group), and all of the faculty for small groups or at least 50 percent for larger faculty. For students, try to get at least 30 per group or 25 percent of the total number in a group (such as 1st / 2nd year design, or graduates in each discipline).

By standardizing the coding, all of us can use the full data set to look at it across the full set of schools participating. Individual schools can do their own analysis, and with the standardized coding we can offer help to those who need it. We have omitted the coding for responses to "Other" as these would not be standardized across the schools. As you may want to analyze these, we suggest that you add them as separate columns to the end of the appropriate data set.

Each column would hold a place for data. If you did not get information for that column, or had non-responses, you would enter a period in that column. That would serve as a place holder for that column. Two asterisks (**) below represent some kind of instructions. There would be three related data sets. For each we give a label for the particular data and what data would go in the rows under that label. Due to space constraints, this appendix cannot show all of the columns at once. Instead, it shows subsets of them in the order they would occur. The first row labels the variable, and subsequent rows (the charts show one) would have the responses. The following sections describe the coding for the exterior data, then the background data, and then the interior data.

Background Data

**For the background data, columns would include, in the following order:

UNIV	START	END	TYPE	SF	NTGSF	COST	OCOST

UNIV less than eight-letter code for your city or university
  (i.e., USYDNEY, OSU, UCINC)
START start of construction year (just two digits)
END completion of construction year (just two digits)
TYPE type of construction (1 = new, 2 = addition, 3 = renovation)
SF total building square footage
NTGSF net to gross square footage
COST total project cost per square foot (POEs in this book adjusted to
  1999 U.S. dollars. You can adjust to the year of construction)
OCOST operating cost per square foot

**Then:

MCOST	ECOST	TCOST	TOCOST	TMCOST	TECOST	SELECT

MCOST maintenance cost per square foot

ECOST energy cost (heating/cooling) per square foot

TCOST typical project cost of buildings on your campus (POEs in this book adjusted to 1999 U.S. Dollars. You can adjust to year of construction.)

TOCOST typical operating cost per square foot

TMCOST typical maintenance cost per square foot

TECOST typical energy cost per square foot

SELECT How designer selected (1 = open competition, 2 = invited competition, 3 = two stage competition, 4 = bidding, 5 = interview process, 6 = other)

** Note we only requested coding on selected data.

Exterior Data

**For the exterior building survey data set, columns would include, in the following order:

UNIV2	SUBJ	POSE	BIRTHE	SEXE	YEARSE

UNIV2 same eight letter code for your city or university

SUBJ subject ID number (from 1 to how many subjects you interview)

POSE question 16 a) position at the campus (student 1st year = 1, 2nd year = 2, third year = 3, fourth year = 4, masters = 5, Ph.D. = 6, faculty = 7, staff = 8, other = 10)

BIRTHE question 16 b) year of birth (last two digits only)

SEXE question 16 c) sex (1 = male, 2 = female)

YEARSE 16 d) number of years on campus (just enter the number of years)

Then enter the ratings from 1 to 7 (where 1 = Strongly Disagree, 2 = Disagree, 3 = Disagree Somewhat, 4 = Neither, 5 = Strongly Agree, 6 = Agree, 8 = Strongly Agree, 99 = Not Applicable) for the following items:

LIKE	EXCIT	DISTRESS	FRIEND	IMPRESS	NOFIT	SAFE

LIKE question 1, I very much like the appearance.

EXCIT question 2, It looks exciting.

DISTRESS question 3, It looks distressing.

FRIEND question 4, It looks friendly.
IMPRESS question 5, It looks impressive.
NOFIT question 6, It does NOT fit the overall campus image.
SAFE question 7, It feels unsafe after dark

Then:

FITWELL	OUTOFWAY	LIKELITE	FUNCT	CONVEN	UGLY

FITWELL question 8, Its appearance fits in well with . . .
OUTOFWAY question 9, I would go out of my way . . .
LIKELITE question 10, I like the lighting after dark.
FUNCT question 11, The exterior clearly indicates . . .
CONVEN question 12, It has convenient entrances and exits.
UGLY question 13, It is one of the ugliest buildings on campus.

**Omit coding answers to open ended questions 14 and 15. You can code them in a separate word or excel file for content analysis. Content analysis could have someone categorize the answers and count frequency of responses in each category.

Interior Data

**For interior data set, the POE responses need not code open-ended responses. You can code them in a separate file for content analysis. The first 6 columns would have:

UNIV	SID	POS	BIRTH	SEX	YEARS

UNIV use the same eight-letter code for your city or university (as above).
SID subject ID (from 1 through however many subjects you have. This may help you catch miscoding of data later on.)
POS question 14 b) your position (student 1st year = 1, 2nd year = 2, third year = 3, fourth year = 4, masters = 5, Ph.D. = 6, faculty = 7, staff = 8, other = 10)
BIRTH question 14 c) year of birth (last two digits)
SEX question 14 d) sex (male = 1, female = 2)
YEARS question 14 e) number of years at present school (enter years)

**For each of the following 14 items, enter the rating from 1 through 7 for each item on question 3 (where 1 = Very Dissatisfied, 2 = Dissatisfied, 3 = Somewhat Dissatisfied, 4 = Neither, 5 = Somewhat Satisfied, 6 = Satisfied, and 7 = Very Satisfied, and 99 = Not Applicable. The first 7 scales are:

EXT	INT	SPACE	WAYF	EQUAL	VIEW	ADAPT

EXT question 3 a) Aesthetic quality of exterior
INT question 3 b) Aesthetic quality of interior
SPACE question 3 c) Amount of space
WAYF question 3 d) Ability to find your way
EQUAL question 3 e) Environmental quality
VIEW question 3 f) Proximity to views
ADAPT question 3 g) Adaptability to changing uses

Then:

ACCESS	SECUR	MAINT	RELAT	FLOORS	WALLS	CEIL

ACCESS question 3 h) Accessibility
SECUR question 3 i) Security
MAINT question 3 j) Maintenance
RELAT question 3 k) Relationship of spaces/layout
FLOORS question 3 l) (a) Floors
WALLS question 3 l) (b) Walls
CEIL question 3 l) (c) Ceiling

**Leave 3 m) Other uncoded. You can code it in a separate file for content analysis.

**Code each of the 15 spaces listed in question 4 on the scale from 1 to 7, where 1 = Very Dissatisfied, 2 = Dissatisfied, 3 = Somewhat Dissatisfied, 4 = Neither, 5 = Somewhat Satisfied, 6 = Satisfied, and 7 = Very Satisfied. Note: If your building does not have one of the spaces, code the column with a period (.) so that all of the data sets line up. If you have a space that is used for two of the purposes below (such as exhibition gallery and jury/crit space), code the answers twice under each category of use. Label the first 8 spaces as follows:

PUB	SEM	MED	LARGE	LECT	COMP	STUDIO	LIB

PUB question 4 a) Public areas
SEM question 4 b) Seminar rooms
MED question 4 c) Medium size classroom
LARGE question 4 d) Large classroom
LECT question 4 e) Large lecture space
COMP question 4 f) Computer lab
STUDIO question 4 g) Studio
LIB question 4 h) Library

Label the next spaces as:

ADMIN	FACUL	EXHIB	JURY	CIRC	RR	STOR

ADMIN question 4 i) Administrative office area
FACUL question 4 j) Faculty offices
EXHIB question 4 k) Exhibition galleries
JURY question 4 l) Jury/crit space
CIRC question 4 m) Circulation
RR question 4 n) Restrooms
STOR question 4 o) Storage

**For the list of spaces under question 5 (hours per week), code the hours spent in per week as follows: code 0–5 as 2.5, 6–10 as 7.5, 11–15 as 12.5, 16–20 as 17.5, etc. until 50+ coded 55. Label the times for the first 8 spaces as:

TPUB	TSEM	TMED	TLARGE	TLECT	TCOMP	TSTUDIO	TLIB

TPUB question 5 a) Public areas
TSEM question 5 b) Seminar rooms
TMED question 5 c) Medium size classroom
TLARGE question 5 d) Large classroom
TLECT question 5 e) Large lecture space
TCOMP question 5 f) computer lab

TSTUDIO question 5 g) studio

TLIB question 5 h) Library

Label the times for the next seven spaces as:

TADMIN	TFACUL	TEXHIB	TJURY	TCIRC	TRR	TSTOR

TADMIN question 5 i) Administrative office

TFACUL question 5 j) Faculty offices

TEXHIB question 5 k) Exhibition/Galleries

TJURY question 5 l) Jury/crit space

TCIRC question 5 m) Circulation

TRR question 5 n) Restrooms

TSTOR question 5 o) Storage

**Now comes the coding for questions about the least satisfying spaces. Under LSPACE1, identify one of the two least-satisfying spaces. Do this by substituting the number equivalent to that space's letter in question 5. For example, code "a) public areas" as "1", "b) seminar rooms" as "2," or "o) storage" as "15."

LSPACE1

**In the next nine columns, enter each rating (question 7) of the quality of that least-satisfying space.

LADEQ	LLIGHT	LACOUS	LTEMP	LODOR

LADEQ question 7 a) Adequacy of space

LLIGHT question 7 b) (note the two L's) Lighting

LACOUS question 7 c) Acoustics

LTEMP question 7 d) Temperature

LODOR question 7 e) Odor

Then,

LESTH	LSEC	LFLEX	LACC

LESTH question 7 f) Aesthetic appeal
LSEC question 7 g) Security
LFLEX question 7 h) Flexibility of use
LACC question 7 i) Accessibility for disabled

**In LSPACE2, identify the other least-satisfying space. As with LSPACE1, substitute the number equivalent to the letter of the space from question 5.

LSPACE2 question 6 b) least satisfied space from 6 b)

**In the next nine columns, enter the ratings (question 8) of the qualities of that least-satisfying space.

LADEQ2	LLIGHT2	LACCOU2	LTEMP2	LODOR2

LADEQ2 question 8 a) Adequacy of space
LLIGHT2 question 8 b) Lighting
LACCOU2 question 8 c) Acoustics
LTEMP2 question 8 d) Temperature
LODOR2 question 8 e) Odor

Then:

LESTH2	LSEC2	LFLEX2	LACC2

LESTH2 question 8 f) Aesthetic appeal
LSEC2 question 8 g) Security
LFLEX2 question 8 h) Flexibility of use
LACC2 question 8 i) Accessibility for disabled

**Now come the questions about the most-satisfying spaces. In MSPACE1, identify one of the two most-satisfying spaces. Code it by the number equivalent to its letter in question 5.

MSPACE1

MSPACE1 question 9 a) most satisfying space. Note question 9 b) comes after ratings on items under question 10.

** In the next nine columns, enter the ratings (question 10) of the qualities of that most-satisfying space

MADD1	MLIGHT1	MACOU1	MTEMP1	MODOR1

MADD1 question 10 a) Adequacy of space
MLIGHT1 question 10 b) Lighting
MACOU1 question 10 c) Acoustics
MTEMP1 question 10 d) Temperature
MODOR1 question 10 e) Odor

Then:

MESTH1	MSEC1	MSEC1	MFLEX1	MACC1

MESTH1 question 10 f) Aesthetic appeal
MSEC1 question 10 g) Security
MFLEX1 question 10 h) Flexibility of use
MACC1 question 10 i) Accessibility for disabled

**For MSPACE2, identify the other most-satisfying space. Code it by the number equivalent to its letter in question 5.

MSPACE2 Most satisfying space from question 9 b)

** In the next nine columns, enter the ratings (question 11) of the qualities of that other most-satisfying space.

MADD2	MLIGHT2	MACCOU2	MTEMP2	MODOR2

MADD2 question 11 a) Adequacy of space
MLIGHT2 question 11 b) Lighting

MACCOU2 question 11 c) Acoustics
MTEMP2 question 11 d) Temperature
MODOR2 question 11 e) Odor

Then:

MESTH2	MSEC2	MFLEX2	MACC2

MESTH2 question 11 f) Aesthetic appeal
MSEC2 question 11 g) Security
MFLEX2 question 11 h) Flexibility of use
MACC2 question 11 i) Accessibility for disabled

**Note, for questions 10 and 11, omit the open-ended responses from coding. Also omit open-ended responses to question 12 and 13 (facilities that are currently lacking), and 13 (suggestions for physical improvements). You can code these in a separate file for content analyses.
**Also leave out room no./building area.

POE ANALYSES

For analyses, you should at least calculate means and standard deviations (SDs) for each item. If skewed, calculate the median. You should also create a histogram or histograms to show the general pattern of evaluations. You can also run analysis of variance and pairwise comparisons of the responses to each item to see which differ at a statistically significant level from one another. For some sets of related items, such as those items on questions 3, 4, 5, 7, 8, 10, or 11, and, on the exterior survey, questions 1 through 13, you can run separate factor analyses to condense the data. Then, as was done for the full data set, you can report means (or medians if skewed) and standard deviations for selected index items rather than the full set of scales. You should also count frequencies with which various items are cited in each open ended response—1, 2, 6 a), 6 b), 9 a), 9 b), 12, 13, and, on the exterior survey, items 14 and 15. You should do Chi Square analyses on the frequency with which respondents cite spaces as least satisfying (question 6) and most satisfying (question 9). Finally, you can split out the data by respondent group (faculty, staff, student, year, major, or sex) to see if the groups differ on items. You can create separate histograms for various groups.

APPENDIX B
LESSONS LEARNED

PARTICIPATING SCHOOLS

Of the 16 designs, 10 used the same instruments to obtain responses from passersby, faculty, staff, and students: Dokuz Eylul University, The Ohio State University, and Universities of Cincinnati, Guelph, Hawaii, Illinois, Michigan, Nebraska, Sydney, and Texas. Three schools not represented in the case studies nevertheless supplied post-occupancy evaluation data. Nathan Perkins provided the Guelph data, Samia Rab, the Hawaii data, and Linda Groat provided data on Michigan's exterior.

BUILDING EXTERIOR EVALUATIONS

Participants in the building exterior surveys included 45 for Cincinnati, 33 for Guelph, 64 for Hawaii, 141 for Illinois, 50 for Michigan, 30 for Nebraska, 79 for Ohio State, 34 for Sydney, and 73 for Texas. Dokuz Eylul did not have a separate evaluation of the exterior by passersby.

COMPARISONS BETWEEN EXTERIORS

Factor analysis of the exterior ratings yielded three factors. Each had an Eigen value greater than 1.0, and the combined factors accounted for 66.7 percent of the variance. Comparisons of the factor scores revealed statistically significant differences between the designs on the factors ($F(2, 16\ df) = 26.60$, $p < 0.01$) and a large effect size associated with those differences (0.49). In addition, Pairwise comparisons with Bonferonni adjustments for multiple claims found statistically significant differences between schools in the different the groups.

INTERIORS

The analysis compared scores on each factor—*Quality of Materials, Accessibility,* and *Appearance / Functionality*—across nine universities: Dokuz Eylul University, The Ohio State University, and Universities of Cincinnati, Guelph, Hawaii, Illinois, Nebraska, Sydney, and Texas. With 1,046 observations, the results revealed significant differences between the universities on each factor ($F(2, 16) = 44.32$, $p < 0.01$). The large effect size for those differences (0.34) suggests that people would notice these differences.

The factor analysis of spaces yielded three factors, each with an Eigen value greater than 1.0. They accounted for 23.33 percent, 19.12 percent, and 18.89 percent of the variance respectively for a total of 62.33 percent.

The comparisons of spaces across the nine buildings (with 830 individuals rating the spaces) found statistically significant differences between the buildings on each factor (F (2, 16 df) = 11.41, $p < 0.01$), with a small to medium sized effect (0.08), meaning that people would likely notice the differences.

THE PROGRAM

Useful guides to programming include Cherry (1999), Duerk (1993), Hershberger (1999), Palmer (1981), Pena, Parshall and Kelly (1987), Preiser (1978, 1993), Sanoff (1977, 1989), White (1972).

TAKEMI SUGIYAMA, ROHAN LULHAM,
AND GARY T. MOORE

EXTERIOR RATINGS

The analysis compared each rating of the Wilkinson Building exterior with the midpoint of the scale (4 = neither disagree nor disagree). The results revealed that no item scored significantly above the midpoint, and all but two items scored below the midpoint at statistically significant levels.

- Like lighting ($p < 0.05$)
- Fits Campus ($p < 0.05$)
- Not Ugliest Building on Campus ($p < 0.05$)
- Not Distressing ($p < 0.05$)
- Safe after Dark, Friendly ($p < 0.01$)
- Like Overall Appearance ($p < 0.01$)
- Impressive ($p < 0.01$)
- Indicates Functions ($p < 0.01$)
- Exciting ($p < 0.01$)
- Go Out of Way ($p < 0.01$)

INTERIOR QUALITY RATINGS

Figure 17.4 shows the mean scores for various aspects of the interior. Additional analysis compared each of those mean scores with the midpoint of the scale (4 = neither disagree nor disagree). Five items scored above the midpoint at a statistically significant level:

- Floor ($p < 0.001$)
- Space ($p < 0.001$)
- Security ($p < 0.001$)
- Maintenance ($p < 0.001$)
- Accessibility ($p < 0.001$)

Three items scored below the mid point at statistically significant levels:

- Ceilings ($p < 0.01$)
- Wayfinding ($p < 0.01$)
- Interior Aesthetics ($p < 0.001$)

INTERIOR SPACE RATINGS

Figure 17.5 shows the mean satisfaction scores for each interior space. Comparisons of each of those means with the scale midpoint (4 = neither disagree nor disagree) found that nine spaces scored above the midpoint at statistically significant levels (five with scores above 4.5, Library (AV Center), Public areas, Lab/Tech workshop, Gallery, and Art workshop:

- Library (AV Center) ($p < 0.001$)
- Public areas ($p < 0.001$)
- Lab/Tech workshop ($p < 0.001$)
- Gallery ($p < 0.001$)
- Art workshop ($p < 0.001$)
- Large lecture space ($p < 0.001$)
- Administrative offices ($p < 0.001$)
- Faculty offices ($p < 0.001$)
- Medium Lecture space ($p < 0.05$)

Four spaces scored below the midpoint at statistically significant levels:

- Jury/crit space ($p < 0.05$)
- Design studios ($p < 0.05$)
- Computer labs ($p < 0.05$)
- Restrooms ($p < 0.001$)

COMPOSITE SPACE RATING

The estimated overall satisfaction with the interior of the Wilkinson Building was 4.19 (standard deviation = 0.91). This came from the mean satisfaction score for each space weighted by the reported time spent in each space. This result supports the view that participants are neutral with the overall quality of interior spaces.

DISLIKED SPACES

For each disliked space, the POE obtained ratings of its qualities (from 1 = Strongly Dissatisfied to 7 = Strongly Satisfied). The restrooms had low satisfaction scores for aesthetics (mean = 1.93 on a scale from 1 to 7) and odor (mean = 1.98). The computer labs had low scores for aesthetics (mean = 2.62), adequacy of space (mean = 2.87), and temperature (mean = 2.95). The architectural, urban design, and urban planning studios received low ratings for aesthetics (mean = 2.27), security (mean = 2.54), adequacy of space (mean = 2.68), and lighting (mean = 2.71).

LIKED SPACES

The POE obtained satisfaction scores (1= Strongly Dissatisfied to 7 = Strongly Satisfied) for qualities of each Liked Space. The Library received high scores for quality of lighting (mean = 5.07) and acoustics (mean = 5.03). The public areas received high scores for lighting (mean = 4.80), aesthetics (mean = 4.79), adequacy of space (mean = 4.73). Flexibility (mean = 4.39) also received a fairly high score. The galleries received high ratings for aesthetics (mean = 4.74) and lighting (mean = 4.61); and fairly high scores for flexibility (mean = 4.45) and adequacy of space (mean = 4.33).

Table C.1

PERCEPTUAL DIMENSIONS OF THE WILKINSON INTERIOR
(PRINCIPAL COMPONENT ANALYSIS WITH VARIMAX ROTATION,
CUT-OFF LOADING POINT = 0.5)

Components	1	2	3	4
Component Labels	Material Aesthetics	Functional Requirements	Layout of Spaces	Security/ Care
Items				
Wall material	0.85	—	—	—
Ceiling material	0.79	—	—	—
Floor material	0.75	—	—	—
Interior aesthetic quality	0.57	—	—	—
Proximity of views	—	0.79	—	—
Adaptability to uses	—	0.69	—	—
Environmental quality	—	0.65	—	—
Ability to find your way	—	—	0.85	—
Relationship of spaces	—	—	0.65	—
Amount of space	—	—	0.57	—
Security	—	—	—	0.88
Maintenance	—	—	—	0.62
PERCENT OF VARIANCE	33.30	10.63	8.65	8.22

Table C.2

PERCEPTUAL DIMENSIONS CONTRIBUTING TO
OVERALL SATISFACTION WITH THE WILKINSON
INTERIOR (REGRESSION ANALYSIS)

Perceptual Dimensions	Standardized Coefficient
Functional Requirements	0.25***
Material Aesthetics	0.24***
Layout of Spaces	0.15**
Security/Care	0.11*

Model summary: $R^2 = 0.31$
*$p < .05$, ** $p < .01$, *** $p < .001$

REFERENCES

Abu-Ghazzeh, T. M. (1996). Movement and wayfinding in the King Saud University built environment: A look at freshman orientation and environmental information. *Journal of Environmental Psychology, 16,* 303–318.

Abu-Obeid, N. (1998). Abstract and sceneographic imagery: The effect of environmental form on wayfinding. *Journal of Environmental Psychology, 18,* 159–173.

Ahrentzen, S., Jue, G. M., Skorpanich, M. A., & Evans, G. W. (1982). School environments and stress. In. G. W. Evans (Ed.), *Environmental stress* (pp. 224–255). NY: Cambridge University Press.

Alexander, C, Ishikawa, S., & Silverstein, M. (1979). *A pattern language.* New York: Oxford University Press.

Allen, S., & Corner, J. (2003). Urban natures. In B. Tschumi, & I. Cheng (Eds.), *The state of architecture at the beginning of the 21st century* (pp. 16–17). New York: The Monacelli Press and Columbia Books of Architecture.

Altman, I., & Chemers, M. (1980). *Culture and environment.* Monterey, CA. Brooks / Cole.

American Heritage Dictionary, 3d ed., s.v. architect and arche-.

Andersen, L. M. (1993). Undergraduate students and the design education experience: An exploration in landscape architecture. Unpublished master's of landscape architecture thesis, University of Guelph, Guelph, Canada.

Anthony, K. (1991). *Design juries on trial: The renaissance of the design studio.* New York: Van Nostrand Reinhold, reprinted by CPS, University of Illinois Printing Services.

Aronoff Center POE Study Group (ACPSG). (1998 Team Leader Sansalone, A.). Post-occupancy evaluation: The Aronoff Center. Unpublished Report, University of Cincinnati, School of Architecture and Interior Design.

A School for the Arts at Yale (February 1964). *Architectural Record, 136,* 111–120.

Association of Collegiate Schools of Architecture (2003). Guide to architecture schools (7th edition). Washington, DC: ACSA.

Austin, R. (1988). Building dedication and alumni reunion. *Dimensions: Journal for Architecture, Planning, and the Design Arts, 8,* 19–31.

Bataille, G. (1992, p. 11). *Theory of Religion* (R. Huxley Trans.). New York: Zone Books.

Becker, F. D. (1986). *Workplace: Creating environments in organizations.* NY: CBS Educational and Professional Publishing.

Beauman, C. P. (2005). Auditory distraction from low intensity noise: A review of the consequences for learning and workplace environments. *Applied Cognitive Psychology, 19,* 1041–1064.

Bennett, N., Andreae, J., Hegarty, P., & Wade, B. (1980). *Open plan schools.* Atlantic Highlands, NH: Humanities.

Bergdoll, B. (1994). *Karl Friedrich Schinkel: An architecture for Prussia.* New York: Rizzoli International, Inc.

Berlyne, D. E. (1971). *Aesthetics and psychobiology.* New York: Appleton-Century-Crofts.

Bernstein, P. G., & Pittman, J. H. (2004). Barriers to the adoption of building information modeling in the building industry. Autodesk Building Solutions White Paper. Retrieved April 7, 2006 from http://images.autodesk.com/adsk/files/BIM_Barriers_WP_Mar05.pdf.

Berry, M. C. (1993). *Brick by golden brick: A history of campus buildings at the University of Texas at Austin, 1883–1993.* Austin, Texas: L. B. Co. Publishing.

Bishop, J. (1977). CRIG Analysis. *Bulletin of Environmental Education, 73,* 3–8.

Bothwell, S. E., Andrés M., Duany, A. M., Hetzel, P. J., Hurtt, S. W., & Thadani, D. A. (2004). Windsor forum on design education: Toward an ideal curriculum to reform architectural education. Miami, FL: New Urban Press.

Boucher, J., & Osgood, E. E (1969). The pollyana hypothesis. *Journal of Verbal Learning and Verbal Behavior, 8,* 1–8.

Boyer, E., & Mitgang, L. (1996). *Building community: A new future for architecture education and practice.* Princeton, NJ: The Carnegie Foundation for the Advancement of Teaching.

Boyle, B. (1984). Taliesin then and now. *AIA Journal, 74,* 129–133.

Brill, M. (1984). *Using office design to increase productivity.* Buffalo, NY: Bosti Studies.

Bronzaft, A. L., & McCarthy, D. P. (1975). The effects of elevated train noise on reading ability. *Journal of Environmental Psychology, 6,* 215–222.

Brown, D. (2005). *Noise orders: Jazz, improvisation, and architecture.* Minneapolis: University of Minnesota Press.

Bussel, A. (1995). Searching for Siza. *Progressive Architecture, 76,* 54–65.

Carpman, J. R., & Grant M. A. (2002). Wayfinding: A broad view. In R. B. Bechtel, & A. Churchman (Eds.), *Handbook of environmental psychology.* (pp. 427–443). New York: John Wiley and Sons, Inc.

Cherry, E. (1999). *Programming for design: From theory to practice.* New York: John Wiley and Sons, Inc.

Cobb, H. (1985). Architectural education: Architecture and the university. *Architectural Record, 173,* 43–51.

Cobb, H. (1992). Ethics and architecture. *Harvard Architecture Review, 8,* 44–49.

Cooper Marcus, C., & Francis, C. (Eds.). (1990) *People places: Design guidelines for urban open space.* New York: Van Nostrand Reinhold.

Cramer, J. (2005). Informal presentation to AIA Chicago board members on August 16, 2005. Chicago.

Crinson, M., & Lubbock, J. (1994). *Architecture—Art of profession.* New York: Manchester University Press.

Crosbie, M. (1985a). Building on a humanistic base: Department of Architecture, University of Pennsylvania. *Architecture: The AIA Journal, 74,* 64–71.

Crosbie, M. (1985b). A place of pluralism and change: College of environmental design, University of California, Berkeley. *Architecture: The AIA Journal, 74,* 38–45.

Crosbie, M. (1988a). Close-knit band of individualistic, 'feisty' students. Yale University School of Architecture. *Architecture: The AIA Journal, 77,* 50–55.

Crosbie, M. (1988b). Competition winner built as designed: Roger Williams College architecture building, Kite Palmer Architects. *Architecture: The AIA Journal, 77*, 84–85.

Cubukcu, E., & Nasar, J. L. (2005). Relation of physical form to spatial knowledge in large-scale virtual environments. *Environment and Behavior, 37*, 397–417.

DAAP (College of Design, Architecture, Art and Planning). (1996). Roundtable Discussion with Peter Eisenman. Cincinnati, OH: University of Cincinnati (Videotape), November 21. a. 1:28:7 User needs are unimportant; b. 1:34:8 User input is useless.

Deleuze, G., & F. Guattari. (1987). *A thousand plateau: Capitalism and schizophrenia.* Trans. Brian Massumi. Minneapolis, MN: University of Minnesota Press.

Department of Architecture (1996). *Architectural program report.* College Station, TX: Department of Architecture, Texas A&M University.

Derrida, J. (1996). *Archive fever: A Freudian impression.* Trans. Eric Prenowitz. Chicago: University of Chicago Press.

Dewey, J. (1963). The process of thought. In R. M. Hutchins, & M. J. Adler (Eds.), *How we think.* In *Gateway to the Great Books* (pp. 88–213). Chicago: Encyclopedia Britannica, Inc.

Dewey, J. (1997). *Education and experience.* New York: Free Press.

Dillon, D. (1990). Best laid plans: Goldsmith Hall, University of Texas, Austin, Thomas and Booziotis Architects and Chartier Newton and Associates, Architects. *Architecture: The AIA Journal, 79*, 84–89.

Dixon, J. M. (1991). College of Design, Architecture, Art, and Planning Architectural Design Award, *Progressive Architecture, 72*, 82–84.

Dixon, J. (1991). Book cage, *Progressive Architecture, 72*, 90–95.

Duerk, D. P. (1993). *Architectural programming: Information management for design.* New York: Van Nostrand Reinhold.

Duffy, F. (1997). *The new office.* London: Conran Octopus.

Egbet, D. D. (1980). *The Beaux-Arts traditions in French architecture.* Princeton, NJ: Princeton University Press.

Evans, G. W. (1980). Environmental cognition. *Psychological Bulletin, 88*, 259–287.

Evans, G., & Cohen, S. (1987). Environmental stress. In D. Stokols, & I. Altman (Eds.) *Handbook of environmental psychology. Vol. 1* (pp. 571–610). New York: Wiley.

Federal Facilities Council (2001). *Learning from our buildings: A state-of-the-practice summary of post-occupancy evaluation.* Washington, DC: National Academy Press.

Fenton, E. (2000). *Carnegie Mellon 1900–2000: A centennial history.* Pittsburgh: Carnegie Mellon University Press, pp. 62–79.

Fisher, T. (1985). An energy education: Florida A&M Architecture School, Tallahassee. *Progressive architecture, 66*, 74–77.

Fisher, T. (1990). Case study: Arizona State University College of Architecture and Environmental Design, Tempe. *Progressive Architecture, 71*, 82–91.

Francescato, G. (2002). Residential satisfaction research: The case for and against. In G. Aragones, G. Francescato, & T. Garling (Eds.) *Residential environments: Choices, satisfaction and behavior.* (pp. 15–34). Westport, CT: Bergin and Garvey.

Friedman, D. (2004) *In Any Case: Ten Questions for the Large Firm Round Table*. Keynote remarks (revised for publication) 2004 ACSA/AIA Cranbrook Teachers Seminar. Online at http://www.aia.org/SiteObjects/files/Keynote%20Address.pdf

Gannon, T., Fletcher, M., & Ball, T. (2005). *Mack Scogin Merrill Elam Knowlton Hall. Source books in architecture 6*. New York: Princeton Architectural Press.

Garvin, D. A. (2003). Making the case: professional education for the world of practice. *Harvard Magazine, 106*, 58–107.

Gaskie, M. (1982) A sophisticated campus precinct. *Architectural Record, 170*, 108–113.

Gibson, W. (1991). Text(v)oid. In C. Davidson (Ed.), *Anyone*. (pp. 162–63). New York: Rizzoli.

Gifford, R. (1997). Environmental perception and cognition. In R. Gifford, *Environmental psychology: Principles and practices*. (2nd ed.), 79–110. Needham Heights: Allyn and Bacon.

Giovannini, J. (1996). Campus complexity. *Architecture, 85*, 8, 114–125.

Giovannini, J. (2003). Southern California Institute of Architecture. *Architectural Record, 191*, 136–141.

Glass, D. C., & Singer, J. E. (1972). *Urban stress*. New York: Academic.

Glass, D. C., Singer, J. E., Leonard, H. S., Krantz, D., Cohen, S., & Cummings, H. (1973). Perceived control of aversive stimulation and the reduction of stress responses. *Journal of Personality, 41*, 577–595.

Gragg, C. (1954). Because wisdom can't be told. In M. P. McNair, & A. C. Hersum (Eds.), *The case method at the Harvard Business School: Papers by present and past members of the faculty and staff*. (pp. 6–14). New York: McGraw-Hill.

Gutman, R. (1988). *Architectural practice: A critical view*. Princeton, N.J.: Princeton Architectural Press.

Gutman, R. (2006). Redesigning architecture education. In T. Fisher, J. L. Nasar, & W. F. E. Preiser (eds.). *Designing for designers*. New York: Fairchild Books.

Hancock, J. E., & Sawyers, K. (Eds.). (1979). College of architecture facilities design competition. *Architecture Nebraska, 2*, 6–23.

Hargrove, R. (1997). *Mastering the art of creative collaboration*. New York: McGraw-Hill.

Hart, S. (2005). At Ohio State University, Mack Scoggin Merrill Elam's new Knowlton Hall brings the design process to the larger academic community. *Architectural Record, 193*, 202–209.

Harwood K. Smith and Partners Architects (1973). *Program of requirements for an addition to the College of Architecture and Environmental Design, Texas A&M University, College Station, Texas*. Dallas, TX: HKS.

Hayden, D. (1976). *Seven American utopias*. Cambridge, MA: MIT.

Hershberger, R. G. (1999). *Architectural programming and pre-design manager*. NY: McGraw-Hill.

Hoffman, G. (1989). Confirmation of contexts: The renovation and expansion of Goldsmith Hall at UT-Austin. *Texas Architect, 39*, 6, 82–85.

Huang, R. (1998). An exploration of an open-plan design studio: A conceptual model of the physical and social-psychological environment. Unpublished master's of landscape architecture thesis, University of Guelph, Guelph, Canada.

Inter-University Consortium for Political and Social Research. www.icpsr.umich .edu.

James C. (2005, August 16). Informal presentation to AIA Chicago board members. Chicago.

Jensen, R. (1972). Gund Hall. *Architectural Record, 11*, 95–104.

Judd, C., Smith, E., & Kidder, L. (2005). *Research methods in social relations.* (6th ed.). New York: Holt Rinehart and Winston.

Kamin, B. (1995, November 26). Architecture school boasts human qualities. *Chicago Tribune,* Section 7, p. 16.

Keegan, E. (1996). Prairie companion. *Architecture, 85,* 96–103.

Kieran, S., & Timberlake, J. (2004). *Refabricating architecture.* New York: McGraw-Hill.

Krell, D. F. (1990). *Of memory, reminiscence, and writing: On the verge.* Bloomington, IN: Indiana University Press.

Kristal, M. (2005). Aronoff Center for Design and Art—University of Cincinnati. *AIA J (The AIA Journal of Architecture),* Sept. 30. Retrieved May 1, 2006, from http://www.aia.org/nwsltr_aiaj.cfm?pagename=aiaj_a_20051020_aranoff

Kumlin, R. (1995). *Architectural programming: Creative techniques for design professionals.* New York: McGraw-Hill.

Lawrence, R. (1994). Type as an analytical tool: Reinterpretation and application. In K. A. Franck & L. H. Schneekloth (Eds.) *Ordering space: Type in architecture and design.* New York: Van Nostrand Reinhold.

Lawton, C. A. (1994). Gender differences in wayfinding strategies: Relationship to spatial ability and spatial anxiety. *Sex Roles, 30,* 765–779.

Levine, M. (1982). You-are-here maps: Psychological considerations. *Environment and Behavior, 14,* 221–237.

Levine, M., Marchon, I., & Hanley, G. (1984). The placement and misplacement of you-are-here maps. *Environment and Behavior, 16,* 139–157.

Litt, S. (1996). Big chill. *Architecture.* 85, 8, 108–113.

Logan-Peters, K. (1999). Unpublished interview by A. Johnson with Kay Logan, architectural librarian at University of Nebraska. September 24, 1999. Lincoln, NE.

Lynch, K. (1960). *The image of the city.* Cambridge, MA: MIT Press.

Lyndon, D. (1966). Big happening in Berkeley, *Architectural Forum, 124,* 56–63.

Lynn, G. (1996). Peter Eisenman: Aronoff Center for Design and Art, Cincinnati. *Domus, 718,* 18–25.

Making a Space for Architecture (1995). *Progressive Architecture, 76,* 12, 31.

Malnar, J. M., & Vodvarka, F. (2004). *Sensory design.* Minneapolis, MN: University of Minnesota Press.

Marans, R. L. (1976). Perceived quality of residential environments. Some methodological lessons. In K. H. Craik & E. H. Zube (Eds.) *Perceiving environmental quality: Research and applications* (pp. 123–147). New York: Plenum.

Marans, R. L., & Spreckelmeyer, K. E. (1981). *Evaluating built environments.* Ann Arbor: Institute for Social Research, The University of Michigan.

Markus, T. (1994). Social practice and building typologies. In Franck, K. A., & Scneekloth, L. H. (Eds.) *Ordering space: Type in architecture and design.* New York: Van Nostrand Reinhold.

Mathews, K. E., & Canon, L. K. (1975). Environmental noise level as a determinant of helping behavior. *Journal of Personality and Social Psychology, 32,* 571–577.

Mies van der Rohe, Vol. 2. (1998). *Kenchiku Bunka. 53, 616,* 21–205.

Muckenfuss, L. (1997). Lost in America. *Planning, 6,* 15–17.

Nasar, J. L. (1979). *The impact of visual aspects of residential environments on hedonic response, interest and fear of crime.* Dissertation, Pennsylvania State University. 160 pages; AAT 7922320.

Nasar, J. L. (1983). Environmental factors, perceived distance and spatial behavior. *Environment and Planning B, 10,* 275–281.

Nasar, J. L. (Ed.). (1988). *Environmental aesthetics: Theory, research and applications.* New York: Cambridge University Press.

Nasar, J. L. (1994). Urban design aesthetics: The evaluative quality of building exteriors. *Environment and Behavior, 26.* 377–401.

Nasar, J. L. (1996) Campus architect e-mail survey.

Nasar, J. L. (1998). *The evaluative image of the city.* Thousand Oaks, CA: Sage Publications.

Nasar, J. L. (1999). *Design by competition: Making design competition work.* New York: Cambridge University Press.

Nasar, J. L. (2004, May 17). Quoted from a meeting with consultant on signage with the University Architect's office at The Ohio State University.

Nasar, J. L., & Cubukcu, E. (2005). Influence of physical characteristics of routes on distance cognition in virtual environments. *Environment and Planning B., 32, 777–785.*

Nasar, J. L., & Fisher, B. (1993). "Hot Spots" of Fear of Crime: A Multiple-Method Investigation. *Journal of Environmental Psychology, 13,* 187–206.

Nasar, J. L., & Yurdakul, R. (1990). Patterns of behavior in urban public spaces. *Journal of Architectural and Planning Research, 7,* 71–85.

National Architectural Accrediting Board (NAAB). Retrieved November 11, 2005 from http://www.naab.org/usr_doc/2004_CONDITIONS.pdf/

National Council of Architectural Registration Boards, NCARB. (2003). *Improving building performance.* (Wolfgang F. E. Preiser, author). Washington, D.C.: NCARB.

New Architecture School by Barton Myers. (1994). *Progressive Architecture, 75,* 21.

North, C., & Hatt, P. (1949). Jobs and occupations: A popular evaluation. In L. Wilson, & W. Kolb (eds.) *Sociological Analysis* (466). New York: Harcourt Brace.

Nunez, F. (1999). *The Story of Langford Architecture Center.* Unpublished manuscript, Texas A&M University at College Station.

O'Brien, G. (2004, May 22). Beauty of the beast. *Sydney Morning Herald.* Retrieved September 1, 2006 http://www.smh.com.au/articles/2004/05/21/1085120119665.html.

Office of Institutional Studies and Planning. (2001). *Room inventory by building, Langford Architecture Center.* Texas A&M University, College Station, TX.

O'Mara. M. (1986). *Casey, Kovacs and Associates: The Broyton University Graduate School of Business.*

O'Neill, M. J. (1991a). Evaluation of a conceptual - model of architectural legibility. *Environment and Behavior, 23,* 259–284.

O'Neill, M. J. (1991b). Effects of signage and floor-plan configuration on wayfinding accuracy, *Environment and Behavior, 23,* 553–574.

Oxford English Dictionary, 2d ed., s.v. architect and arch-.

Palmer, M. (Ed.). (1981). *The Architects' guide to facility programming.* Washington, DC: Architectural Record Books.

Papademetriou, P. (1982) Stirling at Rice: School of Architecture, Rice University, Houston, Texas; architects: James Stirling, Michael Wilford Associates. *Architectural Review, 171, 1021,* 50–57.

Passini, R., Pigot, H., Rainville, C., & Tetreault, M. H. (2000). Wayfinding in a nursing home for advanced dementia of the Alzheimer's type. *Environment and Behavior, 32,* 684–710.

Pearson, C. (1991). Design for learning: College of Architecture, University of North Carolina at Charlotte, Charlotte, North Carolina. *Architectural Record, 179,* 118–125.

Pearson, C. (2003). Bernard Tschumi creates an academic village in suburban Miami for the FIU School of Architecture. *Architectural Record. 191,* 102–107.

Pena, W., Parshall, S., & Kelly, K. (1987). *Problem seeking: An architectural programming primer.* Washington, D.C.: A.I.A. Press.

Physical Plant Office (2001). *Maintenance and service orders for Langford Architecture Center.* Texas A&M University, College Station, TX.

Picon, A. (2003, p. 302). Architecture, science, technology, and the virtual realm. In A. Picon, & A. Ponte (Eds.), *Architecture and the sciences: Exchanging metaphors.* (pp. 292–313). New York: Princeton Architectural Press.

Plattus, A. (1990). The architecture of architecture schools. *Progressive Architecture, 71,* 92–93.

Pound, E. (1960). *ABC of reading.* New York: New Directions.

Preiser, W. F. E. (Ed.). (1978). *Facility programming: Methods and applications.* Stroudsburg: Dowden, Hutchinson, and Ross.

Preiser, W. F. E. (Ed.). (1993). *Professional practice in facility programming.* New York: Van Nostrand Reinhold.

Preiser, W. F. E. (2003). *Improving building performance.* Washington, DC: NCARB.

Preiser, W. F. E. (2005). Building performance assessment-from POE to BPE, a personal perspective. *Architectural Science Review, 48,* 201–12.

Preiser, W. F. E., & Ostroff, E. (Eds.). (2001). *Universal Design Handbook.* New York: McGraw-Hill.

Preiser, W. F. E., Rabinowitz, H. Z., & White, E. T. (1988). *Post-occupancy evaluation.* New York: Van Nostrand Reinhold.

Preiser, W. F. E. and Schramm, U. (1997). Building performance evaluation. In D.

Watson, M. J. Crosbie, and J. H. Callender (Eds.), *Time-saver standards for architectural design data (7th Edition)*. New York: McGraw-Hill.

Preiser, W. F. E., & Vischer, J. C. (Eds.). (2005). *Assessing building performance*. Oxford, UK: Elsevier.

Presier, W. F. E., Vischer, J. C., and White, E. T. (Eds). (1991). *Design intervention: Toward a more human architecture*. New York, NY: Van Nostrand Reinhold.

Project for Public Spaces, PPS. (2000). *How to turn a place around: A handbook for creating successful public spaces*. New York: PPS.

Project for Public Spaces, PPS. (1984). *Managing downtown public spaces*. Washington, DC: American Planning Association.

Pundt, H. (1972). *Schinkel's Berlin: A study in environmental planning* (p. 181). Cambridge. MA: Harvard University Press.

Purcell, A. T. (1986). Environmental perception and affect—A schema discrepancy model. *Environment and Behavior 18*, 3–30.

Rapoport, A. (1975). Toward a redefinition of density. *Environment and Behavior, 7*, 133–158.

Ratliff, B. (2005, December 26). Review of *The Cellar Door Sessions, 1970* (compact disc recording). *New York Times*, p. B1.

Readings, B. (1998). *The university in ruins*. Cambridge, MA: Harvard University Press.

Reese, C. M. (1983). *Paul Cret at Texas: Architectural drawing and the image of the university in the 1930's*. Austin, Texas: Archer M. Huntington Art Gallery, College of Fine Arts, the University of Texas at Austin.

Rorty, R. (1998). *Achieving our country*. Cambridge, MA: Harvard University Press.

Royal Institute of British Architects. (1962). *The architect and his office*, London: RIBA, p.48.

Russell, J. (1998). Affective appraisals of environments. In J. L. Nasar (Ed.), *Environmental aesthetics: Theory, research, & applications*. (pp. 120–129). New York: Cambridge University Press.

San Francisco Public Library Commission. (2000, January). *San Francisco public library post occupancy evaluation*. San Francisco, CA.

Sanoff, H. (1977). *Methods of architectural programming*. Stroudsburg, PA: Dowden, Hutchinson and Ross.

Sanoff, H. (1989). Facility programming. In E. H. Zube, & G. M. Moore (Eds.), *Advances in environment, behavior, and design, Vol. 2* (pp. 239–286). New York: Plenum.

Sanoff, H. (1990). *Visual research methods in design*. New York: Van Nostrand Reinhold.

Sanoff, H. (1994). *School design*. New York: Van Nostrand Reinhold.

Sanoff, H. (2000). *An analysis of student responses to architecture schools*. http://www.crp.ohio-state.edu/archpoe/sanoff/htm.

Santos, A. (1991). Jury comments, College of Design, Architecture, Art, and Planning. Architectural Design Award. *Progressive Architecture, 72*, 83.

School of Architecture (1996, Fall). *Architecture at Illinois: A Newsletter for Alumni, Donors, and Friends, School of Architecture*. University of Illinois at Urbana-Champaign.

Sharp, D. (1993). *Bauhaus Dessau:Walter Gropius.* London: Phaidon Press.

Seidel, A. (1983) Way-finding in public spaces: The Dallas/Fort Worth, USA Airport. In D. Amedeo, J. B. Griffin, & J. J. Potter (Eds.), *EDRA 1983 Proceedings of the Fourteenth International Conference of the Environmental Design Research Association* (pp. 129–138). Lincoln, NE.

Smith, D., Ferguson, J., Henderson, S., Hewer, R., Morgan, Sansalone, J. A., & Waitz, K. (1999) *The vital signs project.* Retrieved September 1, 2006 from http://www.daap.uc.edu/~smithdl/VitalSignsWeb/v_s/index.html.

Spiry, D. (1999). Unpublished interview by A. Johnson with Dan Spiry. September 27, 1999. Lincoln, NE.

Stamps, A. E. (1999). Demographic effects in environmental preferences: a meta-analysis. *Journal of Planning Literature. 14, 2,* 155–175.

Steven Holl, (2003). *GA Document, 74,* 66–77.

Strong, A. L., & Thomas, G. E. (1990). *The book of the school: 100 years.* Philadelphia: The University of Pennsylvania.

Stubbs, S. (1988). Bright-eyed challenger in a blue collar city. *Architecture, 77,* 68–73.

Sundstrom, E. (1986). *Work places: The psychology of the physical environment in offices and factories.* NY: Cambridge University Press.

Surowiecki, J. (2004). *The wisdom of crowds:Why the many are smarter than the few and how collective wisdom shapes business, economies, societies and nations.* NY: Doubleday.

Tesor, P. (1989). Architectural form: Four frames of mind. Unpublished manuscript, North Carolina State University.

Texas Architect. (1990). Goldsmith Hall. *Texas Architect, 40, 1,* 32.

Thorne, P., & Ballard, N. (2004). The AEC industry, building information modeling and the 3 Rs. Retrieved December 11, 2005 from http://www.cambashi.co.uk/research/articles/AEC_ind_3Rs_Mar04.htm/.

Tibbit, W. (2005, May 20). Building information modeling and the future of practice. Paper presented at National AIA Convention and Expo panel. Las Vegas, NV.

Tureyen, M. N. (1999). *Üniversite Yapıları.* Dokuz Eylül Üniversitesi Yayınları, D.E.Ü., İzmir,Türkiye.

Tureyen, M. N. (2000). Dokuz Eylül Üniversitesi, Mimarlik Fakultesi, Kaynaklar, İzmir. *Tasarim, 99.*

Tureyen, M. N. (2003). *Yüksek Öğretim Kurumları—Kampuslar.* Tasarım Yayın Grubu, İstanbul,Türkiye.

Turner, D. (1990). School of Architecture at University of Miami 1986–89, *Zodiac, 31,* 170–201.

Ulmer, G. L. (1994). *Heuretics: The logic of invention.* Baltimore: The John Hopkins University Press.

Under Hyperbolic Parasols. (1961). *Progressive Architecture, 42,* 152–155

University of Illinois at Urbana-Champaign, *Temple Hoyne Buell Hall Program Statement.* School of Architecture, University of Illinois at Urbana-Champaign archives.

University of Illinois Foundation (1991, October 11). *Temple Hoyne Buell Hall including the Lawerence J. Plym Auditorium* (Urbana-Champaign). Pamphlet produced for the groundbreaking for the Temple Hoyne Buell Hall and the Lawrence J. Plym Auditorium.

van Zanten, D. (1987). *Designing Paris: The architecture of Duban, Labrouste, Duc, and Vaudoyer* (pp.77). Cambridge, MA: MIT Press.

Vinsel, A., Brown, B., Altman, I., & Foss, C. (1980). Privacy regulation, territorial displays, and effectiveness of individual functioning. *Journal of Personality and Social Psychology, 39,* 1104–1115.

Vitruvius, P. (1960). Vitruvius: The Ten Books of Architecture (M. H. Morgan, Trans. 1914). New York: Dover Publications.

Von Foerester, H., and Poerksen, B. (1998). Truth is invention of a liar: Conversations for skeptics. Heidelberg: Carl-Auer-Systeme Verlag.

Ward, L. B. (1995, July 23). UC building soars $16 million over plan. *The Cincinnati Enquirer,* p. 1.

Weisman, J. (1981). Evaluating architectural legibility: Wayfinding in the built environment. *Environment and Behavior, 13,* 189–205.

Welsh, F. (2000). *Philip Johnson and Texas* (pp.214). Austin TX: University of Texas Press.

White, E. T. (1972). *Introduction to architectural programming.* Tucson, AZ: Architectural Media.

Whyte, W. (1980) *The social life of small urban spaces.* New York: Project for Public Spaces.

Whyte, W. (1988). *City: Rediscovering the center.* NY: Doubleday.

Williamson, R. K. (1965). *A history of the campus and buildings of the University of Texas with Emphasis on the sources for the architectural styles.* Austin, Texas: University of Texas Report.

Wilson, A. M. (1996, October 13). What's doing in Cincinnati. *New York Times,* Section 5, p. 10.

Within a Disciplined Envelope. (1961). *Progressive Architecture, 42,* 146–151.

Wohlwill, J. F., Nasar, J. L., & DeJoy, D. (1976). Behavioral effects of a noisy environment: Task involvement vs. passive exposure. *Journal of Applied Psychology, 61,* 67–74.

Wood, E. (1978). S.O.D.A. *North Carolina Architect, 25,* 30–31.

Woolham, A. R. (1999). Students and the design education experience: An exploration on the nature of social interaction in a design school. Unpublished master's in landscape architecture thesis, University of Guelph, Guelph, Canada.

Zacharias, J., Stathopoulos, T., & Hanqing, W. (2004). Spatial behavior in San Francisco's plazas: The effect of microclimate, other people, and environmental design. *Environment and Behavior, 36,* 638–658.

CONTRIBUTORS

Cara D. Andersson, Master Landscape Architecture and Bachelor of Arts, University of Guelph. Her research is recently in the area of sustainable development. She practices in Pickering and Toronto, Ontario.

Kathryn H. Anthony, Ph.D. 1981, B.A. 1976, University of California at Berkeley, has conducted numerous post-occupancy evaluations (POEs) for over 30 years. She is a Professor and past Chair of the Design Program Faculty in the School of Architecture at the University of Illinois at Urbana-Champaign, where she also holds a faculty appointment in the Department of Landscape Architecture and the Gender and Women's Studies Program. She wrote *Design Juries on Trial: The Renaissance of the Design Studio* (1991), *Designing for Diversity: Gender, Race, and Ethnicity in the Architectural Profession* (2001), and, with Barry D. Riccio, *Running for Our Lives: An Odyssey with Cancer* (2004). She teaches in Temple Buell Hall but maintains her faculty office in the Architecture Building, where she has been for 23 years.

John Carmody, Bachelors and Masters in Architecture, University of Minnesota, is Professor of Architecture, Director of the Center for Sustainable Building Research in the College of Architecture and Landscape Architecture, and Director of the HUD-sponsored Community Outreach Partnership Center at the University of Minnesota. His research covers building design and construction, sustainable design, and includes books such as *Window Systems for High Performance Buildings* (2003), and *Residential Windows: A Guide to New Technologies and Energy Performance* (2000). John helped develop the *Minnesota Sustainable Design Guide* (a web-based tool for use by public agencies in Minnesota to improve their buildings).

Galen Cranz, Ph.D. 1971 University of Chicago, teaches social and cultural processes in architecture at U.C. Berkeley. POEs from this class include Cranz, G. et al. (1997) Community and complexity on campus. A post-occupancy evaluation of the University of California, Berkeley, Haas School of Business; *Places, 11, 1,* 38—51; and Cranz, G. (2006), The role of design in inhibiting or promoting use of common open spaces, *Journal of Housing for the Elderly, 19, 3/4* and reprinted in S. Rodiek & B. Schwarz (Eds.). (2006). *The Role of the Outdoors in Residential Environments for Aging,* (pp. 71—94). NY: Haworth Press, and Cranz, G. with Cha, EA. (2006). Body conscious design in a "teen" space: Post-occupancy evaluation of an innovative public library. *Public Libraries,* Sept./Nov., 48—56. Other publications include *The Chair: Rethinking Culture, Body, and Design* published by W.W. Norton in 2000.

Ebru Cubukcu, Ph.D. 2003 The Ohio State University, is an Assistant Professor of City and Regional Planning at Dokuz Eylul University, in Izmir, Turkey. She conducts research in the area of environmental perception, spatial cognition, virtual reality, and wayfinding. Her research has appeared in environmental psychology and urban planning journals, including *Environment and Behavior,* and *Environment and Planning B: Planning and Design.*

Thomas Fisher, M.A. 1980 Case Western Reserve University, is Professor and Dean of the College of Architecture and Landscape Architecture at the University of Minnesota. Former Editorial Director of *Progressive Architecture* magazine, he has published 3 books, 25 book chapters, and 247 major articles in various magazines and journals.

Daniel S. Friedman, FAIA, Ph.D. 1999 University of Pennsylvania, is dean of the College of Architecture and Urban Planning at the University of Washington, Seattle. He writes frequently on professional ethics and education, public architecture, and twentieth century theory.

Mark Gillem, Ph.D. Architecture, University of California at Berkeley, is an assistant professor of architecture and landscape architecture at the University of Oregon at Eugene.

Robert Gutman, Ph.D., is a sociologist of architecture. In 1965, under the sponsorship of the Russell Sage Foundation, he explored ways in which the social sciences could be utilized in architectural education and architectural practice. In 1969, he joined the Faculty of the School of Architecture at Princeton, where he continues to teach and conduct research. Gutman is also Professor Emeritus of Sociology at Rutgers. He is the author of 125 articles and 6 books in the fields of environmental sociology, planning, and architecture. Gutman is an honorary member of the American Institute of Architects.

Kathleen A. Harder, Ph.D. Cognitive Psychology, Dartmouth, M. Sc. Experimental Psychology, Stockholm University, Sweden, is a Senior Research Associate and Director of the Center for Human Factors Systems Research and Design in the College of Design at the University of Minnesota. In her research program, she investigates how various systems (or environmental contexts) can be designed to enhance human performance.

Nancy Kwallek, Ph.D. 1978 Purdue University, is a Professor of Architecture in The University of Texas at Austin's School of Architecture and the Gene Edward Mikeska Endowed Professor of Interior Design. Her research examines human response to the interior ambience of office environments. She has studied subjects working on office tasks to assess the well-being, productivity, performance, and satisfaction of workers. Presently Dr. Kwallek is expanding her environmental research by preparing to test the health, well-being, and worker productivity relative to green (sustainable) interior products versus conventional versus recycled interior finish materials, furniture, and products on human subjects in office environments.

Philip Langdon is senior editor of *New Urban News,* a national newsletter on community design and planning. He has written several books, including *A Better Place to Live: Reshaping the American Suburb* (University of Massachusetts Press, 1994) and co-edited *The CRS Team and the Business of Architecture* (Texas A&M University Press, 2002). He was a senior editor at *Progressive Architecture,* and has guest-lectured at many schools of architecture.

Rohan Lulham, Ph.D. Candidate at University of Sydney, is currently completing his dissertation in environment, behavior, and society. He has conducted research and consulted on POEs and applying control theory to environment-behavior issues in juvenile justice centers. He has been published internationally, and has been a regular contributor to EDRA and international conferences.

Gary T. Moore, B.Arch (hons), M.A., Ph.D. 1982 Clark University, *RAIA, PIA, FAPA,* one of the founders of design methods and environment-behavior studies, is Foundation Professor of Environment-Behaviour Studies and past Dean of the Faculty of Architecture, Design and Planning at the University of Sydney. Previously he was Professor of Architecture at the University of Wisconsin-Milwaukee, and Director of the NASA Wisconsin Space Grant Consortium. He has conducted research and published extensively on POEs, facility programming, environmental cognition, EB theory, children's environments, and housing for the elderly. He co-edited the four-volume *Advances in Environment, Behavior and Design* (Plenum, 1987–97); and with colleagues from Sydney, he is completing a new book on *Environment, Behaviour and Society* (being published by Springer).

Jack L. Nasar (FAICP), Ph.D. 1979 Man-Environment Relations, Pennsylvania State University, is a Professor of City & Regional Planning, a member of the Graduate Faculty in Landscape Architecture at The Ohio State University, and the editor of the *Journal of Planning Literature.* He studies environmental meanings, cognition, fear, crime, and spatial behavior. His books include *Environmental Aesthetics: Theory, Research, & Applications; The Evaluative Image of the City; Design by Competition: Making Design Competitions Work;* and *Universal Design and Visitability: From Accessibility to Zoning* (with J. Evans-Cowley). An invited lecturer around the world, he has received the EDRA Career Achievement Award, Ethel Chattel Fellowship from University of Sydney, and the Distinguished Alumni Award from the School of Architecture at Washington University, St. Louis.

Jon Norman, M.Sci. Architecture, University of California at Berkeley, is a Ph.D. candidate in the Department of sociology at the University of California at Berkeley.

Hilal Ozcan, Ph.D. Texas A&M University, M.S. in Urban Design, and B. Arch Middle East Technical University, is a Visiting Assistant Professor at the School of Architecture at Prairie View A&M University. She received her architectural training in Turkey and specializes in research on pediatric intensive care units and other healthcare environments. She was the Tradewell Fellow with WHR Architects in Houston, Texas.

Marina Panos, B.S. in Architectural Studies, University of Illinois at Urbana-Champaign, 2001; Master of Architecture, Illinois Institute of Technology, 2003; LEED Accredited Professional, participated in Kathryn Anthony's seminar course evaluating Temple Buell Hall and worked on academic design studio projects seeking to enliven the building. Marina is currently employed at the Chicago firm of VOA and working on the renovation of the University of Illinois Intramural Physical Education Building and ten LEED Certified consulting projects.

Nathan H. Perkins (ASLA), Ph.D. 1990 University of Wisconsin-Madison, is an Associate Professor of Landscape Architecture at the University of Guelph in Ontario, Canada. He conducts research in the areas of digital applications in environmental assessment and participatory decision-making as well as the application of environment and behavior research in design for children and psychiatric patients.

James J. Potter, Ph.D. Man-Environment Relations, Pennsylvania State University, is the Douglass Professor of Architecture in the College of Architecture at the University of Nebraska-Lincoln. For much of his academic career, his basic research goal has been to expand our knowledge about the impact of physical and social change, especially rapid development, on people's well-being. However, more recently, he and a colleague have been developing a database (Architecture in the Humanities) that associates events from history, film, literature, theater and art with the architectural structure in which the event occurred or was portrayed. You can access the site at: http://libtextcenter.unl.edu/aith/

Wolfgang F. E. Preiser, Ph.D. Man-Environment Relations, Pennsylvania State University, is a Professor of Architecture at the University of Cincinnati. He also holds an M. Arch. in Environmental Systems from Virginia Tech, a Diploma in Engineering in Architecture from the Technical University of Karlsruhe in Germany, and an undergraduate degree in

Architecture from the Technical University in Vienna, Austria. As re-
searcher and consultant, he has lectured globally and is published widely,
with many articles in refereed journals, book chapters, and 16 books. He
has won many awards and honors, including a Fulbright Fellowship, a
Progressive Architecture Applied Research Award and Citation, and the
EDRA Career Achievement and the EDRA Achievement Awards.

Henry Sanoff, AIA, Professor Emeritus, College of Design, North Carolina
State University, is widely published and known for his many books—including 53 *Research Papers in Social Architecture: 1963–2005*; *Programming
and Participation in Architectural Design*; *Three Decades of Design and Community*; *Community Participation in Design and Planning*; *Creating Environments
for Young Children*; *School Design*; *Integrating Programming Evaluation and Participation in Design*; and *Visual Research Methods in Design*. He has been a
visiting lecturer at more than 85 institutions in the U.S. and abroad. He
received the NCSU Holladay Medal of Excellence, Phi Kappa Phi Faculty
Achievement Award, ACSA Architecture Distinguished Professor, ACSA
Community Design Award, Fulbright Senior Specialists Award and the
EDRA Honor and Service Awards. Henry also won a Design award and a
Post Occupancy Evaluation award for the Davidson School, and the Millis
Elementary School from the School Construction News/Design Share
Awards program.

Mardelle McCuskey Shepley (AIA), D. Arch. University of Michigan, M.A.
Psychology, University of Michigan, M.Arch. and B.A., Columbia University, is a Professor, and center director at the College of Architecture
at Texas A&M University. Co-author of *Healthcare Environments for Children
and their Families,* she is a registered architect with 20 years experience in
practice.

Virajita Singh, M.Arch. 2000, University of Minnesota, serves as a Research
Fellow in the Center for Sustainable Building Research, as an Adjunct
Faculty member in the School of Architecture and as a part-time Facilities Coordinator, all at the College of Design, University of Minnesota.
Her passion lies in the area of sustainability and culture, and her research
and teaching strive to make the connection between knowledge and action. She is also leading the effort to green the College of Design.

Dr. Takemi Sugiyama, M. Arch., Ph.D. 2003 University of Sydney, is Research Fellow in the School of Population Health, University of Queens-
land, Brisbane, Australia, following a post-doctoral fellowship at the
OPENspace Research Centre, Edinburgh College of Arts in Scotland. He
has published research on POEs, physical activity and the enviroment,
aging and the environment, children's environments, and environnment-
behavior aspects of sustainabilty.

Iris Tien is an undergraduate student in Engineering at the University of California at Berkeley.

Jess Wendover received a Masters of Architecture from the University of California at Berkeley and is currently Director at the Mayors' Institute on City Design in Washington DC.

CREDITS

Foreword
Figure F.1 — Courtesy of Bill Rydberg

Chapter 3
Figure 3.1 — Courtesy of École des Beaux Arts
Figure 3.2 — Courtesy of Sammlung Architektonisher Entwurfe
Figure 3.3 — Courtesy of Oliver Radford
Figure 3.4 — Photograph from Andrew Saint, *The Image of the Architect*, (1983), p. 75. New Haven: Yale University Press.
Figure 3.5 — Photograph from Dorothy Spencer, *Total Design* (1991), p. 133. San Francisco: Chronicle Books.

Chapter 4
Figure 4.1 — Courtesy of Sammlung Architektonisher Entwurfe
Figures 4.2a, b, and c — Courtesy of Cerney Associates
Figures 4.3a and b — Courtesy of Smith Carter Searle Architects
Figures 4.4a and b — Courtesy of Hillier Group
Figures 4.5a and b — Courtesy of McCarty Bullock Holsaple
Figures 4.6a and b — Courtesy of Philip Johnson
Figures 4.7a and b — Courtesy of Perkins & Will
Figures 4.8a and b — Courtesy of Gwathmey Siegel & Associates
Figures 4.9a and b — Courtesy of Kite Palmer Associates
Figures 4.10a and b — Courtesy of Bernard Tschumi
Figure 4.11 — Courtesy of Felix Duban
Figures 4.12a and b — Courtesy of Alvaro Siza
Figure 4.13 — Courtesy of Aldo Rossi
Figure 4.14 — Courtesy of Barton Meyers Associates
Figures 4.15a and b — Courtesy of James Stirling
Figures 4.16a and b — Courtesy of Schwartz Silver Associates
Figures 4.17a and b — Courtesy of Gary Paige, Kappe Architects Planners, and Studio Works
Figures 4.18a and b — Courtesy of Walter Gropius
Figures 4.19a and b — Courtesy of Paul Rudolph
Figures 4.20a and b — Courtesy of Joseph Esherick, Vernon DeMars, and Donald Olsen
Figures 4.21a and b — Courtesy of Steven Holl
Figures 4.22a and b — Courtesy of Eisenman Architects
Figure 4.23 — Courtesy of Frank Lloyd Wright
Figures 4.24a and b — Courtesy of John Andrews
Figures 4.25a and b — Courtesy of Mack Scogin & Merrill Elam
Figures 4.26a and b — Courtesy of Mies van der Rohe

Chapter 6

Figures 6.1a, 6.5a, 6.7a, and 6.9a — Photographs by Kokyung Soon

Figures 6.1c, 6.3c, 6.5b, 6.7c, and 6.9c — Photo credit: Kathryn H. Anthony

Figure 6.3a — Photograph by Nancy Kwallek

Figures 6.4a, 6.6a, 6.8a, and 6.10a — Photographs by Takemi Sugiyama, University of Sydney

Chapter 8

Figures 8.1a, b, c, and d — Source: Architectural Program Report, 1996

Figure 8.3 — Photo: Mardell McCuskey Shepley

Figure 8.5 — Photograph courtesy of the Cushing Memorial Library, Texas A&M University

Figure 8.7 — Photo: Hongseok Cha

Chapter 9

Figures 9.1a and b — HPA plan prepared by Space Management & Capital Programs

Figure 9.2a — Photograph by Galen Cranz

Figures 9.2b, 9.3, and 9.4 — Photographs by Iris Tien

Chapter 10

Figures 10.1, 10.3, 10.4, and 10.5 — Photographs and chart: Wolfgang F. E. Preiser

Figures 10.2, 10.8. 10.9, and 10.10 Photographs: Jay Yocis, University of Cincinnati

Chapter 11

Figures 11.1, 11.3, and 11.5 — Photo credit: Larry Kanfer Photography Ltd, www.kanfer.com

Figure 11.7 — Photo credit: Kathryn H. Anthony

Figure 11.8 — Photo credit: Marina Panos

Chapter 12

Figures 12.1 and 12.2 — Courtesy of the College of Design, University of Minnesota

Chapter 14

Figures 14.1, 14.2, 14.4, 14.5, 14.6, and 14.7 — Photograph and charts by Nancy Kwallek

Figures 14.3, 14.8, 14.9, and 14.10 — Photographs by Kokyung Soon

Chapter 15

Figure 15.2 — Photograph by FAMU School of Architecture students

Figure 15.4 — Photograph by Nelson Benzing

Figure 15.6 — Photograph by Sherry Ahrentzen

Figure 15.8 — Photo credit: Student POE Research Team, University of Cincinnati, Wolfgang F.E. Preiser, Instructor

Figure 15.10 — Photograph by Henry Sanoff

Figure 15.12 — Photograph by Kathleen Murtagh

Chapter 17

Figure 17.1 — Ricardo Gutierrez © 2007 Faculty of Architecture, University of Sydney

Figures 17.3, 17.5, 17.6, 17.7, and 17.10 — Photographs and chart © Faculty of Architecture, University of Sydney

Figure 17.9 — Photograph by Brett Boardman

INDEX